Gwen and I planted a church 2007. When we started the church, OBX Nation, my friend and confidant, David Baird, suggested that I write a weekly devotional to email to those we were trying to reach. Each week, from the church's beginning, we sent a devotional to our church family and anyone else who requested it. That time each week became an occasion for me to reflect on what I was learning about God and what I was seeing as our young church took shape.

Shortly after the church's beginning Gwen and I were in Williamsburg with our friends Tom and Gail Wells. We awakened one morning and God put a word in my heart about OBX Nation. He said, "I have called you to fish on the other side of the boat." There were people on the Outer Banks no one was reaching. That isn't to the discredit of other churches because each church has its own unique ministry. But, God wanted us to reach people who were "on the other side of the boat."

My life has changed since those days. Our church is a safe place for people who aren't looking for religion but are hungry for a relationship with God through His Son Jesus Christ. I have learned so much more about grace and have observed so much of God's transforming power from this venture. Theological jargon doesn't reach the people we are touching. There is theology, of course, but it is only effective when it is understandable.

I have been guided by two theories in these devotional pieces. First, I believe in the power of God's Word. Second, I believe in the importance of stories that create pictures to help us understand the truth. Jesus told stories. I tell stories, too. I have documented the stories where possible, but mostly they are collected over many years of ministry and I have used them to help people understand what I know about Jesus.

When I look at our congregation, I see individuals who have been transformed, and are being transformed, by God's power. I say, like the disciples who were with Jesus when He calmed the storm, "Who is this? Even the wind and the waves obey Him!" He still calms storms and He still rescues us from danger and gets us where He wants us to go.

1—Hope Keeps Us Alive

Isaac Asimov tells the story of a rough ocean crossing during which a Mr. Jones became terribly seasick. At an especially rough time, a kindly steward patted Jones on the shoulder and said, "I know, sir, that it seems awful. But remember, no man ever died of sea-sickness." Mr. Jones lifted his green countenance to the steward's concerned face and replied, "Man, don't say that! It's only the wonderful hope of dying that keeps me alive."

None of us can overestimate the power of hope. A Scripture that has been a source of strength for many of us is Isaiah 40:31. It says, "But those who hope in the Lord will renew their strength." Those of us who have faced situations we regard as hopeless know the weakening effect it has on us. Biblical hope is more than human optimism. It is based on the reality of a God who is for us and is working in our future to produce an abundant life for us.

One effect of living without hope can be seen in the story of a town in the Northeast region of the United States. Some years ago, a hydroelectric dam was to be built across a valley in New England. The people in a small town in the valley were to be relocated because the town itself would be submerged when the dam was finished. During the time between the decision to build the dam and its completion the buildings in the town, which previously were kept up nicely, fell into disrepair. Instead of being a pretty little town, it became an eyesore. Why did this happen? The answer is simple. As one resident said, "Where there is no faith in the future, there is no work in the present."

The psychology department of Duke University once conducted an experiment. Some of the students wanted to see how long rats could swim. In one container they placed a rat that was given no possibility of escape. He swam a few moments and then ducked his head to drown. In the other container they made the hope of escape possible for the rat. The rat swam for several hours before finally drowning. The conclusion of the experiment was just the opposite of our common conclusion. We usually say, "As long as there is life, there is hope." The Duke experiment proved, "As long as there is hope, there is life."

The word in Isaiah 40:31 that captured my attention and showed the power of hope was the word, "renew." When Isaiah wrote, "Those who hope in the Lord will renew their strength" he used a word that is translated "renew" in Isaiah, but is translated other ways elsewhere in the Old Testament. In Genesis 35:2, it describes a "change" of clothes. Job 14:7 says, "At least there is hope for a tree: If it is cut down, it will sprout again." "Sprout again" translates the word Isaiah used. The Hebrew word means "to change for the better."

Isaiah is literally saying that if we hope in the Lord a "change for the better" will take place. We will give up our weakness and receive His strength. Like a change of clothes or a tree that sprouts again when it seems to be dead, hope in the Lord produces a fresh approach to the future. When we hope in the Lord we exchange our weaknesses for His strength. We may be just about ready to throw in the towel, but if we hope in the Lord we "renew" our strength. When Isaiah invites us to hope in the Lord, he is reminding us that there is never a reason for people of faith to give up on tomorrow.

When a military plane is flying a long-range mission and isn't able to land and refuel, it is refueled in flight. This enables the plane to go beyond the limitations of its fuel tank. A tanker flies close to it and refuels the nearly empty tank of the military aircraft while that aircraft continues on its mission. That is what hope does for us. It enables us to refuel in flight, exchanging our diminishing resources for His provision.

John Ortberg wrote an uplifting book, *If You Want to Walk on Water, You've Got to Get Out of the Boat*. In his book, he explains the power of hope: "In one study, 122 men who had suffered their first heart attack were evaluated on their degree of hopefulness and pessimism. Of the 25 most pessimistic men, 21 had died eight years later. Of the 25 most optimistic, only six had died! Loss of hope increased the odds of death more than 300 percent; it had predicted death more accurately than any medical risk factor including blood pressure, amount of damage to the heart, or cholesterol level. Better to eat Twinkies in hope than to eat broccoli in despair."

The book of Hebrews says that hope is the anchor of our souls. When we have hope, storms can't shake us, adverse circumstances can't break us and we have a confident expectation that God will never let us down.

2–Where Do We Run?

Mrs. Samuel Untermyer, a lawyer's wife, cabled her husband from Europe. She had found a Gobelin tapestry she wanted, but it cost $25,000. She asked, in the cable, if she could buy it. He responded with a cable that said, "No, price too high." When she returned from Europe, she had the tapestry with her. He asked her why she had disregarded his message. She then showed him the cable she had received. It read, "No price too high."

When it came to restoring our relationship with God, it is apparent that God regarded no price as too high. A verse in the Bible with which many of us are familiar is John 3:16: "For God so loved the world that He gave His one and only Son." That is an amazingly high price for anyone to pay, the price of a child, but that is what God was willing to pay for us.

King David, who wrote so many of the Psalms, asks two questions that occur to us as well. In Psalm 8:3-4 (CEV) he ponders, "I often think of the heavens your hands have made, and of the moon and stars you put in place. Then I ask, 'Why do you care about us humans? Why are you concerned for us weaklings?' "

Those are good questions and touch the deepest recesses of our insecurities. Many people feel that God cannot possibly love them because they are not worthy of His attention. We look in our mirrors and ask the same questions David asked, "Why do you care?" and "Why are you concerned?"

G. K. Chesterton, the brilliant English writer who also was an outstanding defender of Christian faith, wrote, "All men matter. You matter. I matter. It is the hardest thing in theology to believe."

One of the great challenges we have as believers today is to convince men and women that they matter and that God loves them. No matter what we think of ourselves, the Bible is clear in telling us that we are important to God, that He values us and loves us with an immeasurable love.

God's love is shown in His sending Jesus to save us and bring us into His family. While we were still sinners, the apostle Paul says in the book of Romans, Jesus died for us. Each of us knows what it means to fall short of God's plan for our lives and live only for ourselves. However, while we were still in that selfish pursuit of our own interests, Jesus died for us because God loved us even then.

My wife, Gwen, found an amazing example of love on the internet. She saw a photo with its accompanying story. There was a picture of infant twins who were lying in the same crib. They had been born prematurely and one of them was very weak. Babies were not to be placed in the same crib, but a nurse had violated regulations and put them together in the same bed. While they were lying side by side the strong one had placed its arm around the weak one. Then an amazing series of improvements began in the weaker infant. When the weak one was embraced by the strong one it immediately became stronger and its vital signs improved dramatically.

That is what God has done for us. When we were weak, Jesus came and put His arm around us. Because He is concerned and because He cares for us, He has intervened in our lives. For those who accept the love of Jesus, His love brings a continual transformation. Love has power to heal us.

So, what about those of us who have found that life is difficult and that we have weaknesses? What about those of us who need a loving arm to support us? We have a Father who loves us and He sent His Son to die for us. Jesus still puts His arm around the weak and brings health to those who have been broken.

Kay Arthur had a friend who went hunting in Oregon with her father. They were walking through the woods when they heard a loud racket and out of the bushes came a brown rabbit, running out its last bit of energy. It ran to the man and leaned against his boot—exhausted. Wild rabbits don't do that and they were amazed. Then they heard more noise and out of the same bushes raced a weasel. It stopped and looked at the rabbit that leaned closer to the man's boot. The hunter fired his gun in front of the weasel which ran off and the rabbit loped away to play another day.

Where do we run when pursued by problems that threaten to overwhelm us? I suggest that we run to a Father who loves us, and to His Son who loves us so much that He laid His life down for us.

3—We Are Living Witnesses

Roger Simms was discharged from the military and was hitchhiking home when Mr. Hanover picked him up. Simms felt impressed to share his faith in Jesus, to his surprise, Mr. Hanover pulled the car to the side of the road. Roger thought he was going to be put out of the car, but instead, Mr. Hanover prayed and accepted Christ as his Savior.

Five years later Simms was going to Chicago and found Hanover's business card. He called the office and was told he couldn't see Mr. Hanover, but Mrs. Hanover was available. Roger met with Mrs. Hanover and told her the story of his meeting with her husband five years earlier. He explained that it had all begun when Mr. Hanover gave him a ride.

"What was the date?" she asked. He said, "May 7th, five years ago, the day I was discharged from the army." He then felt that he should tell her about Mr. Hanover pulling to the side of the road and praying. Suddenly, she began to sob uncontrollably. After several minutes, she regained enough control to explain what had happened.

"I grew up in a Christian home, but my husband did not. I had prayed for my husband's salvation for many years, and I believed God would save him. However, just after he let you out of his car, on May 7th, he was killed in a terrible head-on collision. He never arrived home. I thought God had not kept His promise, and I stopped living for the Lord five years ago because I blamed Him for not keeping His word."

Don't ever underestimate the power of your prayers for someone's salvation, or the power of telling someone about Jesus.

It is important that we share our faith with others. That doesn't mean, by the way, hitting them over the head with the biggest Bible we own. It means that we share our faith in a tactful way and, mostly, live a Christian life in front of them.

Benjamin Franklin learned that plaster sown in the fields would make things grow. He told his neighbors, but they did not believe him and they argued with him trying to prove that plaster could be of no use at all to grass or grain. After a little while, he allowed the matter to drop and said no more about it. However, he went into the field early the next spring and sowed some grain. Close by the path, where men would walk, he traced some letters with his finger, put plaster into them, and then sowed his seed in the field.

After a week or two, the seed sprang up. His neighbors, as they passed that way, were very much surprised to see, in brighter green than all the rest of the field, the writing in large letters, "This has been plastered." Benjamin Franklin did not need to argue with his neighbors any more about the benefit of plaster for the fields. For as the season went on and the grain grew, these bright green letters just rose up above all the rest until they were a kind of relief-plate in the field–"This has been plastered."

People will always look past our words to see what kind of life we really live. Let your life be part of your witness. It would be wonderful if people observed our lives and could see, "This life is touched by Jesus."

That doesn't mean that we never speak about what God has done for us. George Sweeting, in his book *The No-Guilt Guide for Witnessing*, tells of a man by the name of John Currier who in 1949 was found guilty of murder and sentenced to life in prison. Later he was transferred and paroled to work on a farm near Nashville, Tennessee.

In 1968, Currier's sentence was terminated, and a letter bearing the good news was sent to him. However, John never saw the letter, nor was he told anything about it. Life on that farm was hard and without promise for the future. Yet John kept doing what he was told even after the farmer for whom he worked had died. Ten years went by. Then a state parole officer learned about Currier's plight, found him, and told him that his sentence had been terminated. He was a free man.

Sweeting concluded that story by asking, "Would it matter to you if someone sent you an important message—the most important in your life—and year after year the urgent message was never delivered?" We who have heard the good news and experienced freedom through Christ are responsible to proclaim it to others still enslaved by sin. We have the best news that anyone could ever hear. God loves them, Jesus died for them and they don't have to live in bondage any longer. Let's not keep good news like that to ourselves.

4—The Power of Water Baptism

Pastor Charles Foster told this delightful story about water baptism: "As a minister, I conduct many baptismal services. My denomination baptizes in the name of the Father, the Son and the Holy Ghost. One Sunday, my family and I went to a friend's home in the country. Our four children went outside to play with the others. After a short while, we heard only silence and wondered what the children were up to. We found them behind a barn quietly playing 'church.' Our 4-year-old daughter Susan was conducting the baptismal service. She held a cat over a barrel of water. Trying to be as solemn as her father, she repeated the phrase she had heard many times: 'I baptize you in the name of the Father, the Son, and in the hole you go!' "

Because our church is located near the ocean, that is where we baptize new converts. It is exciting to be part of a baptismal service, and there is nothing more invigorating spiritually than seeing believers publicly declare their faith by water baptism. Baptizing at the beach is about as public as it gets.

The story is told about the baptism of King Aengus by St. Patrick in the middle of the fifth century. Sometime during the rite, St. Patrick leaned on his sharp-pointed staff and inadvertently stabbed the king's foot. After the baptism was over, St. Patrick looked down at all the blood, realized what he had done, and begged the king's forgiveness. "Why did you suffer this pain in silence," Saint Patrick wanted to know. The king replied, "I thought it was part of the ritual."

While physical pain is not "part of the ritual," there is a sense in which baptism represents death. Romans 6:3-4 says, "Don't you know that all of us who were baptized into Christ Jesus were baptized into his death? We were therefore buried with him through baptism into death that, just as Christ was raised from the dead through the glory of the Father, we too may live a new life."

When we are baptized, the immersion is a picture of our death and burial. We bury our old life, our past mistakes and our sinfulness. When we are brought back out of the water, it pictures our spiritual resurrection to a new life. In Jesus' last command, He told us to "make disciples of all nations, baptizing them in the name of the Father, and of the Son and of the Holy Spirit." Water baptism doesn't save us, faith in Jesus is the only requirement for salvation. But, water baptism is a public expression of our faith.

Baptism marks a significant change in a believer's life. Martin Marty in his "Context" letter quoted Yale professor-preacher Halford Luccock: "You remember that among the Franks, whole armies were sometimes given baptism at one stroke, and many warriors went out into the water with their right hands held high, so they would not get wet. Then they could say, 'This hand has never been baptized,' and they could swing their battle axes as freely as ever."

When we are baptized our whole nature is buried in faith and is changed by God's power. We bring our hands, our minds, our feet, our eyes—everything—to God in faith.

It is a wonderful experience to see individuals make a public profession of their faith. It keeps the rest of us excited about God's power to change lives.

Haddon Robinson is one of the preaching giants of our generation. He quotes the well-known author, Gordon MacDonald, in a brilliant description of baptism. MacDonald describes Jesus' baptism in water in the following way:

"Several management types were at the River Jordan as the crowds came to John, and they decided they needed to get things organized. So, they set up tables and begin to give tags to those coming for repentance. On the tag is written the person's name and chief sin. Bob walks up to the table. The organizers write his name on the tag and then ask, 'What's your most awful sin, Bob?' 'I stole some money from my boss.' The person at the table takes a marker and writes in bold letters, 'embezzler,' and slaps it on Bob's chest. The next person comes forward. 'Name?' 'Mary.' 'Mary, what's your most awful sin?' 'I gossiped about some people. It wasn't very much, but I didn't like these people.' The organizers write, Mary—slanderer, and slap it on her. A man walks up to the table. 'Name?' 'George.' 'George, what's your most awful sin?' 'I've thought about how nice it would be to have my neighbor's Corvette.' George—coveter. Another man approaches the table. 'What's your name?' he is asked. 'Gordon.' 'What's your sin?' 'I've had an affair.' The organizer writes, Gordon—adulterer, and slaps the sticker on his chest. Soon Christ comes to be baptized. He walks down the line of those waiting to be baptized and asks them for their sin tags. One by one, he takes those tags off the people and sticks them on his own body. He goes to John, and as he is baptized, the river washes away the ink from each name tag he bears."

As each believer is baptized in water, it is a visible presentation of the fact that his or her sins have been washed away. Why be baptized? Because Jesus said to do it, the early church faithfully practiced it and it makes a spiritual difference any time we obey God's Word. Hopefully, there will be many baptismal services ahead for me. I will never get over the thrill of seeing believers publicly declare their faith.

5—The World Needs Love

Love is risky. It is impossible to go through life loving others without being disappointed. When Paul, near the end of his life, wrote his second letter to Timothy, he mentioned three individuals with whom he had experienced a close relationship. He said that Demas had deserted him, having fallen in love with the world. He wrote about his friend, Luke, who had stayed with him through all the challenges of imprisonment. He then asked Timothy to do something that is a bit surprising. He asked Timothy to bring Mark with him to visit Paul in his Roman prison. Mark, the deserter described in Acts 13, had not only been restored to a loving relationship with Paul but Paul called him "helpful to me in my ministry" (2 Timothy 4:9).

Paul is telling us an important truth about relationships. Some people will disappoint you, some will never let you down and others will surprise you—so don't give up on anyone.

I came across a rhyme that describes the challenge of being open to others: "To dwell above with saints we love, that will be grace and glory. To live below with saints we know; that's another story!"

Paul would advise us to continue taking the risk of loving in spite of the past disappointments we experience. You never know whether a person who hurts you now will change and become a valued friend and helper.

There are three principles to keep in mind when dealing with people. First, it is important that we live with a desire to help others. That keeps us healthy.

In his book *Open the Door Wide to Happy Living*, T. Huffman Harris told of a young man named Eddie who became tired of life and decided to leap from a bridge into a turbulent river. Jim, a total stranger, saw Eddie being swept downstream and plunged into the water in an effort to save him. Eddie, a good swimmer, noticed the man floundering desperately in the strong current and knew that without his help he would drown. Something stirred within him. With all of his strength, Eddie swam over to the man and rescued him. Saving that stranger, who had attempted to save him, brought new hope and meaning to Eddie's life. When we do something to help someone else, we can begin to see once again our value to God and to others.

The second principle is just as important. What others think of us doesn't have to determine what we think of them or how we treat them. We aren't responsible for what someone else does, but we are responsible for our own actions and attitudes.

When Robert E. Lee was the highest-ranking Confederate General, he gave a glowing recommendation of another officer to the president of the Confederacy, Jefferson Davis. A man who heard the recommendation said, "General, do you know that the man of whom you speak so highly to the President is one of your bitterest enemies, and misses no opportunity to malign you?" "Yes," replied Lee, "but the President asked my opinion of him, he did not ask for his opinion of me." Be big enough to speak well of others no matter what treatment you have received from them.

The third principle involves our enlarging the boundaries of our hearts to be more inclusive of other people. William Barclay, in his commentary on Ephesians, refers to an incident that helps us see this principle in action.

During the war in France, some soldiers with their sergeant brought the body of a dead comrade to a French cemetery to have him buried. The priest told them gently that he was bound to ask if their comrade had been a baptized adherent of the Roman Catholic Church. They said that they did not know. The priest said that he was very sorry but in that case he could not permit burial in his churchyard. So, the soldiers sadly took their comrade and buried him just outside the fence.

The next day they came back to see that the grave was all right and to their astonishment could not find it. Search as they might they could find no trace of the freshly dug soil. As they were about to leave in bewilderment the priest came up. He told them that his heart had been troubled because of his refusal to allow their dead comrade to be buried in the churchyard; so, early in the morning, he had risen from his bed and with his own hands had moved the fence to include the body of the soldier who had died for France.

The popular song from a few years ago has the lyrics, "What the world needs now is love, sweet love." That is still true and it is God's desire that we, who know Him, love the people He died to save.

6—Don't Miss Your Moment

Teri Leinbaugh, in *Christian Reader*, recited a story that shows the value of taking advantage of unexpected opportunities. She wrote: "My mother and I arise early on Saturday mornings to catch all the garage sales. One typical Saturday we spotted a garage sale that seemed to be just opening for business. We quickly walked into the man's garage and began looking over his wares. After a few minutes and several stern looks from the solemn-faced garage owner, he asked if there was anything he could do for us. 'This is a garage sale, isn't it?' my mother asked timidly. The gentleman chuckled, somewhat relieved. 'No,' he said. 'I was just cleaning out my garage. But if there's something you want, let me know.' We did—and now he's five dollars richer."

One of the keys to any success is our ability to seize unexpected opportunities when they come. An ambitious young man asked an experienced salesman for the secret of his success in selling. The salesman said, "There's no great secret, you just have to jump at every opportunity that comes along." The young man replied, "But how can I tell when an opportunity is coming?" The salesman responded, "You can't. You have to keep jumping."

One of the exciting facts of the Christian life is that we awaken each day to unplanned opportunities. Someone crosses our path and God has placed us where we need to be to have the right word of encouragement. Isaiah says, in the fiftieth chapter, verse four: "The Sovereign LORD has given me an instructed tongue, to know the word that sustains the weary." What a blessing it is to meet someone who is weary and give that person a word that keeps him or her going. It's not that we see the occasion beforehand, we are simply ready when the right time comes.

Opportunities are serious. Never underestimate the value of doing the right thing at just the right time. One of the great disasters of history took place in 1271. In 1271, Niccolo and Matteo Polo (the father and uncle of Marco) were visiting the Kublai Khan. Kublai Khan at that time was a world ruler, for he ruled all China, all India, and the entire East. He was attracted to the story of Christianity as Niccolo and Matteo told it to him. In 1271, he sent a request from Peking to Rome asking for "a hundred men of the Christian religion. I shall be baptized, and when I am baptized all my barons and great men will be baptized, and their subjects will be baptized, and so there will be more Christians here than there are in your parts."

The Mongols were then wavering in the choice of a religion. It might have been, as Kublai forecast, the greatest mass religious movement the world has ever seen. The history of Asia would have been changed. But, what actually happened? Pope Gregory X answered by sending two Dominican friars. They got as far as Armenia, could endure no longer and returned home. Because of that failure to act, Asians lived for long centuries without a knowledge of Jesus Christ.

Only God knows how important it is that we take advantage of the opportunities that come our way.

Of course, there is always the person who says either, "I'm too old," or "It's too late." Don't let the enemy rob you of your moments by telling you those lies.

Bruce Thielemann told one of my favorite stories in a sermon entitled, "Dealing with Discouragement." He told of a man who was sitting on his front porch in Kentucky. He had recently retired from the post office, and was sitting there when his first Social Security check was delivered. He was discouraged. He thought to himself, "Is this what life is going to be from now on—sitting on the porch waiting for my check to arrive?"

He decided he wouldn't settle for that, and so he made a list of all of the things he had going for him—all the blessings and the abilities, the things that were uniquely his. The list was long because he listed everything he could think of. On his list was the fact that he was the only person on earth who knew his mother's recipe for fried chicken. It contained eleven different herbs and spices. So, he went to a nearby restaurant and asked if he could cook the chicken. They said, "Yes." It soon became the most popular item on the menu.

Encouraged by that, he opened his own restaurant, and then others, and ultimately a string of restaurants across all of America. Harland Sanders had created the Kentucky Fried Chicken franchises.

He finally retired a second time (all this happened, you remember, after he had retired from the postal service), and he continued in the service of the company as a public relations representative, earning $250,000 per year until his death. Not only that, but in his retirement years he accepted Jesus Christ as his Savior.

Don't ever let anyone tell you that it is too late for you to seize your opportunities. Begin each day with the excitement that precedes discovery. God has planned golden moments of opportunity for each of us and it is our joy to discover them and act upon them.

7—Don't Worry!

Worry is an enemy of faith. Most of us have had occasions to worry over circumstances that never occur. We feel the anxiety and heart palpitations of worry, only to realize that it was wasted. Bishop R. C. Trench, the renowned Bible scholar, was also the Protestant Archbishop of Dublin. He had a morbid fear of becoming paralyzed. One evening at a party, the woman sitting next to him heard him muttering to himself, "It's happened at last—total insensibility of the right limb." "Your Grace," said the woman, "it may comfort you to learn that it is my leg you are pinching."

What a waste of energy with its damage to faith when we worry! Some of us may remember the Wallenda family and their exploits on the high wire. I watched on television as Karl Wallenda plunged to his death from a tightrope in San Juan, Puerto Rico, in 1978. His widow explained that he had never known fear, but that before that walk he had been worried. Instead of putting his focus on walking the wire, he had focused on not falling. Motivational speakers call this the Wallenda Factor. Beware of being so afraid of failure that you dwell on the negatives. Be careful in a prudent way, but don't be paralyzed by fear of failure.

There are several reasons for recognizing that worry is an enemy. First, it is physically dangerous. Dr. Charles H. Mayo said, "Worry affects the circulation, the heart, the glands, the whole nervous system." We pay a physical price when we allow ourselves to worry.

Also, worry wears us down emotionally. The Greek verb for worry in the New Testament, *merimnao*, means literally "to divide the mind." We are torn in two directions: "God will, maybe He won't; I can, maybe I can't." The result is mental anguish. The original Old German root of the English word "worry" means "to choke." That is exactly what worry feels like. It is a choking sensation. We are torn with anxiety.

Not only that, worry affects us spiritually. In His parable of the different soils, Jesus describes the condition of some people: *"The one who received the seed that fell among the thorns is the man who hears the word, but the worries of this life and the deceitfulness of wealth choke it, making it unfruitful"* (Matthew 13:22). Worry actually chokes the Word of God that we hear so that it does not produce fruit in our lives.

Steve Chandler says, in *100 Ways to Motivate Yourself,* "But when we worry, we don't worry a thing to death, we worry it to life. Our worrying makes the problem grow. And most of the time, we worry it into a grotesque kind of life, a kind of Frankenstein's monster that frightens us beyond all reason."

It doesn't take much worry to cripple our faith. According to the National Bureau of Standards, a dense fog covering seven city blocks to a depth of 100 feet is composed of something less than one glass of water. That is, all the fog covering seven city blocks 100 feet deep could be, if it were gotten all together, held in a single drinking glass; it would not quite fill it. This can be compared to the things we worry about. If we could see into the future and if we could see our problems in their true light, they wouldn't blind us to the world–to living itself–but instead could be relegated to their true size and place. And, if all the things most people worry about were reduced to their true size, you could probably stick them all into a water glass, too.

The question arises, "Do believers ever worry?" Sadly, we do! That is why the Bible not only warns us of its dangers, but gives us ways to defeat it before it takes its painful toll on our lives, robbing us of our joy.

In the Gospels we find the apostle Peter worrying. In Matthew 14:30 he worried about sinking when he began walking on water toward Jesus. He worried about paying taxes (sound familiar to anyone?) in Matthew 17:24. That is why it is significant that he wrote, in 1 Peter 5:7, *"Cast all your anxiety on him because he cares for you."* Peter's word "anxiety" is the same word that is consistently translated "worry." When worry tries to invade your life, carry it immediately to Jesus. Don't allow it to eat away your faith and keep God's Word from being fruitful in your life.

Maybe the best advice about worry comes from Jesus in the Sermon on the Mount. He says, *"Therefore I tell you, do not worry about your life, what you will eat or drink; or about your body, what you will wear. Is not life more important than food, and the body more important than clothes?"* (6:24). That seems easier said than done, doesn't it?

But, He gives us the secret in the following verses. After describing the things we need like clothes, food and drink, He says: *"But seek first his kingdom and his righteousness, and all these things will be given to you as well"* (verse 33).

That is the key. Seek first his kingdom and his righteousness. Remember that in the Lord's Prayer we are taught to pray, *"Our Father in heaven, hallowed be your name, your kingdom come, your will be done on earth as it is in heaven. Give us today our daily bread"* (Matthew 6:9-11).

He is telling us not to start with a request for our daily bread. We'll get to that but begin with "Hallowed be your Name." God isn't saying, "Don't mention the bread." He is saying, "Put me first and the bread will be provided."

8—The Challenge of Forgiving

I was reading my devotional Scriptures this week and came across an interesting exchange between Jesus and His disciples. In Luke 17:4-5 Jesus says about forgiveness, *"If he [your brother] sins against you seven times in a day, and seven times comes back to you and says, 'I repent,' forgive him."* The apostles said to the Lord, *"Increase our faith!"* I see a clear connection between forgiving someone and needing more faith. It is a spiritual challenge for any of us to forgive someone else. It takes faith for miracles and, according to the disciples' response, more faith to forgive someone.

This Scripture caused me to pause and reflect on a few reasons for forgiving others.

First, it is an attractive quality. Bitterness and unforgiveness can mar a person's character and make him or her unpleasant to be around. We have all known people carrying offenses over past hurts and have seen how it hinders them from moving forward. They are chained to some event in the past and are missing the joys of a life free from resentment.

One day when Stan Mooneyham was walking with some friends along a trail in East Africa, he detected a pleasant aroma in the air. He looked up in the trees and around at the bushes in an effort to discover its source. His friends saw what he was doing and told him to look down at the small blue flower growing along the path. Each time someone crushed the tiny blossoms under their feet, more of its sweet perfume was released into the air. His friends then informed him, "We call it the forgiveness flower."

Second, forgiveness can keep us from destroying ourselves. I may think that I am punishing someone else by withholding forgiveness, but it is quite likely that my attitude doesn't faze that person. Gwen and I heard a Christian counselor say something to a group of pastors that I have never forgotten: "Unforgiveness is like taking poison and waiting for the other guy to die."

A friend of mine who was skilled in personal ministry told me that more than 90 percent of the cases of oppression he dealt with were rooted in unforgiveness. Unforgiveness doesn't hurt the other person nearly as much as it will destroy you.

Another reason for forgiving others is that our forgiveness can help someone understand the forgiveness God has for him or her.

In the collection of stories, *Chicken Soup for the Christian Soul*, the account is given of Father O'Malley. He served in the foothills of the Sierra Nevada in a small town called Grass Valley, California. On a Saturday night, he received a call from the Auburn hospital. A patient was dying and the nurse on duty thought he might want last rites. There was a fierce storm blowing and it took Father O'Malley until past midnight to make the 30-mile journey. No one passed him on the way, the roads were so bad.

When he arrived at the hospital, the nurse who had called met him and said, "I'm so glad you're here. The man I called you about is slipping fast, but he is still coherent. He's been an alcoholic for years, and his liver has finally given out. He's been here for a couple of weeks this time and hasn't had one single visitor. He lives up in the woods, and no one around here knows much about him. He always pays his bill with cash and doesn't seem to want to talk much."

Father O'Malley went into the room and asked the patient, a man named Tom, "Would you like to make your confession?" Tom responded forcefully, "Absolutely not." Then he added, "But I would like to talk with you a bit before I go." They talked until dawn.

Just before the sun came up Tom said, "Father, when I was young, I did something that was so bad that I haven't spent a single day since without thinking about it and reliving the horror. I worked as a switchman on the railroad all my life, until I retired a few years ago and moved up here to the woods. Thirty-two years, two months and 11 days ago, I was working in Bakersfield on a night kind of like tonight. It was two nights before Christmas and to push away the gloom of a stormy night the whole yard crew drank all through swing shift. I was drunker than the rest of them, so I volunteered to go out in the rain and wind and push the switch for the northbound 8:30 freight. I guess I was more drunk than I thought I was because I pushed the switch in the wrong direction. At 45 miles an hour that freight train slammed into a passenger car at the next crossing and killed a young man, his wife and their two daughters."

Father O'Malley put his hand on Tom's shoulder and said, "If I can forgive you, God can forgive you, because in that car were my mother, my father and my two older sisters."

There is power in our forgiveness because it helps people understand that God is able and willing to forgive all our sins.

The most compelling reason for forgiveness, to me, is the example of what Jesus has done for us. He is willing to forgive all our sins if we simply ask Him.

Sir Walter Scott, the noted author (and Christian) had difficulty with the idea of "turning the other cheek." However, one day Scott was taking a walk when a stray dog began running toward him. Scott picked up a rock and threw it toward the dog to chase it away. His intent wasn't to hit the dog, but to startle it. His aim was straighter and his delivery stronger than he had intended, however, for he hit the animal and broke its leg. Instead of running off, the dog limped over to him and licked his hand. Sir Walter never forgot that touching response. He said, "That dog preached the Sermon on the Mount to me as few ministers have ever presented it."

No matter how we have sinned against God and no matter what we have done to offend Jesus, He forgives when we ask Him. That is what He wants us to do for others. And, we say, when confronted with the challenge, (in the words of the New Living Translation) *"We need more faith. Tell us how to get it."*

9—Amazing Grace

As a Christian, I believe many things. I believe that God wants me to be the best person I can be and has provided the resources I need to achieve that goal. I believe that He loves me enough to walk with me through any tough times I experience. But, the foundation of all that I believe is my strong confidence in the grace of God. As Ephesians puts it, *"For it is by grace you have been saved, through faith"* (2:8).

God's grace comes to us when we are sinners and have a broken relationship with Him. In the Garden of Eden, with man's first sin, we are told that it was God who came looking for Adam and Eve when they were hiding in the bushes. Our human tendency still, when we are wrong, is to hide from Him. But, He sent His Son, Jesus, to find us. That journey to where we are took Him through the Cross. Our salvation cost Him plenty, but it is free to us if we just trust Him and surrender our lives to Him.

It is naturally hard for us to accept something that is free. Peter Lord, who pastored in Florida, told the story of a new convert in his church. Lisa lived at Cape Canaveral and had just received Jesus as her Savior. People would park in her neighborhood to watch the launching of missiles. She decided to use the occasion of one rocket launch to witness to others about her newfound faith.

Her neighbors had signs in their yards: Parking $5 and Parking $10. She put up a sign: "Free Parking, Free Coffee and Donuts." She got up very early that morning to make coffee and donuts. She was excited about telling others of her experience with Jesus. That morning her neighbors' yards were full of cars. But, no one parked on her property. Puzzled and upset she was complaining to God. Why would people pay for parking when she offered parking for free? God said to her, "Lisa, that's how I feel. I offer you grace for free and you still try to pay for it."

Here is good news for all of us. We don't have to pay for salvation. Jesus did that. All God asks of us is to believe in and trust His Son, Jesus.

An often-overlooked truth about grace is that it enables us to live a life of victory. That doesn't mean we never make a mistake but it does mean that we can grow and improve. Grace means that our failures have been paid for and we can continually come to Christ and find Him willing to pick us up from whatever ditch we have fallen into so we can keep going in the right direction. We don't have to stay in a pit for the rest of our lives and we don't have to be defeated by human weakness. The apostle Paul once heard these words from the Lord: *"My grace is sufficient for you, for my power is made perfect in weakness"* (2 Corinthians 12:9). Those words are a comfort to us who, in our weaknesses, still need to draw on God's grace.

When we become what God wants us to be we won't be able to boast about the improvement we have experienced. We will still be thankful for God's grace. John Stott, the former Rector of All Souls Anglican Church in London, told of a time when he was in seminary. The head of the seminary retired. At his retirement, a portrait of him was unveiled. He looked at the portrait and commented that in the future people looking at the portrait would not ask, "Who is that man?" but rather, "Who painted that portrait?" Stott remarked that it is that way with grace. God's grace, not our glory, will be on display.

What, though, of the moment when each of us stands before God. What difference will grace make? Billy Graham told of a time when he was driving through a small southern town and was stopped for speeding. Graham readily admitted his guilt, but was told by the officer that he would have to appear in court.

When Graham went to court the judge, hardly looking up, asked, "Guilty, or not guilty?" When Graham pleaded guilty, the judge replied, "That'll be ten dollars—one dollar for every mile you went over the limit." Suddenly the judge looked up and recognized the famous minister. "You have violated the law," he said. "The fine must be paid—but I am going to pay it for you." He took a ten-dollar bill from his own wallet, attached it to the ticket, and then took Graham out and bought him a steak dinner! "That," said Billy Graham, "is how God treats repentant sinners!" God found us guilty because we were guilty. But, Jesus paid the penalty for us and invites us to enjoy fellowship with Him forever. That's grace.

A few years ago, a young woman handed me a small article she had found. It describes what grace can do for each of us. The short article said: "Longfellow could take a worthless piece of paper, write a poem on it, and instantly make it worth thousands of dollars—and it's called genius. Rockefeller could sign his name to a piece of paper and make it worth millions of dollars—and it's called wealth. A mechanic can take material worth only five dollars and make it worth five hundred—and it's called skill. An artist can take a fifty-cent piece of canvas, paint a picture on it, and make it worth thousands of dollars—and it's called art. Jesus Christ can take a worthless, sinful life, wash it in His blood, put His Spirit in it, and make it valuable to God—and that's called grace."

No matter where we've been or what we've done, God has grace for us. We'd be crazy to pass up a deal like that.

10—A Turned-Around Life

There is good news for each of us. Jesus can change our lives. The greatest miracle any of us can ever experience is the encounter with Jesus that takes us from who we used to be to who we can be because of His power.

In the ninth chapter of Acts, Saul the persecutor met Jesus on the road to Damascus and was changed into Paul, the greatest missionary in the history of the Church. Thomas, the disciple who was filled with questions and doubt, became the apostle who brought the good news to India.

The examples of God's ability to change us are too many to mention. Those of us who have believed on Jesus can witness to the fact that He is continually changing us. As one man said, "I'm not yet what I'm going to be, but I'm sure not what I was."

When we look at people who display godly qualities we often think we could never become who they are. Especially, when we look at Jesus, His character seems far out of our reach. We are like the two caterpillars that were crawling across the grass when a butterfly flew over them. They looked up, and one nudged the other and said, "You couldn't get me up in one of those things for a million dollars." What God does with us is certainly beyond our own power, but He specializes in the miracle of change.

The change begins with a decision to trust Jesus for salvation. Going to church is important, but going to church can't substitute for a decision to believe on Jesus. Garrison Keillor once said, "You can become a Christian by going to church just about as easily as you can become an automobile by sleeping in a garage."

Sam Shoemaker, in a speech celebrating the founding of Alcoholics Anonymous, pointed out the same truth. "You know what a lot of religious people are like? They are like a lot of people sitting around a railroad station thinking they are on a train. Everybody is talking about travel, and you hear the names of the stations and you have got the tickets, and there is the smell of baggage around you and a great deal of stir, and if you sit there long enough you almost think you are on a train. But, you are not. You only start to get converted at the point where you get on the train and get pulled out of the station. And you do get pulled out; you do not walk out."

The transformation we seek, the desire to become a person who lives like Jesus, can only begin when God touches us and performs the miracle that we call being "born again." It is the fresh start in life that means our sins are forgiven and we can begin to grow into the person God created us to be.

When translator Des Oatridge, working in Papua New Guinea, came to the words "born again" in John's Gospel, he asked his native co-translator to think of a good way to express it. The man explained this custom: "Sometimes a person goes wrong and will not listen to anybody. We all get together in the village and place that person in the midst of us. The elders talk to him for a long time. 'You have gone wrong!' they say. 'All your thoughts, intentions, and values are wrong. Now you have to become a baby again and start to relearn everything right.' " It was the answer Des was looking for. Today the words of John 3:3 in Binumarien are translated, "No one can see the Kingdom of God unless he becomes like a baby again and relearns everything from God's Word." Change begins with our willingness to be born again and our desire to take God's Word seriously.

The result of the miracle of new birth is amazing. While Gwen and I were living in Australia I was invited to speak at an Aboriginal conference is West Australia. I was sitting on the front row at one of the meetings, watching the Aboriginal musicians lead in our time of worship. The head of the Aboriginal ministry touched me and motioned to one of the singers. "See that man. He used to steal ten cars per night." That might be what he once did, but it wasn't who he was when I saw him. He had experienced the miracle of change.

Sometimes it is frustrating when we realize how far we still have to go in order to be like Jesus. But, the miracle of conversion is that God is able to keep changing us as we grow to be like Him. It is a miracle. There is no question about that. But, God still works miracles in us.

An exciting part of God's good news is that we can affect others as we are changed. As reporter Clarence W. Hall followed American troops through Okinawa in 1945, he and his jeep driver came upon a unique small town. He wrote, "We had seen other Okinawan villages, down at the heels and despairing; by contrast, this one shone like a diamond in a dung heap. Everywhere we were greeted by smiles and dignified bows. Proudly the old men showed us their spotless homes, their terraced fields, their storehouses and granaries, their prized sugar mill."

Hall said that he saw no jails and no drunkenness, and that divorce was unknown in this village. When he inquired about the different nature of this village, he was told that an American missionary had come there some thirty years earlier. While he was in the village, the missionary had led two elderly townspeople to Christ and left them with a Japanese Bible. These new believers studied the Scriptures and started leading their fellow villagers to Jesus. Hall's driver made this insightful comment: "So this is what comes out of only a Bible and a couple of old guys who wanted to live like Jesus."

What a miracle can come from a Bible, a desire to live like Jesus and God's supernatural power to change us. By changing us, God begins to change our world.

11–Success!

I want to be successful. Most of us would share that desire unless we have been so bombarded by negativity that we have stifled our dreams and aspirations. Even more than my personal desire for success, I believe God wants each of us to be successful. After all, He made us and everything He makes is designed to work properly.

That means, of course, that it's important for us to define success. In the Bible, success is simply doing the things that please God. Keep the following requirements in mind when making decisions intended to please Him and lead to success.

First, we want enough light to see what we are doing. For example, I discovered the hard way that if you want to look good, it's essential to have the lights on when you dress. When Gwen and I pastored in Virginia Beach we had an early Sunday morning service. Since I would leave the house before the sun came up, I got in the habit of dressing in our walk-in closet on Sunday mornings. One Easter I dressed in the dark to keep from disturbing Gwen and went to church to face the largest crowd of the year. As we left the church Gwen said, "Just look at your shoes." I had worn one black shoe and one brown shoe to church. Even crazier, one had a tassel and the other one did not. I have never forgotten the lesson. Success in dressing for church requires proper lighting.

It is also important that we practice doing the right things. Bobby Knight once said, "Practice doesn't make perfect; perfect practice makes perfect."

I used to love playing golf. To have control over what you're doing, though, requires disciplined practice. I was playing eighteen holes of golf with a friend of mine (who didn't practice) when he teed off on the first hole. His golf ball, meant for the fairway, went ninety degrees to our right and into the garage where the golf carts were parked. We heard the raucous sound of the ball rattling around inside the building, bouncing off metal. Then two employees came running out looking for the offending party. I knew enough about golf to jump behind a tree and let my guilty friend take the blame. Some acts of wisdom just come naturally.

The most important ingredient for any success on our part, however, is a proper relationship with Jesus. The name, Jesus, is well known around the globe, but is often misunderstood.

C. S. Lewis, in *Mere Christianity*, points out how important it is to know Jesus as He really is. He wrote: "I am trying here to prevent anyone saying the really foolish thing that people often say about Him: 'I'm ready to accept Jesus as a great moral teacher, but I don't accept His claim to be God.' That is the one thing we must not say. A man who was merely a man and said the sort of things Jesus said would not be a great moral teacher. He would either be a lunatic—on a level with the man who says he is a poached egg—or else he would be the Devil of Hell. You must take your choice. Either this man was, and is, the Son of God: or else a madman or something worse. You can shut Him up for a fool, you can spit at Him and kill Him as a demon; or you can fall at His feet and call Him Lord and God. But let us not come with any patronising nonsense about His being a great human teacher. He has not left that open to us. He did not intend to."

If we want to be successful and become what God created us to be, it is important that we embrace Jesus as God's Son and our Savior. Who else can lead us to God? As most of us have discovered, human guides can fail us. Jesus never will.

The story is told of a hunter who hired a guide to lead him through the wilderness. The hunter soon discovered they were walking around in circles. "We're lost," the hunter complained to the guide. "I thought you said you were the best guide in the state of Maine." "I am," said the guide, "but I think we're in Canada now." While that is humorous, it speaks a truth. No one but Jesus is able to guide us from where we are to where God wants us to go.

My success is not just determined by here and now, I want to be like Abraham. *"For he was looking forward to the city with foundations, whose architect and builder is God"* (Hebrews 11:10).

Do you want to be successful? Only Jesus can lead you to your highest destiny!

12—Jesus Seeks the "Lost"

The Gospel of Luke defines the purpose of Jesus' coming to earth: *"For the Son of Man came to seek and to save what was lost"* (19:10). Our salvation is possible because God took the initiative to come and retrieve us. Most of the world's population has no idea how important and loved they are. God held back nothing to reach us, even to the point of sacrificing His own Son.

King Theodore of Abyssinia (now Ethiopia) captured a British subject named Cameron. The British demanded his release, but King Theodore would not comply. Consequently, the British sent 10,000 soldiers by sea and they walked 700 miles inland to the island fortress where the British subject was held. They broke down the prison gate, went to the dungeon and claimed Cameron. Then they escorted him down the mountain to the sea where they placed him on a ship bound for England. The British government invested several months and 25 million dollars (when that was a huge amount of money) to rescue one man. As impressive as that effort was, it pales in comparison with what God has done to reach us.

In the 1980's I went to a seminar conducted by John Wimber, the founder of the Vineyard churches. Wimber did not grow up as a churchgoer and told of riding his bike by a place of worship as a young boy. He saw a sign that said, "Jesus saves." He recalled thinking, "I save rubber bands and paper clips. I wonder what Jesus saves."

When I hear someone speaking of individuals being "lost" I am reminded of Wimber's story and wonder whether we shouldn't clarify what the term means. It is biblical. Jesus used it. But, what does it mean to be lost?

In Jesus' world the word "lost" was used in four ways. First, it meant "misplaced." We still use the word that way. Jesus told a parable about a "lost" coin in Luke 15. He was referring to a coin that was misplaced. I am convinced that the world is filled with misplaced people. Jesus came to find us and put us into the place we belong. If you feel "out of place" Jesus came to find you and reposition you into God's plan for your life.

The Greeks also used the word "lost" in the sense of "overloaded." The word specifically referred to Greek stonebreakers who found their work to be drudgery. I saw a statistic that claimed that eighty percent of American workers do not enjoy their jobs. For those to whom life is no longer exciting but is overwhelming, realize that Jesus came to save us from that. How many of us have seen overloaded people crack under the pressure of life and just give up. No matter what I am doing, if I am a believer, I am doing it for the Lord. That gives dignity to every occupation.

Another use of the word "lost" in the original language of the New Testament is "worn out by misuse." If you have an automobile and do not change the oil regularly or get the scheduled service, it will wear out too soon. One of the reasons Christians go to church, read their Bibles and plan time with each other is the fact that we need regular maintenance.

A car dealer who was part of our church in Virginia Beach, Virginia told me of a man who bought the most expensive sports car he sold. The engine froze on Interstate 64 between Hampton Roads and Richmond. He had driven it 40,000 miles without checking the oil. It had been running on the oil in the engine when it left the dealer's lot. If you are one of those individuals who is wearing out because you aren't taking care of yourself be encouraged. Jesus came to save you. Maybe it's time for maintenance.

The last use of this word "lost" in Jesus' day is connected with a proverb: "He that finds his life shall lose it." That is parallel to a Hebrew proverb: "He who focuses on this life trifles it away." We are "lost" when we trifle our lives away. We are "lost" when we are consumed by the insignificant and unimportant. When we ignore things of eternal value and sacrifice them for things that won't last we are "lost."

We are "lost" when we bury our talents in napkins and miss our opportunities for service.

Once again, the good news is that Jesus came to save us from wasting our lives.

Whether we are misplaced, overloaded, worn out by misuse or just trifling our lives away the good news of the Bible is that God is looking for us to save us. I may be wrong, but I think there are many believers God wants to save from all of the above.

How do I keep from being lost? The answer is in my willingness to walk in relationship with Jesus. An elderly man was out walking with his young grandson. "How far are we from home?" he asked the grandson. The boy answered, "Grandpa, I don't know." The grandfather then asked, "Well, where are you?" Again the boy answered, "I don't know." Finally, the old man said good-naturedly, "Sounds to me as if you are lost." The young boy looked up at his grandfather and said, "Nope, I can't be lost. I'm with you."

Ultimately, that is the answer to our lostness, too. We can't be lost if He is with us. And, He is with us because He came to seek and save us.

13—God Loves His Church

A Sunday School teacher asked her children, as they were on their way to church service, "And why is it necessary to be quiet in church?" One bright little girl replied, "Because people are sleeping."

To some "church" is the short amount of time on Sundays when we gather for singing and teaching and when some (too many really) catch up on lost sleep.

To others the "church" is a building. It is certainly more than that. The Christian Church is made up of those who believe in Jesus. The word "church" in the New Testament is the translation of the Greek word *ekklesia*, and literally means "called out." It is the community of believers who have been called out of the world to come together as a unique fellowship celebrating the Lordship of Jesus Christ.

Elton Trueblood captured the wonder of the Church when he wrote about his reaction to a lecture given by a Buddhist monk. The monk had come from Cambodia. He came to the United States to speak about his culture and religion. He told of the Buddhist shrines, their sacred writings and their focus on human love. But, he surprised many by not talking about his Buddhist church. Then those assembled to hear him realized that he did not have a church. There is nothing in Buddhism like our church. The mark of the "church" is not a shrine or religious temple, but people gathered in community. Many religions can be celebrated by a solitary ritual before an altar or shrine, but not Christianity.

Trueblood explained by referring to the Scripture in Matthew 16:18. Jesus said, "I will build my Church." Trueblood continued, "Once the central idea of changing the world by means of a divinely perpetuated society was clear, the practical problem was that of the makeup of this society. Should it be of men only, of monks only, of scholars only? The answer, as everyone knows, led in a radically different direction. It is one thing to have an architect's plan of a building, but it is quite another to decide upon the materials and to do the actual work of construction. On what kind of stuff, Christ seems to have asked, would He or could He build His church. The shocking answer was that He would build on the poor human stuff that He saw right in front of Him?"

God shapes His wonderful new society, the Church, out of the likes of us. That is a miracle.

Why is it important for us to be connected to each other? Nature provides a perfect example of the power of living in harmony with others who are going in the same direction. While Gwen and I were riding to Ocracoke Island this past week, I witnessed something I had read about. There was a V-shaped formation of geese flying above us. While I observed them, the lead goose fell out of the formation and went to the back of the "V." Another goose took the lead.

Canadian scientists, eager to learn why geese fly this way discovered some interesting facts. Their engineers learned that the flapping of each goose's wings provides an upward lift for the goose that follows. When all the geese are flying in perfect formation, the whole flock has a 71 percent greater flying range than if each bird flew alone. Each was dependent on the other to reach its destination.

It seems obvious that Jesus formed us into a community of "called out" ones known as the "Church" because we can go farther and accomplish more together than we can on our own.

He has also formed us into a "Church" so we can accurately reflect His nature to our world. To be sure, there are times when we may not live up to His standards, but that doesn't change who He is.

A pastor stopped by a house and asked the man who lived there to visit his church on Sunday. The pastor also mentioned that the man's neighbor came to his church.

The man said he would go to no church that had a man like his neighbor in it.

The pastor saw a composition by Beethoven lying on the table and asked the man's daughter, who was taking piano lessons, to play it for him. The girl messed up and the pastor said, "Boy, that Beethoven wasn't much of a composer, was he?" At that point, the girl's father realized he had been judging Christianity by the poor way some people live it, not by the greatness of its Composer.

Though there are times when we fall short, the glory of the Church is that there are times when we get it right. There are occasions when people look at us and see the likeness of Jesus.

On a wall near the main entrance to the Alamo in San Antonio, Texas, is a portrait with the following inscription: "James Butler Bonham—no picture of him exists. This portrait is of his nephew, Major James Bonham, deceased, who greatly resembled his uncle. It is placed here by the family that people may know the appearance of the man who died for freedom." No literal portrait of Jesus exists either. But, the likeness of the Son who makes us free can be seen in the lives of his true followers.

It is a great honor to be part of Jesus' Church. Don't try going solo. Become part of a church in which you can move in harmony with other believers who are going in the same direction. One of them may make up for your deficiencies and, if the engineers are right, you'll go 71 percent farther.

14—How Do I Get Right with God?

Some Scriptures are especially important because they become foundation stones of our faith. Once we grasp the truth of them, they change the way we live. One of those truths, for me, is the message of Romans 5:1. The New Living Translation renders it: *"Therefore, since we have been made right in God's sight by faith, we have peace with God because of what Jesus Christ our Lord has done for us."*

It is difficult for me to explain what it meant to me when I first understood that my peace with God was based on what Christ did for me. Most of us who have grown up with religion have found the struggle to earn God's approval challenging. The constant effort to be good enough for God to approve of us was exhausting (and unsuccessful!).

There may be no one in the world more religious than the individual described in the *Grand Rapids Press*. The article stated, "A West German businessman has completed his conversion to the Hindu faith by piercing himself through the cheeks with a 1/4-inch thick, 4-foot-long steel rod, and pulling a chariot for 2 miles by ropes attached to his back and chest by steel hooks. Others walk through 20-foot-long pits of fire, don shoes with soles made of nails, or hang in the air spread-eagle from hooks embedded in their backs." What a contrast to Christianity. Aren't you glad that conversion to faith in Jesus Christ doesn't require this kind of self-inflicted torture?

From a Christian perspective, two wonderful words that form the basis of our faith are "grace" and "justification." When we go to our cars to ride somewhere we get in vehicles with powerful engines capable of moving us down the road at high speeds. That is grace. It is power to take us faster and farther than we could go on our own. But, we must turn the key and start the engine. That is justification by faith. Starting the car is how I appropriate the benefit of the automobile. Grace gives us the power to live; justification by faith is how we get started.

H. A. Ironside had an ability to put the gospel in terms that anyone could understand. He said that while he was presenting the message of Jesus on the streets of a city in California he was often interrupted with questions such as, "There are hundreds of religions in this country, and the followers of each sect think theirs is the only right one. How can poor plain men like us find out what really is the truth?" His response was something like this: "Hundreds of religions, you say? That's strange; I've heard of only two." The questioner would say, "Oh, but you surely know there are more than that?" His answer would be, "Not at all, sir. I find many shades of difference in the opinions of those comprising the two great schools; but after all there are but two." Then he would explain that one of the religions involved its followers doing what they could to save themselves. The other was Christianity, which consisted of those saved by what someone else had done. His challenge would be, "Can you save yourself, or must you be saved by another? If you can be your own savior, you do not need my message. If you cannot, you may as well listen to it."

That is what sets Christianity apart from every other religion. We realize that we cannot save ourselves and we look to Jesus as our Savior. As the apostle Paul says in Romans 5:1, "We have peace with God because of what Jesus Christ our Lord has done for us."

This means that our salvation is placed in the hands of Jesus. J. Rodman Williams, in *Renewal Theology*, has expressed it clearly: "In Him we are righteous—not we who are godly; not we who have climbed the mountain heights of righteous living, but we who are struggling on the plains, and sometimes in the muck and mire, of unrighteous living. There is nothing, absolutely nothing, in us—whether we be the most moral or immoral of people—that makes this possible. God pronounces us righteous, though we are not: this is the glory and wonder of the gospel message."

Of course, there are always those who object that salvation based on faith alone will produce an inferior brand of Christianity. Joseph M. Stowell said that he was chatting with a man who consults with some of the largest U.S. companies about their quality control. Because ministry is a form of human quality control, he thought he'd ask him for some insights. The expert said, "In quality control, we are not concerned about the product." Stowell was surprised. But, the consultant went on to say, "We are concerned about the process. If the process is right, the product is guaranteed." We have the right process. God has chosen to make us righteous through the work of Jesus. When we believe that, and rely on that, the result is guaranteed.

Terry Virgo, while preaching in Toronto, remarked that if God said to a pig, "Your nature is pig. Your calling is to fly," he would have created an unhappy pig. No matter how fast a pig runs he won't leave the ground and fly. Religion without Jesus Christ is the same kind of frustrating attempt to do what we cannot do—make peace with God. The good news of the Bible is that Jesus has made peace for us.

Maybe the question persists in your mind: How can I, imperfect as I am, approach a holy God, let alone be at peace with Him? In the Old Testament when someone brought a sacrificial animal to the priest so the animal could be offered for his sin, the priest didn't examine the man who had sinned. He examined the animal. If the sacrificial animal was without defect, it was offered to God and the man was forgiven. Our Lamb, Jesus, is perfect and was offered to God for us. That is why we are forgiven and can live at peace with God.

God has made us an offer that we would be foolish to turn down. He has offered to take us as we are, accept what Jesus did for us as payment for our mistakes and bring us peace. After all, isn't peace with God the desire that drives people to pull chariots attached to their backs with steel hooks? Salvation is less complicated than that. We simply believe that what Jesus did for us was enough and surrender our loyalties to Him. I have found some words to live by: "Therefore, since we have been made right in God's sight by faith, we have peace with God because of what Jesus Christ our Lord has done for us."

15—Love Breaks Down Barriers

What does God want from me? Jesus summarized all God's requirements with two commandments: *" 'Love the Lord your God with all your heart and with all your soul and with all your mind.' This is the first and greatest commandment. And the second is like it: 'Love your neighbor as yourself' "* (Matthew 22:37-39).

It is easy to believe that I am supposed to love God. He is the Creator who loved me so much that He gave His only Son for my salvation. It is sometimes far more challenging to love people. My sympathies are with the very honest little girl in a third grade Sunday school class. Her teacher was giving a Bible lesson on one of the Ten Commandments: "Honor your father and your mother." The teacher then went beyond the lesson and challenged the class, "Now, does anyone know a commandment for brothers and sisters?" One sharp girl raised her hand and said, "You shall not kill."

Even those of us who are supposed to be loving and kind have our moments of reality. Psychologist James Dobson reported seeing a sign on a convent in southern California reading: "Absolutely No Trespassing—Violators Will Be Prosecuted to the Full Extent of the Law." The proclamation was signed, "The Sisters of Mercy."

I suspect that you have found the same truth I have learned—I can only love God and love other people with the help of the Holy Spirit. The Bible teaches us that the way the world knows we belong to Jesus is by the fact that we love each other. Only God can help us overcome our natural tendencies to want everything our own way so we can really reach out to others. Billy Graham once described the problem this way: "Our world has become a neighborhood without becoming a brotherhood."

Occasionally it takes a crisis to tear down the barriers between us and others. In *One Church from the Fence*, Wes Seelinger made an astute observation. "I have spent long hours in the intensive care waiting room...watching with anguished people...listening to urgent questions: Will my husband make it? Will my child walk again? How do you live without your companion of thirty years?

"The intensive care waiting room is different from any other place in the world. And, the people who wait are different. They can't do enough for each other. No one is rude. The distinctions of race and class melt away. A person is a father first, a black man second. The garbage man loves his wife as much as the university professor loves his, and everyone understands this. Each person pulls for everyone else. In the intensive care waiting room the world changes. Vanity and pretense vanish. The universe is focused on the doctor's next report. If only it will show improvement. Everyone knows that loving someone else is what life is all about."

Wouldn't it be wonderful if we could learn to live and love like that before we get to an intensive care waiting room. What an impact we could make on our world if we learned to love God and love others. Bert Bacharach's song describes the world's longing: "What the world needs now is love, sweet love. It's the only thing that there's just too little of."

When World War II ended, prisoners of war were being released from a prison camp in Siberia. One of the liberating officers reported, "We did our best to repatriate the men as fast as possible, but many were still there when winter threatened to close up the port."

Only a limited number could board the last small boat and the rest would have to spend the winter in Siberia. Among those waiting to be transported were two men who had been close friends during the war. One of them was selected, but the other seemed doomed to remain behind. Because of space limitations, an order was given that those who were leaving could take only one important item of luggage.

The heart of the man who was chosen went out to his buddy, so he emptied his duffle bag of its prized souvenirs and his personal belongings and told his companion to get into the canvas sack. Then carefully lifting the bag on his shoulders, he boarded the ship with his friend as his single, most precious possession. This man truly loved his neighbor as himself.

It's easy to love a friend, but how can we love someone who is considered an enemy? Tony Campolo related a story told to him by international reporter Peter Arnett. Arnett explained that he was in Israel, in a small town on the West Bank, when there was an explosion. Bodies were blown through the air. In every direction there were signs of death and destruction. A man came running up to Arnett holding a bloodied girl in his arms. The anxious man pleaded: "Mister, I can't get her to a hospital! The Israeli troops have sealed off the area. No one can get in or out, but you're press. You can get through. Please, mister! Help me get her to a hospital. Please. If you don't help me, she's going to die!"

As they got in Arnett's car and got through the sealed-off area the man kept pleading from the back seat, "Can you go faster, mister? Can you go faster? I'm losing her!" When they reached the hospital, Arnett and the man sat silently in the waiting room. After a short while, the doctor came out and informed them that the girl didn't make it.

The man collapsed in tears and Arnett put his arms around him and tried to comfort him. "I don't know what to say. I can't imagine what you must be going through. I've never lost a child." The man looked at Peter Arnett in a startled manner and said, "Oh, mister! That Palestinian girl was not my daughter. I'm an Israeli settler. That Palestinian is not my child. But, mister...there comes a time when each of us must realize that every child, regardless of that child's background, is a daughter or a son. There must come a time when we realize that we are all family."

God loves everyone. He loves our friends and He loves our enemies. Sometimes the only way God can get His love to them is through us. If we really love Him, it will be possible for us to love others as ourselves.

16–Trust In the Lord

Ralph Waldo Emerson said, "All I have seen teaches me to trust the Creator for all I have not seen." Trust is one of the essentials of our relationship with Jesus. I am always exercising trust. I go to a restaurant and eat what comes out of the kitchen—that is trust. Gwen and I have boarded a plane and been carried over the Pacific for more than fourteen hours—that is trust. I walk into a room and sit in a chair I have not seen before, and have not tested—that is trust. Why should it be so hard to trust God?

When I was young, I would attend church with my grandparents. The church they attended had "testimony" time. Members of the congregation would be given an opportunity to stand and offer thanks for something God had done. You could always count on my grandmother to stand and speak out. She would get to her feet and, without exception, quote Proverbs 3:5-6 in the King James Version—*"Trust in the LORD with all thine heart; and lean not unto thine own understanding. In all thy ways acknowledge him, and he shall direct thy paths."* She not only quoted that, but she lived it.

I love football. I read the other day about the very successful football coach, Mike Holmgren. He was reflecting on a moment of deep frustration in his life. As a young quarterback, he was cut from the New York Jets. Now an outstanding coach, he explained that the disappointment of not making the team led him to a greater plan for his life. He said, "I had committed my life to Jesus Christ when I was 11, but in my pursuit to make a name for myself in football, I left God next to my dust-covered Bible. But after getting cut from the Jets, I pulled out my Bible and found comfort in a verse I had memorized in Sunday school: 'Trust in the Lord with all thine heart; and lean not unto thine own understanding. In all thy ways acknowledge him, and he shall direct thy paths.' I asked Jesus Christ to take control again. My priorities in life are faith, family, and football—in that order."

Those verses in Proverbs not only worked for my grandmother and Mike Holmgren, they are true for any of us. If we can just learn to trust God He will direct our paths. When disappointments come and we keep on trusting, He will secure the direction of our lives. If we trust Him God will get us where we're supposed to go.

I admit that trusting is still a challenge for me. God is invisible and I like to see what I'm trusting. A friend of mine, Sam Sasser, once gave an example of what I mean by the challenge of trusting God. He told of the Bailey family in Phoenix. They have a young daughter, Jill. A powerful thunderstorm shook the house one night and Jill cried out, "Mama!" Her mother was tired and said, "Sweetheart, go to sleep. Jesus is in there with you." Again the lightning flashed and thunder roared. Jill called out again, "Mama, please come in here." Her mother, intending to pacify her, said, "Honey, go to sleep. Jesus is in there with you." "Mama," the little girl pleaded once more, "you come in here with Jesus and let me go in your bedroom with Daddy."

Sometimes we find it easier to trust the Dad we see than the God we can't see. But, God is present. And, He is dependable. As Proverbs says, *"Trust in the Lord...."*

There is a caution, though, when it comes to trust. Be careful not to misplace it. Everywhere around me I see people who trust in individuals who will let them down. They trust in "things" that won't last. They risk disillusionment because they put their trust in objects that aren't trustworthy.

A United Press release in a Midwestern city reported the story of a hospital that underwent a safety check by local fire department officials. For 35 years the hospital staff had relied on their system of fire hoses to protect them in case of a fire. They knew that they and the patients were safe in case of an emergency. All they had to do was uncoil the water hoses and they could put out any fire. However, the inspectors discovered that the firefighting equipment had never been connected to the city's water main. The pipe that led from the building extended 4 feet underground—and there it stopped!

The medical staff and the patients had felt complete confidence in the system. They thought that if a blaze broke out, they could depend on a nearby hose to extinguish it. But, theirs was a false security. Although the costly equipment with its polished valves and well-placed outlets was impressive to see, it lacked the most important thing—water!

Again, Proverbs says, *"Trust in the Lord."* Don't place your trust in people or things that may fail. Place your trust in the Lord. Whether the stock market rises or falls, whether the Republicans, Democrats or Independents win the election, whether Iran does or doesn't get the big bomb, the Lord is in control and we can trust Him with our journey. He will direct our paths.

When the time comes that we need help, He is the only One trustworthy enough to deserve our full confidence. D. L. Moody was right when he said, "God never made a promise that was too good to be true." All God's promises are true and He is able to keep every one of them.

I learned a lesson about trusting God from one of those experiences that proves truth is stranger than fiction. In May 1995, Randy Reid, a 34-year-old construction worker, was welding on top of a nearly completed water tower outside Chicago. According to writer Melissa Ramsdell, Reid unhooked his safety gear to reach for some pipes when a metal cage slipped and bumped the scaffolding he stood on. The scaffolding tipped, and Reid lost his balance. He fell 110 feet, landing face down on a pile of dirt, just missing rocks and construction debris.

A fellow worker called 911 and, when the paramedics arrived, they found Reid conscious, moving, and complaining of a sore back. It was a miracle. As paramedics carried him on a backboard to the ambulance,

Reid had one request: "Don't drop me." Doctors later said Reid came away from the accident with just a bruised lung.

Sometimes I resemble Randy Reid. God has protected me from a 110-foot fall, but I get nervous about a three-foot drop. It is important for me to remember that the God who has saved my life from destruction, and has forgiven all my sins, can be trusted to safely see me through the challenges I face daily.

I can still hear my grandmother, who graduated to glory when she was 94 years old, encouraging the church with, *"Trust in the LORD with all thine heart; and lean not unto thine own understanding. In all thy ways acknowledge him, and he shall direct thy paths."*

17—Thank You

Rudyard Kipling at one time was so popular that his writings were getting ten shillings per word. A few college students, having learned that fact, facetiously sent him a letter enclosing ten shillings. It read, "Please, send us your best word." They got back a letter from Kipling. He had simply responded, "Thanks."

"Thanks" is a simple word, but it carries power. If you are wondering what you can be thankful for, just reflect for a moment. Each of us has many reasons to be thankful. One Sunday in a certain church, members were praising the Lord for what he had done in their lives that week. Mr. Segault had said that the roof of his house had caught on fire, but fortunately, a neighbor had seen it, and the possible disaster was averted with only minor damage. A minute later, a woman stood up. "I have a praise, too," she said. "I'm Mr. Segualt's insurance agent."

It is not easy growing up in today's world. Young people have challenges some of us older ones never had to face. Our culture has imposed so much political correctness on us that it even interferes with Thanksgiving. We could easily end up sounding like the fourth grader who, trying to be inoffensive in describing Thanksgiving said, "The pilgrims came here seeking freedom of you know what. When they landed, they gave thanks to you know who. Because of them, we can worship each Sunday, you know where."

The Bible says, in Psalm 100:4—*"Enter his gates with thanksgiving, and his courts with praise. Give thanks to him, bless his name."* Learning to be thankful is one of the first steps in coming into the presence of God. That was the spirit of the Pilgrims who had suffered through a terrible winter and seen the death of many of their companions.

According to Tom Olson in *Now* magazine, they were discussing their hardships and one person suggested that they set aside a special day for fasting and prayer. Another man stood up and said they had been dwelling too much on their problems. It was time, he emphasized, to focus on their blessings. The man pointed out that the colony was making good progress. The harvests were becoming more abundant. The streams were full of fish, and the forests provided plenty of game. But, more important than that, he reminded them that they now had what they had been seeking when they had left their homeland–freedom to worship. He recommended that instead of a day of fasting they have a day of thanksgiving!

We can be thankful even in the midst of adversity. David Seamands tells of a time when severe depression was affecting every family in America. In the worst of those days, the early 1930s, Seamands describes a conversation involving William Stidger. Stidger was seated one day with a group of friends in a restaurant and they were talking about the depression and how difficult circumstances were for everyone. People were suffering, the suicide rate was up and people couldn't find work. A preacher among them expressed his dilemma. He mentioned that he had to preach a Thanksgiving sermon in two or three weeks and he didn't know what to say that was affirmative.

Stidger said that he had an inspired thought as the preacher spoke: "Why don't you give thanks to those people who have been a blessing in your life and affirm them during this terrible time?"

When Stidger spoke those words, he thought of a schoolteacher who had taught English literature and had inspired him in ways that changed his life. So he sat down and wrote a letter to this woman who was now up in years.

A few days later he received a reply. "My Dear Willy: I can't tell you how much your note meant to me. I am in my eighties, living alone in a small room, cooking my own meals, lonely, and like the last leaf of autumn lingering behind. You'll be interested to know that I taught in school for more than fifty years, and yours is the first note of appreciation I ever received. It came on a blue, cold morning, and it cheered me as nothing has done in many years."

Stidger was so moved by that response that he thought of a kindly bishop, now retired, an old man whose wife had recently passed away, leaving him alone. This bishop had been there for him when he first began his ministry. He sat down and wrote a letter of gratitude to the old man. In two days a reply came back. "My Dear Will: Your letter was so beautiful, so real, that as I sat reading it in my study, tears fell from my eyes, tears of gratitude. Before I realized what I was doing, I rose from my chair and I called her name to share it with her, forgetting she was gone. You'll never know how much your letter has warmed my spirit. I have been walking around in the glow of your letter all day long."

Maybe God will drop a memory of someone in your heart. You never know what your gratitude may mean to him or her.

Of course, that is only one expression of being thankful. The Bible talks about coming into God's presence with thanksgiving. It reminds us that being thankful to Him is a key to our successful living. G. K. Chesterton pointed out, when writing about Christmas: "When we were children we were grateful to those who filled our stockings with toys at Christmastide. Why are we not grateful to God for filling our stockings with legs?"

Joel Gregory, a great preacher, drove home the meaning of Thanksgiving with this account: "One Thanksgiving season a family was seated around their table, looking at the annual holiday bird. From the oldest to the youngest, they were to express their praise. When they came to the 5-year-old in the family, he began by looking at the turkey and expressing his thanks to the turkey, saying that although he had not tasted it he knew it would be good.

"After that rather novel expression of thanksgiving, he began with a more predictable line of credits, thanking his mother for cooking the turkey and his father for buying the turkey. Then he went beyond that. He joined together a whole hidden multitude of benefactors, linking them with cause and effect. He said, 'I thank you for the checker at the grocery store who checked out the turkey. I thank you for the grocery store people who put it on the shelf. I thank you for the farmer who made it fat. I thank you for the man who made the feed. I thank you for those who brought the turkey to the store.' Using his Columbo-like little mind, he traced the turkey all the way from its origin to his plate. And then at the end he solemnly said 'Did I leave anybody out?' His 2-year-older brother, embarrassed by all those proceedings, said, 'God.' Solemnly and without being flustered at all, the 5-year-old said, 'I was about to get to him.' "

That is the crucial issue for each of us. With all the blessings God has given us are we going to get to Him this Thanksgiving? Take time to give thanks for the people in your life and, above all, give thanks to the One who gives us life.

18—Disappointments Can't Break You

Have you ever been disappointed? Either someone lets you down or circumstances don't work out the way you thought they would. A woman in Terre Haute, Indiana, called the local police station to report a skunk in her cellar. The police told the woman to make a trail of bread crumbs from the basement to the yard and to wait for the skunk to follow the line of crumbs outside. A little later the woman called back and said, "I did what you told me. Now I've got two skunks in my basement."

We have all experienced the truth of Proverbs 13:12, "*Hope deferred makes the heart sick.*" That kind of disappointment can touch every area of our lives. Jimmy Evans, teaching on marriage, points out that there once were three major causes of divorce: money, sex and power (or control). Now, however, the number one cause of divorce is none of those three. It is disappointment: "You're not who I thought you were."

One of the major causes of disappointment is promises that are not kept. A church choir director was being driven out of his mind at the rehearsals for the Christmas choral concert. It seemed that at least one or more members of the choir was absent at every rehearsal. Finally, they reached the last rehearsal and he announced: "I want to personally thank the pianist for being the only person in this entire church choir to attend each and every rehearsal during the past two months." At this, the pianist rose, bowed, and said, "It was the least I could do, considering I won't be able to be at the concert tonight."

Cartoonist Rob Portlock, in *Leadership Journal,* portrays a pastor making a Sunday morning announcement: "We have a special gift for a lady that hasn't missed a service in forty-five years. Eleanor Smith! Where is Eleanor sitting? Eleanor? Eleanor ..."

Not all occasions of disappointment, though, are due to someone intentionally breaking a promise. Sometimes circumstances beyond anyone's control interfere with our plans. That was the case in one of the most disappointing times of my life.

My dad had bone cancer. He lived two years with the disease. During the last year of Dad's life, we planned to ride Amtrak together to Oregon to see my sister, Rosalie, and my brother-in-law, Mac. Knowing how ill Dad had been I was looking forward to that time with him. In April of his last year, he went into remission. We went to a train station together, planning the trip in August. Then in August, when we thought we would be traveling to Oregon, Dad died. I not only was broken up by his death, but I felt that my last chance to be with him without distractions was stolen. It wasn't Dad's fault. The circumstances were beyond his control.

Here is the problem with disappointments. They can color our outlook on life, and can even change the way we see God.

Jimmy Harris said, "A cynic is not merely one who reads bitter lessons from the past; he is one who is prematurely disappointed in the future."

I have met any number of people who have allowed their disappointments to color their view of God. They see God as an extension of people who are either short on commitment or are short on the power to control things.

Here is the good news. God is faithful. I have often been encouraged by Paul's words to the Corinthians, *"God, who has called you into fellowship with his Son Jesus Christ our Lord, is faithful"* (1 Corinthians 1:9). When I face my weaknesses, whether those weaknesses are character issues I have or are just my powerlessness in the face of events, I am encouraged to know that my destiny rests on the faithfulness of God.

That doesn't mean, of course, that I have no responsibility. I do. But, it does mean that while I am growing in faith and obedience God's faithfulness protects me. As the psalmist says, *"His faithfulness will be your shield"* (Psalm 91:4).

When I understand the faithfulness of God I can rise above every past circumstance that left me disappointed. I can take His promises seriously and can put my life and my future in His hands.

William Penn, the founder of the commonwealth of Pennsylvania, was well liked by the Indians. Once they told him he could have as much of their land as he could encompass on foot in a single day. So, early the next morning he started out and walked until late that night. When he finally went to claim his land, the Indians were greatly surprised, for they really didn't think he would take them seriously. But, they kept their promise and gave him a large area which today is part of the city of Philadelphia. William Penn simply believed what they said. If William Penn found the Indians to be faithful to their words, I can certainly expect God to be faithful to His.

Moses pointed that out to Israel a long time ago: *"God is not a man, that he should lie, nor a son of man, that he should change his mind. Does he speak and then not act? Does he promise and not fulfill?"* (Numbers 23:19). If God said it, His character stands behind it. He is in control of circumstances and will never have to say, "I never saw that coming." He not only intends to fulfill His Word, He is able to fulfill His Word.

God's commitment to us is more extensive than most of us imagine. Author and business leader Fred Smith wrote about an experience that helps us understand this. He wrote, "One of my treasured memories comes from a doughnut shop in Grand Saline, Texas. There was a young farm couple sitting at the table next to mine. He was wearing overalls and she a gingham dress. After finishing their doughnuts, he got up to pay the bill, and I noticed she didn't get up to follow him.

"But then he came back and stood in front of her. She put her arms around his neck, and he lifted her up, revealing that she was wearing a full-body brace. He lifted her out of her chair and backed out the front door to the pickup truck, with her hanging from his neck. As he gently put her into the truck, everyone in the shop watched. No one said anything until a waitress remarked, almost reverently, 'He took his vows seriously.' "

God takes His vows seriously. The apostle Paul wrote to Timothy: *"If we are faithless, he will remain faithful"* (2 Timothy 2:13). When I am weak, and even when my faith is weak, He is faithful. We can depend on that.

19—God Makes It Work Out Right

Have you ever wondered how God could run the universe and still keep track of your life? As students entered the lunch line at Asbury Theological Seminary in Wilmore, Kentucky, they were greeted by a sign over the bowl of apples that read: "Take only one apple. God is watching you." At the other end of the line there was a large pan of cookies with a hastily written sign reading: "Take as many cookies as you want. God is back watching the apples." Many individuals struggle with the mistaken notion that God can't watch the cookies and the apples at the same time.

Gwen and I attended a conference a few years ago at which Bob Mumford was speaking. He described his desire to have God direct every action of his life. He explained that he was standing in front of his closet one morning and, in his sincere desire to obey God, prayed, "God what would you like me to wear today." He told us that God responded, "Wear what you want to wear. I'm your Father, not your mother."

God gives us the freedom to make our own choices. He may not care which shirt I wear, but He has promised to watch over me and use the choices I make to help me become the person He wants me to be.

Life can seem crazy at times, but the underlying truth for every believer is that God is at work in our lives. He is working in things that we call coincidences as well as in the circumstances that clearly reveal His activity. When He brings healing or salvation to someone there is no doubting that He is at work. But, what about the times we are interrupted by an unplanned meeting, or are delayed by a traffic jam? Romans 8:28 gives us an answer. The New Living Translation puts it this way: *"And we know that God causes everything to work together for the good of those who love God and are called according to his purpose for them."* This means, among other things, that when I put my faith in Jesus God begins to work for my good in everything that happens to me. God is causing everything to work for my good—whether or not I understand it at the time.

Harry Emerson Fosdick once pointed out that Whistler, the artist, started out to be a soldier and failed at West Point because he could not pass chemistry. "If silicon had been a gas," Whistler used to say, "I should have been a major-general." It is amazing how God can even use our failures to get us where He wants us to go.

Many of us could testify to the fact that our lives have often been shaped by what seemed at the time to be a chance event. Late one evening a professor sat at his desk working on the next day's lectures. He shuffled through the papers and mail placed there by his housekeeper. He began to throw them in the wastebasket when one magazine—not even addressed to him but delivered to his office by mistake—caught his attention. The magazine fell open to an article titled "The Needs of the Congo Mission."

As the professor read the article, he was touched by the words, "The need is great here. We have no one to work the northern province of Gabon in the central Congo. And it is my prayer as I write this article that God will lay His hand on one—one on whom, already, the Master's eyes have been cast—that he or she shall be called to this place to help us." The professor closed the magazine and wrote in his diary: "My search is over." He committed the rest of his life to the Congo. The professor's name was Albert Schweitzer. His life was changed by an article intended for someone else. A coincidence? Hardly.

God's hand can be seen in our lives if we stop to evaluate those things that we, at first, don't understand. Isn't it amazing how many "coincidences" turn out to be God's guidance? Accidents don't happen to God's children. Romans 8:28 reminds me that God is causing *everything* to work for my good if I love Him and am called to His purpose for my life.

A few years ago, I read a story by Chery Stewart that graphically displays the truth of Romans 8:28. She wrote of her grandfather, a godly man who lived during the Great Depression. Grandpa Nybakken was a carpenter and one day was building some crates for his church. The crates were needed so the church could ship clothes they had collected to an orphanage in China. After building the crates he helped others fill them with clothing and then he nailed them shut.

Having finished his work at the church he left for home. As he was driving away from the church he reached into his shirt pocket to find his glasses, only to discover that they were missing. Certain that he had put his glasses in his pocket that morning, he thought back through the day's events. Then he realized what had happened. As he had leaned over and finished packing one of the crates his glasses must have fallen out of his pocket. Now those glasses were on their way to China!

He was upset. He had just spent twenty dollars for those glasses that morning. The Great Depression was at its height and he had six children. Twenty dollars was a lot of money to spend and now he was going to have to buy another pair. He actually complained to God as he drove home, "It's not fair. I have been working for You and in the process lost my glasses."

Several months later, the director of the orphanage was on furlough in the United States. He wanted to visit all the churches that supported him in China, so he came to speak one Sunday night at Grandpa Nybakken's church in Chicago. The missionary began by thanking the people for their faithfulness in supporting the orphanage. "But most of all," he said, "I must thank you for the glasses you sent last year. You see, the Communists had just swept through the orphanage destroying everything, including my glasses. I was desperate. Even if I had the money, there was simply no way of replacing those glasses. Along with not being able to see well, I experienced headaches every day. Then your crates arrived. When my staff removed the covers, they found a pair of glasses lying on top. Folks, when I tried on the glasses, it was as though they had been custom-made just for me! I want to thank you for being part of that."

Most of the congregation that night thought the missionary had confused them with another church. Eyeglasses weren't on the list of things they had packed for the orphanage in China. But, Grandpa Nybakken knew better. Everything now made sense. God was working in the accidental loss of his glasses to accomplish a miracle for a missionary thousands of miles away.

In all the unexplainable occurrences of our lives, we as believers can live in the confidence that God is causing everything to work for our good. God is working for us and not against us. If we will just love Him and live for His purposes He can handle all the details of our lives.

20—A Savior Has Been Born

Christmas means different things to different people. For many there's some confusion about its significance. From shopping to Christmas cards, it's easy to get lost in the details. I heard of a woman who went to the Post Office to buy stamps for her Christmas cards. She said to the clerk, "May I have 50 Christmas stamps?" The clerk asked, "What denomination?" The woman responded in alarm, "God help us. Has it come to this? Give me 6 Catholic, 12 Presbyterian, 10 Lutheran and 22 Baptists."

Linda Stafford said that one of the proudest moments of her life was when her young son had the role of a wise man in the Christmas play. When it was his turn to speak his line he stepped forward wearing a bathrobe and a paper crown and announced, "We are three wise men, and we are bringing gifts of gold, common sense and fur."

Most of us have Christmas memories. My memories of Christmas are filled with all the trappings I love—the lights, the decorated trees and the carols. I remember the chemistry set my parents gave me, and I remember all of us standing outside the house in the cold that Christmas morning because the directions for creating a "Rotten Egg Smell" worked.

Gwen and I will never forget the one trip we made to the Holy Land. On one of the evenings we went to a field outside Bethlehem. There, where the shepherds first heard the Christmas message, we listened as the story of Jesus' birth was retold. It was impossible to look up at the sky that night and not imagine what it would have been like for those shepherds who saw the evening sky light up with angels declaring that a Savior had been born.

Luke recorded the message that changed the world: *"But the angel said to them, 'Do not be afraid. I bring you good news of great joy that will be for all the people. Today in the town of David a Savior has been born to you; he is Christ the Lord' "* (Luke 2:10-11).

"Good news of great joy...for all the people." What an interesting way to describe Jesus' birth. In many cases, what is good news for one group of people is not good news for others. The next time you watch a football game, notice the different reactions of the fans. Those supporting the winning team are celebrating the news of victory, but those who cheered for the losing team are despondent. Christmas is not like that. It is good news for all the people.

Religious people of Jesus' day had a list of undesirable occupations. Shepherds were on that list. Religious leaders regarded shepherds with contempt and considered them ceremonially unclean. They couldn't keep rules like washing their hands before they ate. Regarded as outcasts by their society, the angels went out of their way to let these isolated and misunderstood shepherds know that a Savior had been born.

Later, Simeon would discover the infant Jesus in the Temple. Simeon never missed church and had a vital relationship with God. The good news of Christmas is for all the people. Whether we grew up attending church or have never been inside church doors, the good news is that Jesus has come to be a Savior for each of us. And, we all need a Savior.

No matter what our background may be, when we come to Christmas, something about it makes us stop and think. An old pioneer traveled westward across the great plains until he came to an abrupt halt at the edge of the Grand Canyon. He gawked at the sight before him: a vast gorge one mile down, eighteen miles across, and more than a hundred miles long! He gasped, "Something musta happened here!" A visitor to our world at Christmas time, seeing the lights, the decorations, the trees, the parades, the festivities, and the religious services, would also probably say, "Something musta happened here!"

Something did happen. God came to our world on the first Christmas. He came for shepherds, wise men, worshipers and sinners. We couldn't reach Him so God came to us. That is good news for everyone.

I read about a Catholic church in San Francisco. The priest went outside the church on December 26 and noticed that the "infant Jesus" was missing from the manger scene. While he was pondering what might have happened to baby Jesus, a little boy came down the sidewalk pulling a red wagon. In the wagon was the baby from the Nativity scene. The small boy explained, "A week before Christmas I prayed to the little Lord Jesus and I told him if he would send me a red wagon for Christmas I'd give him a ride."

On reflection, I am reminded that every good gift I have ever gotten can be traced back to the little Lord Jesus who came long ago. I can't give Him a ride in my red wagon, but I can pause during this holiday season and say, "Thank you for Christmas, Jesus. You're the best gift anyone could ever receive."

21–Who Do You Belong To?

Many of us have, at one time or other, faced a sense of our own inadequacy with a corresponding feeling that we are not valuable to God or anyone else. This feeling can be rooted in our childhood. For example, a young aspiring pitcher knew he was in trouble when the Little League coach approached the mound and said, "Son, I think I'd better have someone relieve you." "But," the pitcher argued, "I struck this guy out last time." "I know," said the coach emphatically, "but this is the same inning."

The Bible teaches that, whether we can pitch well or can't pitch well, we are valuable to God. Philip Yancey, in his book, *The Bible Jesus Read*, explains that truth. He describes the woman at the well in Samaria as "a half-breed woman who had gone through five husbands already and was no doubt the center of the town's gossip industry." He points out that Jesus made her His first missionary. He continues, "Another woman, too full of shame over her embarrassing condition to approach Jesus face to face, grabbed his robe, hoping He would not notice. He did notice. She learned, like so many other 'nobodies,' that you can't easily escape Jesus' gaze. We matter too much." Every one of us matters to God.

When a few of us knew that God wanted us to plant a church on the Outer Banks of North Carolina, we also knew that it was important to give it a name that accurately reflected its purpose. The Scripture God used to mark our church is 1 Peter 2:9–*"But you are a chosen people, a royal priesthood, a holy nation, a people belonging to God, that you may declare the praises of him who called you out of darkness into his wonderful light."* That verse not only announced our church's purpose, but it gave our church its name, OBX Nation.

That one short verse tells us who we are and how valuable we are to God. We have been chosen, we are a holy nation and we belong to God. If you've ever visited a museum, you've observed how valuable simple things can be because they belonged to someone famous. Benjamin Franklin's eyeglasses, which would be very inadequate by today's standards, have great value because Franklin once wore them.

After the lead guitar player for the Grateful Dead, Jerry Garcia, died some of his memorabilia was sold at auction. A cream-colored 1975 Travis Bean electric guitar he had owned sold for $312,000. All together, the Grateful Dead memorabilia sold for $1.2 million. One of Garcia's guitar straps sold for $20,400. His flight case filled with guitar picks, strings and other accessories sold for $16,800. That's a lot of money for a guitar and various accessories, but their worth was established by the fact that they had belonged to Jerry Garcia.

Ordinary things can have great value because of the person who owns them. We, as believers, are owned by God. That makes us more important than we can imagine, no matter how ordinary we feel. Don't allow the devil to run you down. Don't demean yourself. Learn to say about yourself what God says about you. You are chosen, you are royal in God's eyes and you are His possession. You belong to Him.

So, since that is true, what are we supposed to do? We are to declare His praise. The reason God has chosen us is, first, to get us into a right relationship with Himself. He wants us to be His people. Secondly, he wants us to show others how wonderful His is.

It is our privilege to declare to the world how loving and gracious God is. We don't have to be expert theologians and we don't have to master every mystery of the Bible before we talk about Him. He has called us "out of darkness into his wonderful light" and that is enough to give us credibility when we speak about Him to others.

Jim Elliot was martyred in 1956. He was trying to reach the Auca Indians of South America for Jesus Christ. Three years earlier, he had watched an Indian die in a hut and had told God he was willing to die to reach this tribe. He prayed Psalm 71:18 before he was killed. *"Do not forsake me, O God, till I declare your power to the next generation, your might to all who are to come."* Within three years of his death he was known all over the world and his journals were inspiring thousands.

When we commit ourselves to telling others about Him, God will assist us. A Christian in Kentucky tells about a method they used at his church to get people to come to the meetings. Having prepared cards that read, "Get right with God," they gave them to a group of newsboys who attached them to their caps. One day a strange bulldog come along and made friends with these boys. One of the boys ran to the man with the cards and asked for one so he could attach it to the dog. He then fastened the card to the nameplate on the dog's collar.

In the meantime, the people of the church had been praying for a certain man, but had been unsuccessful in getting him to attend church. That night he came to the meeting, and as soon as an invitation was given, went to the front of the church and opened his heart to Jesus.

When asked what had brought about this change, he told an interesting story. He said, "I was not feeling well today, so remained at home from work. I was trying to get some sleep this afternoon, when I was disturbed by a fierce and prolonged barking at the rear of our house. I finally decided to go and see what it was all about. As I opened the rear door, in bounded a fierce, ugly-looking bulldog, entirely strange to our neighborhood. At first I was somewhat frightened by the beast, but soon discovered that he was friendly. So I sat down in a chair, and he immediately and lovingly came and put his big head in my lap. There, staring me in the face, attached to his collar, was one of those 'Get right with God' cards. I decided that if God loved me enough to send that bulldog after me, I'd better give up; and here I am."

When we decide to tell others about Jesus, He will help our methods work—even if our efforts involve a bulldog and a simple card.

I was channel surfing several years ago and I came to C-Span. I don't usually watch that channel. It's mostly boring. However, the station that day was televising Barbara Jordan's funeral. I was immediately captivated by D. Z. Cofield's sermon. I listened to his entire message. I have never forgotten one of his statements: "Some people spend their lives climbing the ladder of success only to find when they get to the top that it's leaning against the wrong building."

If we belong to God, let's spend our lives telling others about His goodness. That ladder is leaning against the right building. That is successful living.

22–A Bumper Crop

There is something exciting about a new year. It hasn't been clouded by failure, frustration or disappointment. A new year is filled with promise because God's Word cannot fail. A few years ago I listened to a radio preacher who flew his own airplane describe what it was like to fly over the Gulf of Mexico from South America. He explained that there would be a long stretch of time over the gulf in which there was no radio communication and, at night, no lights. He described the joy with which he would see the lights of Houston. For those who spent some time in their past in the dark, it is thrilling to see lights on the horizon. It means we are closer to our destination.

In my devotional reading this week, I came to a passage of Scripture that leaped out to me. It was as if God said, "This is My promise to you." The passage is Psalm 107:35-37 (NLT) *"But he also turns deserts into pools of water, the dry land into flowing springs. He brings the hungry to settle there and build their cities. They sow their fields, plant their vineyards, and harvest their bumper crops."*

The promise is for anyone who has been going through a dry spell. The dry land of our lives will be refreshed with flowing springs. I love the way the New Living Translation puts it, *"They...harvest their bumper crops."* If you have been waiting for a bumper crop of blessing, get ready.

Don't treat the promises of God the way Crowfoot, the great chief of the Blackfoot confederacy in southern Alberta, Canada treated the railroad pass he was given. When he gave the Canadian Pacific Railroad permission to cross the Blackfoot land from Medicine Hat to Calgary, he was given in return a lifetime railroad pass. Crowfoot put it in a leather case and carried it around his neck for the rest of his life. There is no record, however, that he ever availed himself of the right to travel anywhere on the Canadian Pacific Railroad. God's promises are not meant to be ornaments we wear proudly, they are to be enjoyed.

We can depend on God to keep His promises to us. When I was young, my father drove my mother, my sister and me to Los Angeles from Virginia several times. It was a grueling trip, with no Interstate highways. We slept in the car while Dad drove. He went on very little sleep, since we didn't have the money to stop in motels. He would travel on about two hours sleep each night until we got to California.

Since we went through Northern Arizona, I pleaded with him one year to take me to Tombstone. I was captivated by the story of Wyatt Earp and the OK Corral and wanted desperately to visit the scene of the action. I didn't know anything about maps apparently, because when I look back I realize it would be equivalent of going from North Carolina to Miami by way of Washington, DC. I had no understanding of the stress it would put on Dad physically, or the cost of the extra gasoline when he was traveling on a very limited budget. I just wanted to see Tombstone. Dad promised that he would take me there the next time we went to California.

He did it. We walked the streets of Tombstone, saw pictures of the members of the Clanton gang who had died there and toured Boot Hill. I'll never forget that visit. More than that, I'll never forget the father who went out of his way to keep his promise to me.

Vic Pentz tells of an experience he had with Nordstrom's department store. He says, "About a year and a half ago, I bought a new navy blazer at Nordstrom. It was one of those cases you may have gone through where you buy an item of clothing and the more you wear it, the more you realize you don't like it. My blazer wasn't the right color, and to make matters worse, it attracted lint like it was going out of style. After wearing it pretty regularly for six months or so, I stuck it in my closet and didn't wear it for a long time.

"Tucked away in the back of my mind all the while was that famous Nordstrom unconditional-return policy. I thought, I've had this thing for a year and a half. I've worn it lots of times, and there's just no way they're going to take it back. About two weeks ago I decided I had nothing to lose. I pulled the blazer out, threw a lot of lint on it to make it look bad, and took it down to Nordstrom's men's department. I walked in, and immediately I felt nervous. I felt like I was about to pull a scam of some sort, but I played it straight. I walked right up to the first salesman I saw and gave this little prepared speech. I said, 'I am about to put your famous unconditional-return policy to its ultimate test. I have here a blazer. I've worn it lots. I've had it for a year and a half. I don't like it. It's the wrong color, and it attracts lint like it's going out of style. But I want to return this blazer for another blazer that I like.'

"Then I stood there. I couldn't believe it. This guy with a big handlebar mustache just looked at me and shook his head. He said, 'For heaven's sake, what took you so long? Let's go find you a blazer.' Ten minutes later I walked out with another blazer that was marked seventy-five dollars more than I paid for the one that I brought in. It was perfect for me. Didn't cost me a penny."

Pentz came to this conclusion: "God is like Nordstrom. God makes all sorts of outlandish promises that we cannot bring ourselves to believe. Can we? When we get up enough courage or we're desperate enough, we finally take Him at his word. He looks at us and he shakes His head. 'For heaven's sake,' He says, 'what took you so long?' "

We have a heavenly Father who will do whatever is necessary to keep His promises to us. Don't take so long to trust Him. He will keep every promise He has made to you. God's promise to us is still the same. God wants us to enjoy "bumper crops" of blessing. We can take Him at His Word. It's better than money in the bank.

23—Never Give Up

We don't exactly know what the future holds for us, but we do know one thing. We can never be defeated if we don't quit. Paul explained it to the Corinthian church this way: *"We are pressed on every side by troubles, but we are not crushed and broken. We are perplexed, but we don't give up and quit. We are hunted down, but God never abandons us. We get knocked down, but we get up again and keep going"* (2 Corinthians 4:8-9 NLT).

A prized characteristic of believers is unquenchable optimism. A salesman saw a young boy trying unsuccessfully to sell a puppy and felt sorry for him. He told the boy the problem was that he didn't think big enough. He needed to raise the price. The next time he drove by the boy had put up a sign, "Puppy–$5,000." Two days later the sign was gone. The salesman was curious about what had happened and stopped to inquire. He said to the young boy, "I never thought you'd sell the puppy at that price." "It was easy," said the boy, "I traded him for two $2500 cats."

Larry Olsen describes optimism. In his *Outdoor Survivor Skills,* he tells of a guy who has been lost in the desert for days. He's out of food and water. His lips are parched and his tongue is swollen. His legs are bruised and bleeding from crawling, his skin is scorched by the sun, bitten by insects, and pricked by cactus thorns. As he pulls himself over the next sand dune, he sees nothing but more wasteland through his bloodshot, sand-peppered eyes. He sighs, "You know, a few more days of this, and I might get discouraged."

There is nothing in our future that can defeat us if we have the confidence that comes from faith in God. When I was in seminary one of our professors, whose family lived in the Soviet Union, said that the favorite book in the Bible for Russian believers was Revelation. I was surprised by that, because I have read the book and have come away with more than a few questions. Put any one hundred

Christians together and we are likely to have one hundred interpretations of some of the difficult passages. When pressed as to why the book was so popular, the professor explained that Revelation was a comforting assurance that Jesus wins at the end of history. Russian Christians needed to hear that—and so do we.

That is the secret, of course, of Christian optimism. The optimism of faith is not our effort to escape reality, it is our recognition that Jesus is in control of the universe no matter what is going on in our lives at any given time.

How does that kind of faith make sense when things are going badly? In her book, *The Hiding Place*, Corrie ten Boom tells about an incident that taught her a major lesson about the life of faith. It was during World War II. Corrie and her sister, Betsy, had been harboring Jewish people in their home, so they were arrested and imprisoned at the Ravensbruck Concentration Camp. The building in which they lived was extremely crowded with people and infested with fleas. One morning they read in their tattered Bible from 1 Thessalonians. In the passage, they read Paul challenged Christians to rejoice in all things.

Betsy said, "Corrie, we've got to give thanks for this barracks and even for these fleas." Corrie replied, "No way am I going to thank God for fleas." But, Betsy was persuasive, and they did thank God, even for the fleas. During the months that followed, they found that their building was left relatively free, and they could do Bible study, talk openly and even pray there. It was their only place of refuge. Several months later they learned that the reason the guards never entered their barracks was because of those blasted fleas.

God is in control even when our circumstances don't make sense. As Paul said, "We are perplexed, but we don't give up and quit. We are hunted down, but God never abandons us." We can face the future with faith and confidence because we serve a God who will never abandon us. He has a destiny and a purpose for each of us and He will enable us to reach our destinations.

I enjoy watching golf. Gwen says it's as exciting as watching grass grow, but I love it. When you've lost as many golf balls as I have lost it isn't hard to appreciate the skill of the men and women who actually know where the ball is going to go before they hit it.

One of the players I have enjoyed watching is Calvin Peete. I didn't know his story, but I admired the fact that this African-American was on the PGA tour and was having a successful career. Later, I learned that Calvin Peete is an outspoken Christian. He grew up in central Florida where his family picked vegetables. Calvin had a dream—to be a professional golfer. His friends laughed at his dream. In the eighth grade, Calvin found it necessary to drop out of school and go into the fields to help his family earn a living. But, he always felt God intended more for him than picking vegetables.

Calvin took up the game as an adult. He not only had the disadvantage of beginning golf at a late age, but he had to play with a left arm that wouldn't straighten out to full extension—the result of a broken elbow when he was a child. Because it wasn't set properly, it remained crooked for his entire career. Professional golfers would say it's impossible to play golf without an extended left arm. But, within six months he was shooting below 80. Eighteen months later, he was shooting below par and joined the mini-tour in Florida. In 1975, he qualified for the PGA tour—the oldest rookie ever, at age 35. With twelve wins on the PGA Tour, he was the winningest African-American golfer until Tiger Woods came on the scene. That's quite impressive company.

Calvin maintained a strong faith in God. "It's been a long road from the fields to the fairways," Calvin says. "One a lot of people said was impossible. But, you see, I knew something maybe they didn't. That God had a plan for me—but I had to be willing to work at it. When you work hard and pray hard, you have a combination that can take you places you've never imagined."

That's some pretty good advice for all of us this year. Work hard, pray hard and watch where God will take us. That, by the way, is the optimism that comes with faith—believing that if we don't quit God will get us where He wants us to go.

24—Hope

My wife, Gwen, introduced me to her favorite Scripture and now it is one of mine. In Paul's letter to the Romans he said, *"May the God of hope fill you with all joy and peace as you trust in him, so that you may overflow with hope by the power of the Holy Spirit"* (15:13). What a way to face life! We can overflow with hope by the power of the Holy Spirit.

Some people seem to be natural optimists. There was a personal notice in the Flint, Michigan, *Weekly Review* that reflected someone's optimism: "Barbershop quartet forming; need bass, baritone and tenor." The author of that ad was apparently an incurable optimist. But natural optimism isn't enough when circumstances are difficult. The Holy Spirit is available to us no matter what life is like. Isn't it good to know that we have a supernatural source of hope for our tough times?

I know a little bit about hope. I loved my time in Bible College, but there were occasions when I would be frustrated by the endless parade of tests, written papers and homework. Sometimes I would feel like quitting. When those times came, I would travel a short distance to Limerick Chapel and listen to an outstanding preacher, Dr. Diddon. His church was in a converted factory in Limerick, Pennsylvania. The building wasn't spectacular, but hundreds of people would flock to it to hear him preach. On Sunday evenings, he would preach through the New Testament. I would sit spellbound and think, "That's who I want to be someday." His ministry gave me hope and kept me going.

Biblical hope is not wishful thinking. It is based on concrete reality. Gwen and I recently went away for three days to one of my favorite spots in the world, Ocracoke Island. We drove to Hatteras village to catch the ferry to Ocracoke and, just as we had hoped, the ferry was there. We crossed the inlet as we have done several times before and, amazingly, the island was still there. Our hope was based on reality. So is our hope as Christians. Christian hope is more than, "I hope I win the lottery." Christian hope is based on the truth that we have a loving God Who is willing to secure our future no matter what surprises we face along the way.

William Sangster, the great English pastor, explained the lasting power of our hope. He read in his local newspaper that some Radium was lost in a London hospital. They found it with a Geiger counter. It had gone through an incinerator and was still sending out its rays. Our hope is like that. When it comes from the Holy Spirit, the fires of affliction cannot put it out.

I must confess that our hope is often a mystery to others. We smile no matter what is happening. We are confident in the midst of adversity. That makes us seem strange to those who don't know our source of hope.

One of our favorite groups of people is the people of Scotland. They are both hardy and friendly. We have many good friends who are Scottish. One of their stories I love comes from the days when they were constantly at war with the English. The English army was besieging a Scottish castle. They sent word to the Scots, asking if the Scots were ready to surrender. They were certain that they were starving out the inhabitants of the castle. In reply, the Scots draped a string of fresh fish over the wall. They had found an underground passage to the sea and were eating fresh fish while the English army was living on rations. The English gave up. We, as believers, are like those Scots. No matter how surrounded we seem, we have hope which links our lives to heaven's resources.

Jamie Buckingham wrote an article in *Charisma* magazine in which he quoted Hugo Gryn, a London rabbi. Gryn had described, in the German magazine *Der Morgen*, a holocaust experience:

"It was the cold winter of 1944 and although we had nothing like calendars, my father who was a fellow prisoner there, took me and some of our friends to a corner of the barrack. He announced it was the eve of Hanukkah, produced a curious-shaped clay bowl, and began to light a wick immersed in his precious, but now melted, margarine ration. Before he could recite the blessing, I protested at this waste of food. He said, 'You and I have seen that it is possible to live up to three weeks without food. We once lived almost three days without water. But you cannot live properly for three minutes without hope.' "

If you are struggling with low levels of hope remember that Paul, in Romans, called God "the God of hope." Remember that you can "overflow with hope by the power of the Holy Spirit." Thankfully, we aren't left to depend on our own resources and we don't have to struggle to keep our chins up. God provides hope just as much as He provides salvation.

Maybe we wonder from time to time about what awaits us after death. To face eternity with hope is a blessing that comes with faith in Christ. John Ortberg, in his book *If You Want to Walk on Water, You've Got to Get Out of the Boat*, wrote of an interesting incident. He says, "I read recently about a woman who had been diagnosed with cancer and was given three months to live. Her doctor told her to make preparations to die, so she contacted her pastor and told him how she wanted things arranged for her funeral service—which songs she wanted to have sung, what Scriptures should be read, what words should be spoken—and that she wanted to be buried with her favorite Bible.

"But before he left, she called out to him, 'One more thing.' 'What?' he asked. 'This is important. I want to be buried with a fork in my right hand.' The pastor did not know what to say. No one had ever made such a request before. So she explained. 'In all my years going to church functions, whenever food was involved, my favorite part was when whoever was cleaning dishes of the main course would lean over and say, You can keep your fork.' It was my favorite part because I knew that it meant something great was coming. It wasn't Jell-O. It was something with substance—cake or pie—biblical food. So I just want people to see me there in my casket with a fork in my hand, and I want them to wonder, 'What's with the fork?' Then I want you to tell them, 'Something better is coming. Keep your fork.' "

What insight! I can say with confidence to anyone (and often have to say it to myself) something better is coming. Keep your fork.

25—God's Word

I love the Bible. Sometimes I read parts of it that cut deeply, but that's because I need the surgery. At other times, it is the healing ointment that cures me where I have been wounded. It is so dependable that any of us can take what it says as absolute truth. It is remarkable to me that God has given us, in His Word, an unvarying standard. Our world changes from day to day, but God's Word never changes. It belongs to the ages.

For some the Bible is a trophy to be admired, but not to be read or obeyed. A pastor called on a family and listened to the lady of the house describe her problems. He suggested that she get her Bible so he could read some Scripture to her. Wanting to impress the pastor, she called to her daughter, "Darling, bring mother that old book she loves so much." The daughter entered with the *TV Guide*.

Thankfully, the Bible is easy to understand. There are parts of it that challenge Bible scholars, but the essential truths about who God is and how we can please Him are made clear. If the Bible could not be understood it wouldn't be of much use to us. Rebecca Self, from New Mexico, tells a story about her young son. They were visiting a church and the minister announced they had both Spanish and English Bibles for use during the service. Her youngest son tugged at her sleeve and whispered, "Mommy, I want one of those Spanish Bibles." "Don't be silly, you can't read Spanish," she quickly responded. Holding out his own Bible to his mom, the kindergartner explained, "Mom, I can't read English either."

I grew up in church. The teachers in charge of explaining the Bible to children (God bless them!) taught us to memorize a few Scriptures. I memorized Psalm 119:105 in the King James Version, and it has been a standby for me through many years and experiences: *"Thy word is a lamp unto my feet, and a light unto my path."* It is dangerous to walk or drive in the dark. It is even more dangerous to live without reference to God's Word.

The time we spend with God's Word can be the most profitable time of any day. It refreshes us, challenges us, encourages and informs us. It is, in fact, God's love letter to us. It speaks of real people with real problems who can find solutions to every crisis in life through God's willingness to communicate with us through His Word.

The importance of spending a lot of time with God's Word is illustrated by a quote from the *National Geographic* magazine about Carl Sharsmith, an 81 year old guide in Yosemite National Park. "Carl was back at his tent quarters after a long afternoon with tourists. His nose was flaked white and red with sunburn; his eyes were watery, partly from age but also from hearing again an old question after a half century of summers in California's Yosemite National Park. A lady tourist had hit him with a question where it hurt: 'I've only got an hour to spend at Yosemite,' she declared. 'What should I do? Where should I go?'

"The old naturalist-interpreter-ranger finally found voice to reply. 'Ah, lady, only an hour.' He repeated it slowly. 'I suppose that if I had only an hour to spend at Yosemite, I'd just walk over there by the river and sit down and cry.' "

A whole lifetime is not long enough to appreciate fully the beauty, learning, and value of the Bible. That's why we must take time to study its truths and make them real in our lives.

I can't begin to describe the number of times when I am reading some passage in the Bible and God begins to whisper His thoughts to me. I see answers to issues I am facing. I am reminded of truths I have neglected. I sense once more how loved I am in spite of my faults and weaknesses.

Scott Harrison shared an experience in *Daily Guideposts* that expresses how I feel about time with God's Word: "Sam was my best dog, ever. A field trial dog who found birds and pointed them with contagious enthusiasm, Sam taught me the joy of becoming part of nature. If his point said a bird was hiding in a clump of bushes, it was there. He was so much more than a bird dog, though. Often we'd share together lazy lunches in an abandoned apple orchard, and the snooze that followed.

"Late one afternoon, Sam and I became separated. Neither of us was familiar with the area. I called and whistled. No sign of Sam. I had to get back to town for an important appointment. But how could I leave Sam? If he finally came back and I wasn't there, would I lose him for good? Then I remembered a trick an old dog trainer had passed on. I unbuttoned my jacket, removed my shirt and laid it on the ground under the branches of a small bush.

"I worried all night. But when I returned the next morning there was Sam curled up with his nose under the sleeve of my shirt. He looked up and wagged his tail. 'Where've you been friend?' his eyes seemed to say. 'I've been waiting for you all night. But I knew you'd come back.' Later I wondered. When I get lost, do I have the trust to look for some part of God's word and curl up in it? To wait patiently, knowing that my Friend will find me if I just have faith in him"

I love that thought. We can curl up with God's Word and He will meet us there.

When I want to give up His Word encourages me to persevere. When I am discouraged, His Word gives me courage. When my faith falters, His Word helps me believe again. When I feel inadequate, His Word tells me of His great power at work in me. When I am broken, His Word repairs me. When I don't know what to do His Word is a *"lamp unto my feet and a light unto my path."*

A small factory had to cease operations when a vital piece of machinery broke down. The firm's own mechanics couldn't get it working again so an outside expert was called in. He looked the situation over for a couple of minutes and then took a hammer and tapped the machine in a certain spot. It started running beautifully. When he submitted a bill for $100 the plant owner figuratively hit the ceiling and demanded an itemized bill. The expert submitted the following: "$1.00 for hitting machine; $99.00 for knowing where to hit it." God uses His Word to "hit" us where we need fixing.

Don't neglect your Bible. It will not only light your way in this life, its truth will last through eternity.

26—Grace

My mother's father lived until his late sixties. Most of my life was spent separated from him. He and my grandmother were divorced before I was born. He loved my mom but we weren't close. Most of my grandfather's years were spent not only living apart from us, but also living apart from God. He wasn't a bad man, he was a good man (very successful in many ways) but he didn't have time for God.

When he was in his sixties he came to faith in Christ, attended a Presbyterian church in east Tennessee and taught a Sunday School class. It was an amazing turn-around. My parents sent me to spend some time with him in the summer because we wanted to make up for lost time in the relationship. He had married a very sweet woman and it was great being with them. I still remember Saturday night when Granddaddy was getting ready for his Sunday School class the next day.

When Granddaddy passed away shortly after that summer we went to the funeral. His pastor said that he had gone to see my grandfather just before he died, when he was too weak to talk much. He noticed that Granddaddy seemed to be saying something and he leaned closer to hear what it was. My grandfather was softly singing, "Amazing grace, how sweet the sound, that saved a wretch like me. I once was lost but now am found. Was blind but now I see."

There is only one word to describe what happened to my grandfather in his sixties, after ignoring God for decades—grace. Paul describes it this way in Ephesians 2:8, *"For it is by grace you have been saved, through faith—and this not from yourselves, it is the gift of God."*

If we are honest with ourselves, the only hope any of us have is for God's grace. Adrienne Cranor describes a scene that depicts the human condition. "At the hospital where my mother works, patients' food and drug allergies are posted on a large sign above the beds. One day a visitor approached the nurses' station to say, 'You people sure do call them as you see them.' My mother went into a nearby room and saw that instead of writing that the patient was allergic to shellfish and nuts, the nurse had written in bold letters: 'Selfish and Nuts.' "

For some reason that description fits too close to home for my comfort. The bottom line is that we all need grace. The reason some have a hard time with the idea of grace is that it is a confession about the human condition. God's grace means that I can't please God on my own.

Mark Twain was certainly no theologian, but he caught the idea of grace. He once said, "Heaven goes by favor. If it went by merit, you would stay out, and your dog would go in."

I read of a leading manufacturer that developed a new cake mix. It was such a simple formula that it required only water to be added. Pre-launch taste tests were run and the cake mix was found to be of superior quality to the other similar products. It tasted good, it was easy to use, and it made a moist, tender cake. The company spent large sums of money on an advertising campaign and then released the cake mix to the general market.

However, few people bought the new cake mix. The company then spent more money on a survey to find out why it didn't sell. Based on the results of this survey, the company recalled the mix, reworked the formula, and released the revised cake mix. The change required that, in addition to the water, an egg had to be added. It sold like hot cakes and is now a leading product in the field. You see, the first cake mix was just too simple to be believable. Something in human nature wants to "add an egg." Then we *deserve* the cake.

The great Swiss-German theologian Karl Barth delivered one of the closing lectures of his life at the University of Chicago Divinity School. At the end of the lecture, the president of the seminary told the audience that Dr. Barth was not well and was very tired, and though he thought Dr.

Barth would like to be open for questions, he probably could not handle the strain. Then he added, "Therefore, I'll ask just one question on behalf of all of us."

He turned to Barth and asked, "Of all the theological insights you have ever had, which do you consider to be the greatest of them all?" This was a remarkable question to ask of a man who had written tens of thousands of pages of some of the most sophisticated theology ever put on paper. The students sat with pads and pencils ready. They wanted to jot down the premier insight of the greatest theologian of their time. Karl Barth closed his eyes and thought for a while. Then he smiled, opened his eyes, and said to the young seminarians, "The greatest theological insight I have ever had is this: Jesus loves me, this I know, for the Bible tells me so." Something so complicated as theology can be reduced to the simple truth of God's grace.

Newspapers carried the tragic story of Arnold Dobson, Harold Most and Harold Most, Jr. They died in Death Valley. One had made it seven miles, another fourteen miles and the third seventeen miles. Thirty miles before their car broke down they had passed a ranch house and were trying to get back to it. A mile in the other direction was a grove of willow trees and a spring of fresh water. Life was in easy reach but they went the wrong way and perished.

The problem with all of us is that we were going in the wrong direction. Grace is God sending His Son to find us and lead us to safety. "It is by grace you have been saved."

27–Saying "Amen" to God's Promise

One of the most difficult challenges to my faith is learning to distinguish between God's part and my part in seeing His promises become reality. I have met people who are like the farmer who waited for everything to happen without his effort. He was sitting on the porch of his house when a stranger came by and asked, "How's things?" "Tolerable," came the reply. The farmer continued, "Two weeks ago a tornado came along and knocked down all the trees I would have had to chop down for this winter's firewood. Then last week lightning struck the brush I had planned to burn to clear the fields for planting." The stranger responded, "That's remarkable, what are you doing now?" The farmer answered, "Waiting for an earthquake to come along and shake the 'taters out of the ground." Guess what the farmer learned. The earthquake never came and, without his effort, the 'taters stayed in the ground.

In my walk of faith I sometimes feel like the little girl who was struggling with the problem of what to do after she prayed. She learned that her brothers had set traps to catch little birds. When someone asked what she did when she found out, she responded, "I prayed that the traps would not catch the birds. Then I asked God to keep the birds out of the traps. Then I went and kicked the traps all to pieces." How often, when we pray, does God expect us then to do something? It could be that after we have prayed and believed God expects us to "kick the traps all to pieces."

In his second letter to the Corinthian church Paul explains, to some degree, how faith works. He wrote, *"For no matter how many promises God has made, they are 'Yes' in Christ. And so through him the 'Amen' is spoken by us to the glory of God"* (1:20).

The answer to our questions about God's promises is "Yes." Will He heal me? Yes. Will He provide for me? Yes. Will He walk with me through every difficulty I face? Yes. Is my eternal destiny secure when I trust Him for my salvation? Yes. The answer to every one of those questions, and more, is "Yes" in Christ. He is the key to every promise God has made.

Had Jesus never come we might have doubted the promises. They seemed too good to be true. "Can I make it?" Without Jesus, I wouldn't have a clear answer to that. "Can I be happy?" Without Jesus, I could never be sure. But, in Christ, the answer to every question about our provision is "Yes!"

If we want to experience the good things God promises it's important for us to put our faith in Jesus Christ. Louis Banks, a great Methodist pastor at the turn of the Twentieth century, came home from a vacation, turned on his faucet and got no water. He went to the basement and turned a valve, still no water. He called a plumber who checked the house and figured the problem must be in the street. The city must have turned the water off. He called the Water Works office—Banks' bill had not been paid. The reservoir was there but he couldn't use it. A person can live next to the reservoir and have no water if the pipes aren't connected. We can also live near the presence of God and miss the benefits if we don't trust Jesus.

It's an undeniable truth that God will keep His promises, but what is my responsibility? I still remember the exciting moment when I understood the last part of that verse. God's part is to keep His promises to us. Our part is to say "Amen." There are many benefits of God's promises that we may not enjoy until we learn to say "Amen."

To most people "Amen" is the way we close our prayers—not much more than a religious ending to a religious petition. The Hebrew root that underlies this Greek word is *aman*. It means "certainty," "firmness," "reliability." It's an Old Testament word for faith. We believe because the object of our trust is reliable and sure. God's promise is reliable and sure. Our saying "Amen" is an expression of our confidence in the faithfulness of God. God makes a promise and when I say "Amen" I am expressing my faith in what He said.

It's not enough for God to give the promise. It's not enough for Jesus to answer our questions by reminding us that God says "Yes." The benefits are not received until we say "Amen." It is important for me to say, "I believe. I will trust God." God's promises are "Yes" in Christ. What God wants from me is "Amen, I believe that and will trust it."

What happens when we begin to say "Amen" to the promises of God? Jesus' thirty years of ministry provides a living example of what to expect. In Revelation 3:14 the apostle John records a letter from Jesus to the church at Laodicea: *"To the angel of the church in Laodicea write: These are the words of the Amen."*

Jesus lived and ministered with a constant appropriation of the promises of God. To the blind, crippled, neglected, suffering and morally wounded He was the Divine "Yes" to God's promises and the Divine "Amen" for those who came to Him. He says in Revelation: "I am the perfect Example of anyone who says 'Amen' to God's 'Yes.'"

When we pray we are to lay hold of the promises of God. There are too many of them to mention here. After praying, we aren't to just mouth a religious word, "Amen." We are to mean what we say. We are saying, "Jesus, I trust that the answer to this promise is 'Yes.' I believe that and will place my faith in what You have said."

All of that is available to us because of Jesus. Per Nilsen, a father in Minnesota, told of the night his young son, Bjorn, got sick. He took the boy's temperature and it was 102.5 degrees. After a dose of children's Advil, it went down to 100 degrees. That night the father woke up and checked him again. His temperature was 104 degrees. When Nilsen called the local emergency care they said, "Bring him in as soon as possible." The father stayed with the other child while his wife started the van and prepared to take Bjorn to the emergency room.

As the father jostled the little boy awake and told him his mother was going to take him to the emergency room, the child asked, "Daddy, am I going to die?" The father said, "I told him no, that we just needed to get his fever down." Then I thought of the conversation that had once taken place between Jesus and His Father. When Jesus asked, "Daddy, am I going to die?" in His heart the Father knew the answer was "Yes." That, though, was the only way we could have access to the promises of God.

Jesus paid a great price so that God's promises would be available to us. Now it's our responsibility to say "Amen."

28—God Loves Us

Charlotte Mortimer described her adult-education creative-writing class. The teacher asked all the students to write, "I love you" in twenty-five words or less, without using the words "I love you." The class was given fifteen minutes to complete the assignment. Charlotte wrote that one woman spent about ten minutes looking at the ceiling and wriggling in her seat. Then the last five minutes she wrote frantically. Later she read her composition to the class. It consisted of three loving statements: "Why, I've seen lots worse hairdos than that, honey." "These cookies are hardly burned at all." "Cuddle up-I'll get your feet warm." It tells us something about her husband. It also tells us something about the practical side of love.

I don't know if anyone else spends much time wondering why God loves us, but sometimes His love is a mystery to me. I know my inadequacies and shortcomings. I also know that God loves me in spite of them. Moses' words to Israel in Deuteronomy 7:7-8 comfort me. He explains God's love for them to the Israelites: *"The LORD did not set his affection on you and choose you because you were more numerous than other peoples, for you were the fewest of all peoples. But it was because the LORD loved you and kept the oath he swore to your forefathers that he brought you out with a mighty hand and redeemed you from the land of slavery, from the power of Pharaoh king of Egypt."* Our might and importance have nothing to do with God's affection for us. He just loves us. John 3:16 may be the most memorized verse in the Bible: *"God so loved the world...."*

A book that touched me was *Love Beyond Reason*, by John Ortberg. In the book, Ortberg describes a doll, Pandy, that belonged to his sister, Barbie. By the time he knew Pandy he says, "She had lost a lot of hair, one arm was missing and she'd had the stuffing knocked out of her." Not impressed with Pandy's beauty he felt that she was too damaged to be even given away.

He remembers his family going to Canada from Illinois for vacation. On the return trip, they realized that they had left the doll in Canada and had to drive all the way back to Canada to retrieve her. Pandy was that important to his sister.

When Barbie married and had a little girl of her own, Courtney, his sister had Pandy restored and kept her as Courtney's doll. Ortberg's reflection on Pandy's story affected me deeply. He wrote, "When Pandy was young, Barbie loved her. She celebrated her beauty. When Pandy was old and ragged, Barbie loved her still. Now she did not simply love Pandy because Pandy was beautiful, she loved her with the kind of love that made Pandy beautiful."

That's what God's love has done for us. He doesn't love us because we are beautiful, His love makes us attractive.

Sometimes it is hard for us to receive undeserved love, so we try to earn it. Richard Bellinger, a young boy in South Carolina, was the son of a Baptist minister. One Saturday night Richard decided to shine his father's shoes. The following night his father put a silver dollar on the bureau of his son's room with a note commending his son for what he had done, and telling him that the dollar was his reward. The next morning, when the father put on his shoes, he felt something hard and metallic in one of them. When he took the shoe off and reached inside, he found the silver dollar he had given to his son the night before. Along with the dollar was a note that simply read, "I did it for love!"

What God has done for us He did for love. Instead of trying to understand it, deserve it, or pay for it, He just wants us to receive it and say "Thank you." When we do that, His love begins to change us. And, does His love ever have the power to change us!

Gwen and I pastored outside Baltimore, Maryland early in our ministry. I was drawn to a story I read about a college in that area. One of the local college professors gave an assignment to his class. He asked them to go into the economically impoverished communities to get case histories of two hundred young boys. They were asked to write an evaluation of each boy's future. In every case, the students wrote something like, "He hasn't got a chance."

Twenty-five years later another sociology professor came across the earlier study. He decided to use his class to follow up on the previous survey in order to see what had happened to those boys. With the exception of twenty boys who had moved away or died, the students learned that 176 of the remaining 180 had achieved more than ordinary success as lawyers, doctors and businessmen.

The professor was astounded at the results and decided to pursue the matter further. Fortunately, the 176 men still lived in the area and his class interviewed each of them. They were asked the question, "How do you account for your success?" In each case the reply came with feeling, "There was a teacher."

Investigating, the professor learned that the teacher was still alive. He personally went to speak with her. He asked her what magic formula she had used to pull these boys out of the slums into successful achievement. The teacher looked at him, broke into a smile, and said, "It's really very simple, I loved those boys."

God loves us. When we are about to step into heaven because we have believed in Him, if someone asks us why we made it, we can confidently say, "He just loved us."

The kind of love God has for us cost Him dearly. John MacArthur told of an incident that occurred during Oliver Cromwell's reign as Lord Protector of England. A young soldier was scheduled to be executed. The girl to whom he was engaged pleaded with Cromwell to spare the life of her beloved, but Cromwell was resistant to her request. The young man was to be executed when the curfew bell sounded.

However, when the sexton repeatedly pulled the rope to signal the execution the bell made no sound. The soldier's fiancee had climbed into the belfry and wrapped herself around the clapper so that it could not strike the bell. Her body was smashed and bruised, but she did not let go until the clapper stopped swinging. She managed to climb down, bruised and bleeding, to meet those gathered to witness the execution. When she explained what she had done, Cromwell commuted the sentence.

A poet beautifully recorded the story as follows:

"At his feet she told her story, showed her hands all bruised and torn, And her sweet young face still haggard with the anguish it had worn, Touched his heart with sudden pity, lit his eyes with misty light. 'Go, your lover lives,' said Cromwell; 'Curfew will not ring tonight.' "

God loves us. His body still bears the scars from His suffering so we would not die. He wants us to believe that and allow His love to change us. When I know God loves me that much I can never give up on myself.

29–What Business Are We In?

InfoWorld reported an interview with George Morrow of Morrow Systems, a computer company. Morrow made an interesting observation: "An article in the *Harvard Business Review*... talked about how some people didn't understand what business they were in. For example, the railroad people didn't realize they were in the transportation business; they thought they were in the railroad business. Had they realized they were in the transportation business they would have invested in the airplane. The telegraph people thought they were in the telegraph business instead of the communications business. In 1886 or so, they could have bought all the telephone patents for $40,000. So obviously these people didn't know what business they were in. I used to think these guys were really dumb because they didn't know what business they were in. Then I asked myself, 'What business am I in?'"

That insight made me contemplate what business we are in as Christians. Obviously, we are in the business of living for Jesus. Our first responsibility in life is to please Him. That motivates us to worship with our words and our behavior. Believing in Jesus and living for Him will get us to heaven, but is that the only business with which we are to occupy ourselves?

I have often thought that if our goal was simply to get to heaven God would ask whoever baptizes us to shoot us. That would guarantee that we make it to heaven. But, we don't die immediately upon baptism. At least no one I ever baptized has drowned from being immersed. I'm particularly grateful for that.

Why, though, does God leave us here after we have believed in Him? There are several reasons, but one of which I am certain is explained by a statement Paul made in his first letter to the Corinthian church. Paul wrote, *"Though I am free and belong to no man, I make myself a slave to everyone, to win as many as possible"* (1 Corinthians 9:19).

The same expression translated *"make myself a slave"* is used in Titus 2:3: *"Likewise teach the older women...not to be slanderers or addicted to much wine."* I was reflecting on that Scripture and wondered why older women are particularly told not to be addicted to much wine. Then I realized that older women are married to older men. Maybe that subjects them to a greater temptation to drink too much.

The Greek word translated *"addicted"* uses the same verb that occurs in 1 Corinthians 9:19. What Paul says to Timothy is that older women are not to be *addicted* to much wine. Making the connection between those two passages gives me a fresh insight into what Paul says to the Corinthians. He is saying, "I am *addicted* to people." We, as Christians, are in the people business. Paul points out to the Corinthians that some people are religious and some are not. Some are weak and some are strong. Paul was a great teacher and a powerful theologian, but above all he was addicted to people.

It is easy for us to mistake our business as Christians and think it's about buildings, organizations or the details of operating a church. Those things are important, for sure, but are not to be our major focus. Our business is people. The driving purpose of our lives whether we are pastors, engineers, truck drivers or professionals is to win people for Jesus. We need buildings so we can care for people. We want organization so we can effectively minister to people. But, it is all about bringing people into a relationship with Jesus.

Abraham Bininger, a Swiss boy from Zurich, knew his business. Abraham came to America on the same ship that brought John Wesley to the new world. His parents died on the voyage and were buried at sea. He stepped into America knowing no one. He grew to adulthood and asked to be allowed to go to the island of St. Thomas to preach the gospel.

When Abraham arrived on the island, he learned that the only ones allowed to preach to slaves were other slaves. He wrote the governor and asked to be made a slave for the rest of his life so he could preach to the slaves. The governor sent the letter to the king of Denmark, who controlled the island. The king was so touched that he officially authorized Bininger to preach Christ when and where he chose—to black or white, bond or free. Abraham Bininger was addicted to people.

One of my favorite characters from history is Alexander Whyte. Whyte pastored a church in Edinburgh, Scotland, in the late 1800's and early 1900's. During that time, a salesman by the name of Rigby would travel to Edinburgh regularly just to hear him preach. He would often invite other businessmen to accompany him to the services. One Sunday morning Rigby asked a fellow traveler to go to church with him. Reluctantly, the man said yes. When he heard Whyte's message, he was so impressed that he asked Rigby if they could return for the evening service. That night, as Whyte spoke, Rigby's friend believed on Jesus Christ as his Savior.

Because Alexander Whyte had no way of knowing about the new life of his friend, Rigby decided to tell him. The next morning he walked by the home of Pastor Whyte and stopped to share the story of his friend's conversion the previous night.

When Whyte came to the door and learned that his caller's name was Rigby, he became visibly excited. He exclaimed, "You're the man I've wanted to see for years!" He went to his study and returned with a bundle of letters. Alexander Whyte read Rigby some excerpts—all telling of changed lives. They were men Rigby had brought to hear the gospel. Mr. Rigby was addicted to people. Interestingly, he had no idea of how extensive his influence had been.

When we are addicted to people we speak to them, love them and, more important, live out our faith before them. Jim, an elder at a church, was given the responsibility of overseeing the evangelism of new people who moved into the area near his congregation. Sun Lee and his family were Vietnamese refugees who had recently arrived in the community. They had no possessions, knew no one and needed help in every way. Jim began by helping them get food and then spent much time helping Sun Lee find a job.

Jim wanted to tell Sun Lee about Jesus, but he didn't know Vietnamese and the refugee knew very little English. Both men sought to learn the other's language so they could become better friends. One day, Jim felt that he knew enough to tell Sun Lee about Jesus. Jim began to explain about God and the story became frustrated by his inability to communicate in Vietnamese. He gave up, deciding to try again when he knew more Vietnamese. Then Sun Lee blurted out in English, "Is your God like you? If He is I want to know Him." Jim felt he had not been communicating, but he had in the most powerful way—with his life.

We may be in the church business (as I am), in the restaurant business, in real estate business, in the homemaking business or any number of other businesses. But, don't ever forget, our main business is people. I read 1 Corinthians 9:19 differently now: *"Though I am free and belong to no man, I am **addicted to everyone**, to win as many as possible."*

30—Smoke Signals

Max Lucado once wrote about a woman who owned a parakeet named Chippie. Chippie's owner loved everything about Chippie but the job of taking the dirty paper out of the bottom of the cage. She decided to skip the ugly details of cleaning the cage and use her vacuum cleaner. One day while she was vacuuming the mess, with the little bird shrinking back in a corner of the cage, the phone rang. As she picked up the phone, she heard "Sssoppp!" Chippie had been sucked in.

She hurriedly opened the vacuum cleaner and found Chippie in the dirt bag, alive but stunned. His eyes were wide open and he was covered with dirt, so she grabbed him and ran to the bathroom to rinse off the dirt. As she rinsed him under the faucet, he began to shiver. Concerned that the water might not be good for him, she grabbed the hair dryer and hit him with a blast of hot air. Chippie never knew what had happened to him. He had been sucked in, washed out and blown away. A reporter heard about Chippie and called later to see how the little guy was recuperating. "Well," the woman told him, "Chippie doesn't sing much anymore—he just sits and stares."

Life sometimes hits us like that. We are minding our own business when suddenly we are sucked in, washed out and blown away. Times like that leave us just sitting and staring. I frequently speak to congregations of people and there are always a few out there who aren't singing much anymore. Their eyes are like saucers and they are wondering which way the truck went just hit them went.

I am no different from anyone else. I don't like trouble. If I had my way, every road I take in life would be smooth and I would never see a pothole, let alone be jarred by one. But, that isn't the Christian life. Paul says, in Romans 5:3-4, *"We also rejoice in our sufferings, because we know that suffering produces perseverance; perseverance, character; and character, hope."* Those words by Paul are designed to help us face life. The New Living Translation puts it this way: *"We can rejoice, too, when we run into problems and trials, for we know that they are good for us—they help us learn to endure. And endurance develops strength of character in us, and character strengthens our confident expectation of salvation."*

The Greek word translated "character" in this passage was used to describe precious metals that had been proved by testing. Problems and trials are not designed by God to cause us to stumble, they are designed to prove the strength and purity of what is inside us.

I read an article in our local newspaper that expressed the essence of Christian living. A local public figure had gone through a time of severe testing and public scrutiny. I read the article thinking, "I'm glad that's not me." When the reporter interviewed him, he made an insightful observation: "I'm like a tea bag. You don't know how strong I am until I get in hot water."

Trouble doesn't create our character, it simply reveals it. Under pressure, what we are on the inside will become visible to those on the outside. One of my heroes is Winston Churchill. I admire him, not for what he was when things were going well, but for the noble way in which he handled the pressure of World War II. He once said, "Difficulties mastered are opportunities won."

I have been blessed in life with the privilege of knowing many wonderful people. Not one of them has arrived at a place of influence without coming through troubled times with strength of character. Testing is part of God's plan to make us like Jesus.

A customer once asked a shopkeeper, "What makes this set of china more expensive that that one? They look almost the same." The shopkeeper replied, "The costlier set has had more done to it, you see it had to be put through the oven twice because the flowers are on a yellow background. On the less expensive set, the flowers are on a white background. The costly china had to be put through the fire once for the yellow background and then a second time for the design on it." If we want to be the best we can be, we learn to come through trouble with endurance that refuses to quit. That demonstrates character that says we have been tested and approved. That process gives us hope that nothing is able to destroy.

My grandfather was, for a large portion of his life, a railroad man. In the days of steam engines, he was a fireman with the Norfolk and Western Railroad. His job was not to put out fires, but to keep the fire in the engine going by feeding it coal. That fire heated the water and turned it to steam. Some of the steam would go through the whistle and make a lot of noise. That was important because it let people know the train was coming. However, the most important use of the steam was to drive the wheels of the locomotive so the train could be driven up the steep grades of Southwest Virginia. That steam was a lot of pressure but it was channeled into power.

God wants every bit of trouble that comes our way to be channeled into spiritual power. That can happen when we are not driven by our circumstances, but move in the direction of His presence in us. A good picture of that is the phenomenon that often occurs in the North Atlantic. Ice Bergs can be seen moving against the direction of the wind. That is because 90% of the mass of an iceberg is under the surface of the water. It is fixed in the ocean's current and is not directed by the wind. That is what sustains believers who face the pressure of circumstances. Trouble doesn't determine how we react. Under pressure we demonstrate to the world that we are secured in the flow of God's love, grace and provision.

So, does God make sure that trouble always works in our favor? Emphatically, yes. John Yates, in a sermon on gratitude, told of the sole survivor of a shipwreck. He was washed up on a small uninhabited island. He was exhausted and, in desperation, cried out to God to save him. Every day he scanned the horizon, searching for help.

Finally, he managed to build a rough hut and put his few articles in that hut.

One day, coming home from hunting for food, he was overcome with grief at the sight of his little hut going up in flames and covered with a cloud of smoke. The worst had happened. But, early the next day, a ship drew in and rescued him. He asked the crew, "How did you know I was here?" They replied, "We saw your smoke signal."

Gwen and I heard a speaker begin a conference message with the words, "Welcome trouble." He explained, "Trouble gives God a chance to do a miracle." God will see our smoke signals, He will show up and every trial we successfully endure will add to our character and make us more like Jesus.

31—Living in Freedom

When Gwen and I were living in Australia, we met a woman who grew up in a rural community in Queensland. She was describing what it was like to live in a small town with limited electrical power. She told us that there was a local hospital in town and someone from the hospital regularly called every home in town with an emergency message: "Please turn off your ovens. We are about to operate the X-ray machine."

Most of us living in America have not experienced that kind of power limitation. When the occasional storm knocks out our power temporarily, I can't even find the hurricane lamp. Power shortages freeze elevators between floors, leave offices in the dark and stifle public communication (especially for those who get their news by way of television). Thankfully, those shortages usually don't last long.

When it comes to our spiritual lives, we are never in danger of a power shortage. God has given us the Holy Spirit and provided us with all the power we need. The key to successful living lies in our ability to exercise the spiritual power that's available to us.

A few years ago, Mike Kollin left Auburn University to play professional football for the Miami Dolphins. Shug Jordan, his old coach at Auburn University, called him and asked him to recruit football players from the Miami area for Auburn. "Sure coach," Mike said, "what kind of players are you looking for?"

"Well, Mike," said Jordan, "there are guys that you knock them down and they stay down." "We don't want them, do we coach?" said Kollin. "No!" continued Jordan. "Then there are guys who you knock them down and they get up. You knock them down and they get up. You knock them down and they get up." "We want them, don't we coach?" responded Mike. "No, Mike," said Jordan, "we don't want them either. Get the guy who's knocking all these people down. We want him."

God wants us to be the kind of believers who overcome every obstacle life presents. He wants us to live in freedom and not be held captive by the sin and death around us. The problem is that we are all aware of our weaknesses and limitations. We feel inadequate about our ability to live in that kind of freedom. Something had to be done to make us strong enough to win this game called life.

Paul, in Romans 8, gives us God's answer to human weakness. God provides the Holy Spirit. Each of us knows the toll sin can take on us and we only have to drive past a cemetery to know the inevitability of physical death. The good news Paul shares gives us hope: *"Through Christ Jesus the law of the Spirit of life set me free from the law of sin and death"* (Romans 8:2).

That's an amazing statement! As dominating as sin and death seem to be, God has sent, through Jesus, the law of the Spirit of life and the Spirit of life has set us free. Sin and death can't defeat us. The Holy Spirit is more than a match for both of them. God doesn't leave me to battle the forces of sin and death on my own. I have already proved they are too much for me. Instead, He has sent the Holy Spirit to set me free. That's real freedom. I can walk through my life and into eternity knowing that sin and death do not determine my destiny because Jesus has given me the Holy Spirit.

When I was in college, we were taught about a phenomenon called *Bernoulli's Principle*. Simply stated, it means that as a liquid (including air) moves at a higher speed it develops less pressure th
an a liquid (including air) moving at a slower speed. An extension of this principle is used for the design of airplane wings. The wing design, aided by the flaps, forces the air flowing over the top of the wing to move faster than the air flowing under the wind. That creates greater pressure under the wing. That pressure lifts the plane.

It is one thing to know this principle theoretically. It is another thing to sit in a 747 as it speeds to the end of the runway. You're aware that your life depends on old Bernoulli knowing what he was talking about. If the plane doesn't take off there is a good chance that you will see Jesus immediately.

Some believers understand theories of God's power. But, God wants us to experience the power of the Holy Spirit. We are speeding down the runway of life and sin and death are lurking at the end of the pavement. We don't have to doubt. Paul knew what he was talking about. The Holy Spirit will give us the lift we need and enable us to soar above the danger.

Paul continues his hope-filled message in Romans 8 with a verse that expresses the unlimited power God gives us. Whether in life or in death, God gives us the power we need to be successful: *"And if the Spirit of him who raised Jesus from the dead is living in you, he who raised Christ from the dead will also give life to your mortal bodies through his Spirit, who lives in you"* (Romans 8:11). The resurrection power of God is living in us. Death can't defeat us. Sin can't destroy us—not because we are so powerful, but because His Spirit dwells in us.

God has intervened in our lives so that we can be free from the forces that would weaken and hurt us. I saw a television documentary that depicted a Canadian goose that was in dire straits. Someone had thrown away a plastic six-pack holder and the goose had caught its beak in the discarded item. Because its beak was consequently fastened shut, it was unable to eat. Left alone it would have starved to death. A man saw the situation was determined to set the poor goose free. The goose ran away from its rescuer (as we sometimes run away from God), but the man was persistent.

In its flight from the man, the goose reached the middle of a river. It was floating downstream out of reach. The determined pursuer stood on a bridge toward which the goose was floating. He dropped a net from the bridge, capturing the goose, and jumped from the bridge to free the poor bird. In jumping, the man broke his leg, but was able to cut away the plastic death trap and set the handicapped bird free to live as it was designed to live.

That's what Jesus did for us. He came to our rescue at great cost to Himself. In doing so, He not only set us free but also gave us the Holy Spirit so we could continue to be free. Paul got the message: *"The law of the Spirit of life set me free...."*

32—The Week That Shook the World

One of the most frightening events in my childhood took place when I was six years old. We were living in Hollywood, California when an earthquake shook the city. Our family gathered in the doorway leading into the house. We had been told it was the safest place to be if the house collapsed.

I have distinct memories of that night. I actually remember the sounds more than the shaking. We lived two blocks from Hollywood Boulevard and the earthquake set off burglar alarms up and down the boulevard. The noise was frightening to a six-year-old. The screams of a frightened woman who was running up and down the middle of our street didn't help to calm my nerves. In addition to the noise of the burglar alarms and the screams of a frightened woman there was the unsteady motion of the earth beneath our feet. I was shaking with fear. It is an amazing thing when a city is stirred.

Jesus began the last week of His earthly ministry by riding into Jerusalem on a donkey amid the boisterous shouts of praise from the crowds that gathered around Him. The commotion captured the attention of the entire city. Matthew identifies the impact of the moment: *"When Jesus entered Jerusalem, the whole city was stirred and asked, 'Who is this?' "* (21:10). The Triumphal Entry of Jesus "shook" the city of Jerusalem. That is the literal meaning of the word Matthew used when he said the city was "stirred." Now we can see that not only was Jerusalem shaken that day, but also it was the beginning of the week that shook the world.

This wasn't the first triumphal entry in the history of the Roman territories. Rome had observed victory parades many times in the past. This one was different, though. It is certain that the Romans would not have been impressed by a crowd of pilgrims throwing old clothes and broken tree branches in front of a Jewish teacher riding on a donkey. Their celebrations of victory were much more elaborate.

But this King is not a Roman tyrant, this King's name is Jesus.

The whole event was prophesied by Zechariah many years earlier. He had seen this day and described it: *"Rejoice greatly, O Daughter of Zion! Shout, Daughter of Jerusalem! See, your king comes to you, righteous and having salvation, gentle and riding on a donkey, on a colt, the foal of a donkey"* (Zechariah 9:9). Roman emperors were typically arrogant and proud. Jesus was gentle and came bringing salvation.

Martin Luther observed that Jesus is a different kind of King. We did not seek Him, He sought us. For other kings the subjects came humbly to him. Jesus comes humbly to us.

Everyone wants peace. We want peace in the Middle East, we want peace in our communities and our families and we want peace in our own hearts. In those days, the animal a king rode indicated his mission. Kings who were going to war rode horses. Kings who came in peace rode donkeys. Jesus was coming as the King who would bring peace to all who believe in Him.

A few years ago, a family was afraid that someday there would be war where they lived and they made plans to move to a safe place. They exhaustively researched various places in the world and found the one site that would be safe from war. They moved there. That Christmas their former pastor received a letter from them, sent from their new home—the Falkland Islands. That winter war broke out in the Falkland Islands between England and Argentina. No matter how diligently we search for peace, we won't find it in some geographical location. The only safe place to find peace is in the presence of Jesus.

An interesting feature of Jesus' entry into Jerusalem is the fact that the people were throwing their garments in front of Him. It was a symbolic way of saying, "Jesus, You can walk on my stuff." Personally, I am like most people. I defend my "stuff." I don't want anyone walking into my house and walking off with my stuff. That's called burglary. One of the first American flags depicted a coiled serpent with the words, "Don't tread on me." That's the American spirit. The people of that day were saying, as He entered the city, "Jesus you can tread on my property."

It really makes sense, though, to acknowledge Jesus' lordship over our lives and our property. After all, He has blessed us with all that we have. Even more, He has our interests and welfare at heart. Some people are afraid that submitting to Jesus will ruin their lives. The truth is that surrendering to Jesus is the only way to live the abundant life. John quotes Jesus in his Gospel, *"I have come that they may have life, and have it to the full"* (10:10).

If someone gave me a brand new car, I would find an owner's manual in the glove department. It would tell me when to change the oil, what air pressure the tires required and when to get scheduled service. I would be crazy to think, "No one is going to tell me how to run my car" and ignore the manual. Jesus has given us an owner's manual—the Bible. It isn't that He wants to deprive us, He just knows how we best function. The wisest thing we can do with any of our "stuff" is acknowledge His lordship over it.

A friend of ours who attended our church in Virginia Beach owned a car dealership. He told me that he sold an individual their top-of-the-line sports car. The new owner called and informed the dealer that the engine of his sports car had frozen on I-64 between Richmond, Virginia and Virginia Beach. On investigating the problem, the dealership discovered that the car's owner had driven 40,000 miles without changing the oil or putting a drop of oil in the engine. He would have been well advised to pay attention to the suggestions of the ones who made the car.

It is the life surrendered to Jesus that reaches its fullest potential. In the days before automobiles, when the standard mode of transportation was a horse and carriage, a woman was riding in a carriage with a man who held the reins of the horses. She became frightened and grabbed one of the reins. The man explained to her that she had either to take both reins or let the one go. He told her, "We can't both hold the reins."

That's what Jesus says to us, "We can't both hold the reins." That is one of the lessons of His Triumphal Entry into Jerusalem as the crowd threw their garments in His path. He is not a tyrant, but He is a gentle King. Our challenge is to trust Him.

I read a tragic story in our local paper in 1998. A man had drowned in the Powhatan River when his boat capsized. He was not able to swim. He flailed about and was unable to reach a life jacket that was just beyond his grasp. When the rescuers arrived, they found that he had drowned in four feet of water. All he had to have done was stop struggling and stand up with his feet on the bottom.

So many of us have been like that man. We have struggled with all our might when all we need to do is stand on the firm foundation of Jesus Christ. He is the King Zechariah describes: *"See, your king comes to you, righteous and having salvation, gentle and riding on a donkey."* He can be trusted with our lives and all we possess.

33—He is Alive!

It is often interesting to look at events through the eyes of children. One Easter morning as the minister was preaching the children's sermon, he reached into his bag of props and pulled out an egg. He pointed at the egg and asked the children, "What's in here?" "I know," a little boy exclaimed. "Pantyhose!"

We know that Easter is more than colored eggs and chocolate bunnies. It's a celebration of the fact that Jesus defeated death for all of us. As He told Martha on his way to Lazarus' tomb, *"I am the resurrection and the life. He who believes in me will live, even though he dies"* (John 11:25). Every believer has hope of eternal life because Jesus defeated death for all humanity.

When Jesus was crucified none of Jesus' followers thought He would be raised from the dead. The apostle John reports an encounter the resurrected Jesus had with Mary Magdalene in the garden near the tomb. She mistook Him for the gardener. However, when Jesus called her name the light came on and she recognized Him. In her excitement she grabbed Jesus, only to have Him say, *"Do not hold on to me, for I have not yet returned to the Father. Go instead to my brothers and tell them, 'I am returning to my Father and your Father, to my God and your God.' Mary Magdalene went to the disciples with the news: 'I have seen the Lord!' And she told them that he had said these things to her"* (John 20:17-18).

The message Mary carried to the disciples is the message that changed the world and still changes lives. Jesus is alive!

In 1976, Gwen and I made our only trip to the Holy Land. While there, we went to the Garden Tomb and did what thousands of tourists and worshipers have done. We looked inside. We discovered what so many through the centuries have found to be true. Jesus is not there. He is alive.

The discovery of the Garden Tomb is an interesting story in itself. When it was discovered in 1885, the godly General Gordon was convinced that this was the location of Jesus' tomb. There is a traditional tomb inside the walls of modern Jerusalem, but many feel that it doesn't fit the criteria for Jesus' actual burial site.

When Gordon discovered it, the Garden Tomb was covered with rubbish twenty feet high. It had been hidden for centuries. When workmen first cleared the spot they carefully gathered all the dust and debris within the tomb and shipped it to the Scientific Association of Great Britain. Every part of it was analyzed, but there was no trace of human remains. If this is the real tomb of Christ, then Jesus was not only the first to be laid there but He was also the last.

The Resurrection of Jesus makes Christianity unique. 400 million Buddhists reverence a two-inch-long discolored eyetooth as the most sacred object on earth. The tooth is supposed to have been reclaimed from Buddha's funeral pyre in 543 B.C. It was brought to Sri Lanka 800 years later. Today the tooth sets upon a golden lotus in the glorious temple of the tooth in Kandy, Sri Lanka. It is surrounded by rubies and tons of flowers. Each year a hundred thousand faithful Buddhists come from many countries to gaze at the sacred tooth. They bring gifts of gold, silver and jewels to place within the temple.

There's no tooth of Jesus to worship, no occupied grave to which we can make a pilgrimage. He is alive! No other religion can make that claim of its founder.

As horrific as the crucifixion was, it was not God's last word. Even though some don't understand the significance of the Resurrection, it reversed the verdict of the Roman government and nullified the hatred of those who opposed Jesus. The Resurrection is the triumph of life over death, faith over unbelief and hope over despair. The fact that

Jesus is alive is the most exciting truth in history. It means that we who believe in Him shall live.

The sadness that pervaded the disciples' lives for three days was lifted when the resurrected Lord appeared to them. As the cliché states it: Victory was snatched from the jaws of defeat.

The Battle of Waterloo decided the fate of Europe. Napoleon, free from exile, had gathered a mighty army and was intent on conquering Europe. An allied army consisting of Dutch, German and British soldiers stood in his way. On June 18, 1815, the Duke of Wellington led the allied army against the French commander.

The people of England knew that their future hinged on the outcome of the battle. In order to find out the result of the encounter they arranged a system of signals to send the message across the English Channel and from town to town. One of these signal stations was on the tower of Winchester Cathedral. Late in the day, it flashed the signal, letter by letter: *"Wellington defeated..."* Just at that moment, one of those sudden English fogs made it impossible to read the message. The abbreviated message that seemed to signal defeat quickly spread throughout the city. The whole countryside was sad and gloomy when they heard the news that England and its allies had lost the war.

Suddenly the fog lifted, and the remainder of the message could be read. The message had four words, not two. The complete message was: *"Wellington defeated the enemy!"* It took only a few minutes for the good news to spread. Sorrow was turned into joy, defeat was turned into victory!

In the same way, some have only gotten part of the message about Jesus: *"Christ was crucified."* The Resurrection clears away the fog so we can see the entire Christian message: *"Christ was crucified but is now alive forever."*

Winston Churchill, one of my heroes, planned his own funeral. At the end of the service in St. Paul's Cathedral a bugler, high in the dome of the sanctuary, played Taps, the universal signal that the day is over. There was a long pause. Then a bugler on the other side of the dome played Reveille, the military wake-up call. It was Churchill's way of communicating that, while we say "Good night" here, it's "Good morning" up there. Now why could he do that? Because he believed in Jesus Christ, who said, *"I am the resurrection and the life. He who believes in me will live, even though he dies."*

What does the Resurrection mean about Jesus? Robert Russell expressed it this way: "When a man steps out of his own grave, he is anything that he says that he is, and he can do anything that he says he can do." Jesus stepped out of his own grave and showed the world that He truly is the resurrection and life. All of us face obstacles, but we know that we can trust a Man who defeated death to see us through any crisis.

34—The Footsteps of Faith

Faith is a difficult concept for many people to understand but it is central to all our lives. For example, we go to a doctor whose name we cannot pronounce and whose degrees we have never verified. He gives us a prescription we cannot read. We take it to a pharmacist we have never seen before. He gives us a chemical compound we do not understand. Then we go home and take the pill according to the instructions on the bottle. All in trusting, sincere faith.

In the New Testament, Paul portrays Abraham as the model of faith for all believers. *"Therefore, the promise comes by faith, so that it may be by grace and may be guaranteed to all Abraham's offspring—not only to those who are of the law but also to those who are of the faith of Abraham. He is the father of us all"* (Romans 4:16). Abraham's faith sets the pattern for all of us who choose to walk in faith.

By understanding Abraham's faith, I can understand more clearly the kind of faith God wants from me. Abraham's faith began with obedience. He obeyed God when God told him to pack up and move without telling him where he was going. Hebrews 11 makes that clear: *"By faith Abraham, when called to go to a place he would later receive as his inheritance, obeyed and went, even though he did not know where he was going"* (verse 8). I often find it hard to obey God even when I know where I am going. Abraham's faith enabled him to follow instructions without knowing the outcome of his decisions.

In Genesis 12, where the story of Abraham's faith is recorded, there is an aspect of it that stands out to me. His faith was exercised against all the measurable obstacles in his life. The journey from Ur, in what is now Iraq, to the Promised Land would have led Abraham through bandit-infested country. He and his wife are promised a child, but they couldn't have children. God promised him the land, but when his wife, Sarah, died he purchased a burial place and that is the only title deed he possessed at his death.

In addition to those challenges, he arrived at his destination during a famine. His neighbors were a variety of Canaanite tribes that were formidable and powerful. Archaeologists have uncovered massive fortresses from Abraham's time at Hazor and Megiddo. Not only were they imposing militarily, but the morals of that society were decidedly ungodly. Psalm 106:38 states about that culture, *"They shed innocent blood, the blood of their sons and daughters, whom they sacrificed to the idols of Canaan, and the land was desecrated by their blood."*

Here's one of my problems with faith. I want to exercise faith in a perfect environment. I want the ones among whom I live and work to believe with me. That, however, isn't how faith works. Faith calls for us to trust God when everything around us may be out of step with God.

That is the kind of faith Martin Luther exercised. On one occasion he received word that his assistant, Myconius, was sick. In fact, Myconius wrote Luther a tender farewell letter. When Luther received the letter, he penned a response: "I command thee in the name of God to live because I still have need of thee in the work of restoring the Church.... The Lord will never let me hear that thou art dead, but will permit thee to survive me. For this I am praying, it is my will and may my will be done, because I seek only to glorify the name of God."

Maybe we can find fault with some of the assumptions Luther made. But, Myconius was healed when he read the letter. Just to verify Luther's proclamation, "The Lord will never let me hear that thou art dead," Myconius lived six more years and died two months after Luther's death.

Luther's was the faith of Abraham. It was faith that looked in the face of adversity and dared to trust God's provision.

How can we have that kind of triumphant faith when we live in a culture that is largely secular and godless? Abraham found a solution. In the land populated by ungodly Canaanites, he created his own faith-filled environment.

One of the truths of Genesis 12 has sustained me when I have been tempted to question God's promises. Genesis 12:8 says about Abraham, *"From there he went on toward the hills east of Bethel and pitched his tent, with Bethel on the west and Ai on the east. There he built an altar to the LORD and called on the name of the LORD."*

Note the power of these two expressions: He *"pitched his tent...he built an altar."* His tent was movable. He could fold it up, put it on his back and carry it to the next place. His altar was permanent! In a hostile environment, he had an altar to which he could go and commune with God. The place where he met God was more permanent than the location of his dwelling place.

It would be wonderful if everyone around us spoke positive words and encouraged us in our walk of faith. They probably won't; but we have an option. We can do what Abraham did. We can build an altar where we meet God. When we have an altar where we commune with God our faith can be increased even if those around us don't believe.

The first diving bells were shown in a *National Geographic* magazine. They were inverted bells that trapped twenty minutes worth of air inside. If you have ever been submerged in water, you discovered that we can't breathe water. We simply don't have gills to separate the oxygen from the water. The earliest diving bells were the first devices that allowed divers to work underwater. The process is simple. A diver could work under water for an extended period by returning to the diving bell to catch his breath in the air trapped below the surface.

Our altars are our spiritual diving bells. We go there to breathe the air of heaven in the midst of the polluted atmosphere of the world that doesn't sustain faith. Then we can leave our altars to live by faith in a world that doesn't understand what it means to trust God.

A man by the name of Mallory led an expedition to try to conquer Mount Everest in the 1920's. Three attempts failed. On the third try, an avalanche hit the team. It killed Mallory and most of the party. A member of the team, Sir Edmund Hillary, survived. He returned to a hero's welcome in London, England, where a banquet held in his honor was attended by the lords and ladies and powerful people of the British empire. Behind the speakers' platform were huge blown-up photographs of Mount Everest. When Hillary arose to receive the acclaim of the distinguished audience, he turned around and faced the photographs of the mountain and said, "Mount Everest, you have defeated me. But I will return. And I will defeat you. Because you can't get any bigger and I can."

Sir Edmund did return and he did reach the summit of Everest—at 11:30 on the morning of May 29, 1953. When a mountain seems to have mastered you, don't give up. Build an altar. Meet with God. Let Him strengthen your faith. You will find that God is able to make you and your faith more than adequate to face any difficulty.

35—Don't Stay Down

I remember laughing out loud when I heard Rodney Dangerfield going through his routine, "I don't get no respect." He said that when he was born his doctor held him up and slapped his mother. Part of my laughter was that nervous response that comes when humor is too close to the truth.

We hope we are covering our insecurities well, but we aren't fully convinced. So, when someone like Bob Uecker, the baseball commentator and former player, builds his comedy around our fears, it can be very funny. A sportswriter once asked him this question: "How did you handle pressure as a player?" Uecker responded, "It was easy. I'd strike out and put the pressure on the guy behind me."

I can relate to Erma Bombeck's remark about dieting. She wrote in her column that she once prayed, "Lord, if you can't make me thin, make my friends look fat."

A frustration under the surface of many of our lives is rooted in our feeling we aren't good enough. Even some of those we regard as successful had to rise above negative opinions about their abilities. In 1902, the poetry editor of *The Atlantic Monthly* returned a sheaf of poems to a twenty-eight-year old poet with this note: "Our magazine has no place for your vigorous verse." The poet was Robert Frost. In 1905, the University of Bern turned down a Ph.D. dissertation as being irrelevant and fanciful. The physics student who submitted the dissertation was Albert Einstein. In 1894, the rhetoric teacher at Harrow in England said of a sixteen-year-old's speaking skills, "a conspicuous lack of ability." The student was Winston Churchill, whose speeches rallied England to victory in World War II.

One of the beauties of Scripture is that it teaches us to have a positive outlook on what we can do. Paul wrote, in Philippians 4:13, *"I can do everything through him who gives me strength."* That is very different from the feeling of some that failure is inevitable.

There was a boy nicknamed Sparky. He was a miserable failure in school. He failed every subject in the eighth grade. He flunked physics in high school, getting a grade of zero. Sparky also flunked Latin, algebra and English. He was awkward socially, in fact he never asked a girl out the entire time he was in school. It wasn't that the other students didn't like him. They hardly knew he existed.

One thing Sparky enjoyed was drawing. He submitted some drawings to his high school yearbook. The editors rejected them. Convinced that art was his one gift, after graduating from high school he submitted a sample of his work to Walt Disney studios. They, too, turned his drawings down. Another loss for the loser.

Sparky didn't give up. He decided to write his own autobiography in cartoons. He described his childhood self—a little boy loser and chronic underachiever. The cartoon character would soon become famous worldwide. For Sparky, the boy who had such lack of success in school and whose work was rejected repeatedly, was Charles Shulz. He created the *Peanuts* comic strip and the little cartoon character whose kite would never fly and who never succeeded in kicking a football—Charlie Brown.

An important fact about Charles Shulz was that he was a Christian and packed large doses of Christian principles into his comic strip. His life is evidence that, while many may not believe in us, we can do all things through him who gives us strength.

Here is another slice of history that I have found encouraging. An American hero had a checkered past: In 1816, his family was forced out of their home and he had to work to support them. Two years later his mother died. In 1831, his business failed. He tried politics and, in 1832, ran for the state legislature. He lost. That year he also lost his job and applied to enter law school. He wasn't accepted.

One year later, he borrowed some money from a friend to start a business and it went bankrupt. He spent the next seventeen years of his life paying off the debt. In 1834, he ran, once more, for the state legislature and lost. One year later, he was engaged to be married. When his fiancee died before the wedding, he had a nervous breakdown and was in bed for six months.

Always persistent, he tried his hand at politics again and suffered a series of defeats. Over the next fourteen years he was defeated for the state legislature and, having won a seat in Congress, was defeated in his reelection bid. In 1854 and 1856 he was defeated as a candidate for both the U. S. Senate and for the Vice-Presidential nomination. In 1858, he lost again in another race for the U. S. Senate. In 1860, Abraham Lincoln was elected President of the United States. He was arguably the best President in history.

If Paul's words are true, and they are, we should never accept defeat or make light of our potential. *"I can do everything through him who gives me strength."*

It is important, however, that we not overlook the key words in that verse, *"through him."* In *Actions Speak Louder Than Words*, Herb Miller writes: "Two Kentucky farmers who owned racing stables had developed a keen rivalry. One spring each of them entered a horse in a local steeplechase. Thinking that a professional rider might help him outdo his friend, one of the farmers engaged a crack jockey.

"The two horses were neck and neck with a large lead over the rest of the pack at the last fence, but suddenly both fell, unseating their riders. The professional jockey remounted quickly and rode on to win the race. Returning triumphantly to the paddock, the jockey found the farmer who had hired him fuming with rage. 'What's the matter?' the jockey asked. 'I won, didn't I?' 'Oh, yea,' roared the farmer. 'You won all right, but you crossed the finish line on the wrong horse.' In his hurry to remount after the fall, the jockey had jumped on his competitor's horse."

The real measure of our success is whether or not we are achieving our goals *through Him*. The only success that will last through eternity is the success built on faith in Jesus Christ. The arrogant may say, "I can do everything." They can't. Believers say, "I can do everything through him who gives me strength." And we can!

36—We Are Loved

What Jesus did for us is remarkable. Mother Theresa exemplified Jesus' attitude toward us by working with the poorest of the poor in Calcutta, India. A television commentator visited her in Calcutta and saw firsthand her arduous work for the poor in the midst of the filth, disease and suffering of those she helped. He remarked, "I wouldn't do what you're doing for all the money in the world." Her simple reply was, "Neither would I." We do some things for money. Mother Theresa served out of love. There is only one explanation for what Jesus did; He loves us.

We could not have earned His love. No matter how much we have achieved, it isn't enough to deserve the love and sacrifice of the Son of God. A veteran of the Korean War enjoyed telling about the day he was inducted into the United States Army. Having completed his physical, he was interviewed by a sergeant. "Did you go to grammar school?" the sergeant asked. "Yes, sir," answered the draftee. He continued, "I also went through high school, graduated *cum laude* from college, completed three years of graduate studies at Cornell, and then acquired two more degrees at Columbia." The sergeant nodded, reached for a rubber stamp, and slapped it on the questionnaire. It was a single word: "Literate."

When I think I have finally achieved enough for God to love me I am reminded, as Isaiah says, *"All our righteous acts are like filthy rags"* (Isaiah 64:6). God doesn't love me because I have impressed Him with my achievements. He just loves me.

There are landmark moments in most of our lives that remind us of a time when something changed our perspective. We may discover a truth that was always there, but suddenly we "get it." There have been a few of those times in my life. One of them occurred in Bible College many years ago. I was in my first preaching class and was a novice in a class full of novices. One of our assignments was foreboding. We were required to stand in front of our classmates and deliver a five-minute talk on some verse in the Bible.

The teacher didn't expect perfection, so she wasn't surprised by our faltering attempts at preaching. Choosing a verse was as daunting a task to me as the challenge of saying something meaningful. I'm not even sure why I chose the verse I selected, but I'm certain there was no great spiritual reason. After all, it was just a classroom assignment. Yet, I'll never forget the verse or the moment because something awesome occurred while I was speaking. Over the next five minutes, I "got it."

My verse was 1 John 3:1, and since the New International Version was not yet available, I used the King James Version. It read: *"Behold, what manner of love the Father hath bestowed upon us, that we should be called the sons of God."*

My five minutes seemed like an eternity. My classroom assignment became a fresh encounter with God. I learned what can happen when we speak; the text comes alive. I was overwhelmed by God's great love for me and the words, *"What manner of love"* reverberated in my heart. What began as an exercise in front of the class became a moment of inspiration as I realized to a small degree how much God loved me. Wally, with all his faults and inadequacies, was loved by God. I didn't deserve this "manner" of love, and still don't, but He calls me His son.

At the end of my brief talk, I quoted the words of a song we sang in church when I was a child. I had previously heard the words sung without being particularly moved. But as I was speaking the familiar words brought fresh tears to my eyes: "Could we with ink the ocean fill, and were the skies of parchment made, were every stalk on earth a quill, and every man a scribe by trade, to write the love of God above would drain the ocean dry, nor could the scroll contain the whole, though stretched from sky to sky." The words still thrill me.

I have heard for most of my life the words of John 3:16: *"For God so loved the world, that he gave his only begotten Son, that whosoever believeth in him should not perish, but have everlasting life"* (again, the King James Version). But, that day the whole truth came alive for me. God loves me. All He asks is that I believe in Him.

I know so many people who struggle in two ways. First, they feel that they have to perform at a certain level of competence before God will love them. They strive to keep the rules and work hard to earn what they can never deserve. They struggle to impress God but how do we impress the Creator of the universe?

My mother used to tell me that I could never do anything that would stop her from loving me. I now know what she meant. I have three daughters and they don't have to earn my love for them. It's unconditional. Did my mother grieve over my failures? Absolutely. Did she discipline me? Without question. She used to say, before she paddled me: "I'll love you no matter what you do, but I want other people to like you." Still, I never went to sleep doubting her love for me. And, we don't have to fall asleep doubting God's love for us.

The second problem I see people facing is a corollary of the first. Having tried to earn God's love and having failed in some way, they give up. They think, "I'll never be good enough" and they quit. Please, don't ever give up! God doesn't love you because of your performance, He just loves you.

One of my favorite Bible teachers was Fulton J. Sheen, the Roman Catholic archbishop whose television program helped many understand their faith. He once said: "God does not love us because we are valuable. We are valuable because God loves us."

Richard Armstrong, in his book *Make Your Life Worthwhile*, reports the story about a man in Wales who sought to win the affection of a certain woman for 42 years before she said, "Yes." The couple, both 74, finally married. For more than 40 years, the persistent, but rather shy man slipped a weekly love letter under his neighbor's door. But, she continually refused to speak and mend the spat that had parted them many years before. After writing 2,184 love letters without ever getting a spoken or written answer, the single-hearted old man eventually summoned up enough courage to present himself in person. He knocked on the door of the reluctant woman and asked for her hand. To his delight and surprise, she accepted his proposal and married him.

Imagine God's dilemma. Repeatedly He tried to get His message of love through to us with little response. He gave us Scripture and He sent prophets to us. He showed us examples of His love in the lives of those who believed in Him. Finally, when there was no other way, He wrapped up His message in a person, Jesus. When we are tempted to forget the "manner of love" the Father has bestowed on us, all we need to do is remember the Cross. *"For God so loved the world, that he gave his only begotten Son...."*

37—We are Wonderfully Made

Elton Trueblood once said that there must have been a chuckle among the other disciples when Jesus nicknamed unstable Simon, "Rocky." No one could have imagined flighty, foot-in-the-mouth Simon ever becoming the "Rock" who would stand and preach fearlessly on the day of Pentecost. One thing we learn from the Bible is that God is able to look at a person and see more than what that person is at the time. He sees what that person will become.

David, the son of Jesse, was anointed as a king of Israel. He became a mighty leader of Israel, conquering all the nations around his kingdom. One of the identifying descriptions of Jesus in the New Testament is that He was a son of David. Yet, when Samuel showed up to anoint one of Jesse's sons, Jesse didn't even bother to invite David to the tryout. Samuel had to ask Jesse, "Don't you have another son?" Often we don't see the potential in those who are close to us. Jesse didn't see the potential of his youngest son, who was in the backyard watching sheep, but God did.

When we open our hearts to God He enables us to look at others as He does. We don't just see their weaknesses and flaws. We are able to see what He is making of them. Instead of being judgmental, we become encouragers and do what we can to keep them growing spiritually. That is what God has done for each of us. He continually reminds us of our destiny.

London businessman Lindsay Clegg told the story of a warehouse property he was selling. The building had been empty for months and needed repairs. Vandals had damaged the doors, smashed the windows and strewn trash all over the place. As he showed a prospective buyer the property, he took pains to explain that he would replace the broken windows, bring in a crew to correct any structural damage, and clean out the garbage.

The buyer said, "Forget about the repairs. When I buy this place, I'm going to build something completely different. I don't want the building; I want the site." That's God's message to us! Compared with the renovation God has in mind, our efforts to improve our own lives are as trivial as sweeping a warehouse slated for the wrecking ball. When we become God's property, the old life is over. He makes all things new. All He wants is the site and the permission to build. There are still some trying to "reform," but God offers "redemption." All we have to do is give Him the "property" and He will do the necessary "building."

In *Mere Christianity* C. S. Lewis describes the process God uses to change us. He uses the analogy of a house and says we come to God because of some problems we are having. We want our front porch repaired. Then God comes in and begins to knock down walls and tear up the roof. We go, "Wait a minute. I didn't want you to do all this." Then we realize that God isn't just repairing our old cottage, He is working from a different set of plans altogether. He is rebuilding us completely. The old cottage is going to be changed into a mansion.

No matter how much we may have messed up our lives, when we come to Jesus and give Him the keys to our cottage, He begins to remake us so we become everything He originally intended us to be.

Exactly what did God have in mind for us from the beginning? The psalmist wrote, *"I praise you because I am fearfully and wonderfully made; your works are wonderful, I know that full well"* (Psalm 139:14). Sometimes we find that hard to believe because we only see the results of our mistakes and bad choices. We know our weaknesses but God knows what He has in mind for us. God did good work when He made us, He knows the potential that He placed in us and He will work with us to finish what He started.

For those of us who wonder why God went to such extremes to save us, the answer has to be that He values us more than we realize. Why else would He have given

His Son to save us? How else can we explain Jesus dying to bring us salvation?

It's important for us to realize that when Jesus died it was a voluntary act on His part. He told His disciples, before He was executed, that no one could take his life from Him. He was giving it up voluntarily. In the First World War, a young French soldier was seriously wounded. His arm was so badly smashed that it had to be amputated. The surgeon was grieved that the young soldier must go through life maimed so he waited beside his bedside to tell him the bad news when he recovered consciousness. When the young man's eyes opened, the surgeon said to him: "I am sorry to tell you that you have lost your arm." "Sir," said the soldier, "I did not lose it; I gave it–for France."

If we are ever tempted to look at our shortcomings and think we have no value all we have to do is remember the price God paid for us. Not only are we *"fearfully and wonderfully made"* but we have a bright future. God is committed to making us what He wants us to be if we just allow Him to take charge of our lives.

As a young boy, James M. Gray had a friend whose father was very wealthy. Having already made a fortune, the man sought to add to it by purchasing a large tract of real estate in upper Manhattan Island. At that time it was known as Harlem Flats. One day Gray's young companion said, "Let's go up and see the land Dad bought." Dr. Gray, recounting the incident years later, said, "I remember how I laughed when we got there. He couldn't show me a single spot of dry ground. The property was completely covered over with tidewater. I didn't see much of an investment in that for anybody. But, of course, his father did not acquire it for what it was worth then, but for its value in decades to come." Today that land has all been filled in and is heavily populated. It represents millions and millions of dollars to its present owners. What a picture of our redemption! God sees our worth and value even when we don't. He looks ahead to the finished product.

God loves us so much that He purchased our salvation at the cost of His Son's life. We are worth what He was willing to pay for us.

In *Man in the Mirror*, Patrick Morley tells of a group of anglers who landed in a secluded bay in Alaska and had a great day fishing for salmon. But, when they returned to their sea plane, they found it aground because of the fluctuating tides. They waited until the next morning for the tides to come in, but when they took off, they only got a few feet into the air before crashing back into the sea.

While it was aground the day before, one of the seaplane's pontoons had been punctured and was filled with water. Now the flooded pontoon began pulling the plane down and it started sinking. As the seaplane began to sink the passengers, three men and a 12-year-old son of one of the men, prayed and then jumped into the icy cold waters to swim to shore. The riptide was strong, but two of the men reached the shore exhausted. They looked back, and saw the father with his arms around his son being swept out to sea. The boy had not been strong enough to make it. The father was a strong swimmer, but he had chosen to die with his son rather than to live without him.

It is amazing, but it's true. Jesus chose to die for us rather than live without us. Who can resist love like that?

38—You Can Make a Difference

There was an old Mercedes Benz TV commercial that showed their car colliding with a cement wall during a safety test. Someone then asks the company representative why they don't enforce their patent on the Mercedes Benz energy-absorbing car body, a design evidently copied by other companies because of its success. He replies matter-of-factly, "Because some things in life are too important not to share."

The Early Church had a remarkably difficult time following through on Jesus' command to go into all the world. Maybe that's human nature. Change doesn't come easily. The church, in its beginning, stayed clustered around Jerusalem. In Acts 8, though, there was a breakthrough. God allowed the pressure of opposition to scatter the church until it reached Samaria.

In the eighth chapter of Acts one individual stands out, Philip. Philip was introduced in chapter six as one of the seven men appointed to take care of feeding the widows. Here, we see that he was also zealous about spreading the good news of Jesus to others. He was the one-man army who went to the despised Samaritans and sparked a revival. God honored his efforts by accompanying his testimony with conversions and miracles.

The entire city of Samaria was affected by one man's willingness to share the good news. Acts 8:8 explains, *"So there was great joy in that city."* When I read the eighth chapter of Acts, I see what I desire in the place where I live. I want God to visit my community in such a way that there will be joy filling hearts where there has been guilt and anxiety.

The most astounding part of Acts 8, at least to me, is the end of the chapter. God reached into an amazing citywide revival and plucked out the evangelist. He sent him to the desert south of Israel to meet one Ethiopian who was heading home with a scroll containing the words of Isaiah.

The Ethiopian was the treasurer of his country and he had spent a small fortune for the Scripture he was reading. Scrolls were copied by hand and were very expensive. This lone traveler had a problem. He didn't understand what he was reading.

God took Philip out of a powerful crusade to reach one man. I am amazed at God's care for each one of us. Jesus, who had preached to large crowds of people, spent a good part of one day talking to a woman at Jacob's well. This woman had a sketchy background at best, but she was important to Jesus.

It's easy to underestimate the power of one individual. God never does that. He visited the city of Samaria with signs and wonders, but He saw the need of an Ethiopian man riding his carriage through the desert. The Ethiopian needed understanding and Philip was willing to go where God sent him.

When Gwen and I lived in Australia, I became a fan of Cricket. I persuaded Gwen to go with me to a match between Australia and Pakistan. I don't think I'll ever get her to go again. It began at 2:00 PM and we left at 8:30 PM. I loved every minute of it, but Gwen was bored out of her mind. It was there that a story I had heard began to make sense. Skilled Cricket players are rock stars in that part of the world. The same is true in England.

You may have heard of C. T. Studd. He was a national hero as a Cricket player in England. At sixteen years of age he was already an expert at the game. At 19, he was captain of the Eton team and was famous. He had a great career in front of him. But, while he was at Cambridge University he heard Moody preach and was converted. Called from a successful career, he went to China. While there, he inherited the equivalent of $500,000. Within twenty-four hours he had given it all away. He returned to England and then went to Africa. Acquaintances told Studd that he would die in Africa and his response was that he was only looking for an opportunity to die for Jesus. C. T.

Studd believed what God wants each of us to believe, God wants everyone to hear the good news that Jesus died for him or her.

Philip had already left Jerusalem. Now he was willing to leave a successful crusade because God cares about one person. The Ethiopian treasurer was converted and baptized, then continued on his way home. Philip never saw him again. When missionaries first arrived in Ethiopia, they found a church already in existence. One man had gone home and changed his nation.

We never know the potential in the one person God uses us to influence. Luis Palau is an evangelist who is best known for his worldwide contemporary evangelistic festivals. Palau is a native of Buenos Aires, Argentina. He began his preaching ministry at age 18 by sharing the Gospel on the streets of Buenos Aires. More than a billion people worldwide have heard him preach the Good News through festivals, radio, television, and the internet.

He has described the missionaries who came to his part of the world. "The British missionaries who led my family to Christ made all the cultural mistakes in the book. I remember as a little boy sitting in the front row, watching this poor man. It was hot as blazes in the summer. Being a proper Britisher, he not only wore a tweed suit but a vest and thick socks. He would stand there sweating and sweating. I remember looking at the poor fellow and saying, 'Why doesn't he take his coat off?' But, a proper Britisher in those days kept his coat on and toughed it out. He massacred the Spanish language and had strange foreign habits. But because of that fellow, my father went to heaven."

Who would have known that the little boy sitting there listening to a missionary who made numerous cultural gaffes would touch the world? God knew. And, some missionary in heaven is going to receive the reward of a servant who knew the value of one and was willing to go where God sent him.

C. Summer Wemp told of an experience that affected him deeply. "While at the beach in Jacksonville, Florida, one summer, I saw a lifeguard suddenly jump to his feet in his tower. He took the Red Cross flag out of its standard and waved it frantically so they could see him at the main lifeguard station. He then threw it to the ground, jumped down, grabbed a life buoy and rushed out into the water. With strong strokes, he swam toward a man waving for help. In a few seconds, an ambulance came up and three other guards swam out to help.

"They rescued the man. The same scene was repeated several times that day, for the undertow was unusually strong. Late that afternoon I went to the main station to say thanks for the dedication of these lifeguards. When I walked into the station I was struck by a sign on the wall in large red letters which read: If in doubt, go! It struck me that this ought to be on the wall of every church and on the table of every heart as we see the multitudes around us."

Each of us would love to influence large crowds for Jesus. But, it may be that He has called us to touch one person who will change the world.

39—God is My Compass

A survey some years ago revealed the number one question believers were asking. Their most puzzling problem was, "How do I know God's will for my life?" There are critical moments when we may have to choose a career, a spouse, a place to live or a car to purchase. We don't have to be convinced that God's will for us is important at those times. We know that understanding God's will is important when facing those decisions. Major crossroads, though, aren't the only occasions when knowing God's will is important. We have choices to make every day and it is important that we know what God wants us to do on a daily basis. Every morning we are confronted with knowing what God's will is for that day.

When we face decisions, we have a variety of ways by which we determine what to do. Bob Kuechenberg, formerly a professional football player for the Miami Dolphins, told *Newsweek* magazine why he went to college. He explained, "My father and uncle were human cannonballs in carnivals. My father told me, 'Go to college or be a cannonball.' Then one day my uncle came out of the cannon, missed the net and hit the Ferris wheel. I decided to go to college."

When we face options that affect our destinies, it is important for us to follow the right leader. A man driving through the Black Hills of South Dakota, near Mount Rushmore, ran into a snowstorm and lost all sense of direction. Frustrated, he peered out his side window and saw a snowplow. Relieved, he kept as close to the vehicle as he could while it removed snow from the pavement. At times the heavy snowfall made it difficult to follow the machine. After a while, the plow stopped and the operator got out and walked over to the car. "Mister, where are you headed?" the driver asked. "I'm on my way to Montana," the man responded. "Well, you'll never get there following me. I'm plowing out this parking lot!" I know a lot of people who have gone miles and miles, yet have never left the parking lot.

There is a better method of guidance than that. The Psalmist said, *"I will instruct you and teach you in the way you should go; I will counsel you and watch over you. Do not be like the horse or the mule, which have no understanding but must be controlled by bit and bridle or they will not come to you"* (Psalm 32:8-9).

For those of us who have been controlled by God's bit and bridle there is hope. We can be guided by His eye. That is the literal meaning of verse 38. The New American Standard version reads: *"I will counsel you with My eye upon you."* When I was a child, my parents guided me that way. They would look at me and I would know whether or not they approved of what I was doing.

Bob Mumford, when commenting about the way God guides us, said, "God wants to bring us beyond the point where we need signs to discern His guiding hand. Satan cannot counterfeit the peace of God or the love of God dwelling in us. When Christ's abiding presence becomes our guide, then guidance becomes an almost unconscious response to the gentle moving of His Holy Spirit within us."

Still, it is sometimes hard to know what God wants us to do. Gwen and I were staying with friends and they showed us a video of Adrian Plass, an Englishman with a humorous way of describing church life. We laughed as he narrated the following dilemma, but we identified with what he was saying about "open doors" as a means of direction: "Well, I thought the Lord was opening one door for us, but when I pushed the door I found it was shut. So, I tried another door and this one did open so I passed through and on the other side found another door. But, this door was shut like the first door. And, when I tried to turn around and go back through the previous door by way of the other door I found that that had shut behind us.

"So we were, as it were, stuck between the two doors. And, I had to climb up as it were through a skylight and down a skylight and we found ourselves in front of a fourth door.

And, this door was slightly ajar so I pushed it, but it was on a very strong spring and it swung back and hit me quite hard in the face. So, I did rebuke that door, and in fact all other doors as well, and we did wonder whether doors were opening through which something demonic might come. So we decided to ask the Lord to show us guidance by laying a fleece, but He shut that door."

Does that sound familiar to anyone? We sometimes go through contortions to find God's will because, as believers, we instinctively know that His plan for us is the best way we can live.

According to C. S. Lewis, there are two kinds of people: those who say to God, "Thy will be done," and those to whom God says, "All right, then, have it your way." Those of us who have had it our way are learning to say, "Your will be done."

When I began pastoring last century (that sounds old, doesn't it?) I read a book by Robert Schuller and he made a statement that I have never forgotten. He said, "I'd rather be right than have my own way." When I realize that my way is not necessarily God's way I remember the wisdom of Robert Schuller's words. It is always better to be right than to have our own way.

Learning to trust God's guidance is part of our experience as Christians. Before the days of modern navigation aids, a traveler made the Atlantic crossing in a boat equipped with two compasses. One was fixed to the deck where the man at the wheel could see it. The other compass was fastened up on one of the masts, and often a sailor would be seen climbing up to inspect it.

One of the passengers asked the captain, "Why do you have two compasses?" "This is an iron vessel," replied the captain, "and the compass on the deck is often affected by the metal. That isn't the case with the compass on the mast. It always reads our heading correctly. We regularly check it so we can make sure that we're going in the right direction.

We live on the move and often look at our circumstances to determine what to do next. There is nothing wrong with that. Just make sure that you "climb the mast" regularly to check the compass that never deviates from the truth. Let God guide you with His eyes. That's the surest way to reach your destination safely.

40—Mothers Deserve a Day

I have never seen anyone exceed the love and patience of a good mother. The now-defunct *Saturday Evening Post* once ran a cartoon that showed a young boy about five or six years old talking on the telephone. He was saying, "Mom is in the hospital, the twins and Roxie and Billie and Sally and the dog and me and Dad are all home alone." That is more serious than it is funny. It's a lonely feeling when Mom isn't home.

Sometimes we take for granted all the things they do. A teacher had just given a lesson on magnets and followed it with a test. One question read, "My name starts with 'M,' has six letters and picks up things. What am I?" She was surprised when half the class responded, "Mother."

A Spanish proverb is a sobering reminder for pastors like me of our relative influence: "An ounce of mother is worth a pound of clergy." As much as we want to influence the lives of those we serve, nothing can approach the effect a godly mother has on her children. Children learn about the world, themselves and God from their mothers.

In my Bible readings, I love Paul's letters. Most of his letters were addressed to churches, but a few were addressed to individuals. The last letter he wrote, in fact, was addressed to a young man he mentored in the ministry. Timothy's father was Greek and, as far as we know, not a believer. Paul nurtured Timothy's faith, but never forgot the origin of that faith. As Paul awaited execution, he wrote his last letter to Timothy. He said, *"I have been reminded of your sincere faith, which first lived in your grandmother Lois and in your mother Eunice and, I am persuaded, now lives in you also"* (2 Timothy 1:5).

Timothy, when he met Paul, was already living out the faith he had seen in his mother and his grandmother. That faith, in the original language of the New Testament, is called "sincere." Literally, the word is *anhypokritos*—"not hypocritical." The word *hypokritos* was used of the masks

Greek actors wore in the theater. The mask was essential to Greek theater because men played female roles as well as male roles. The thought of *hypokritos* is that someone can hide his identity behind a false front. It is easy to put on a mask for those we see occasionally, but we can't fool our families. They see us as we really are. Paul credits Timothy's faith to the "unhypocritical" faith he saw at home. His mother and grandmother didn't put on masks, their faith was genuine. And, genuine faith is contagious.

My mother had that kind of faith. When she was wheeled into surgery for cancer several years before she passed away, a nurse asked if she was nervous. She said, "I'll either wake up here or in heaven and either one is fine with me." That kind of faith is contagious.

For those of us who have been blessed with mothers who love us and show us the way to live, we can identify with the little girl who was in a church program. She had a simple verse to quote but, faced with the congregation looking at her, went blank. She had memorized the Scripture for the occasion but the sight of hundreds of eyes peering at her caused her to forget her line. In the front row, her mother was almost as desperate as the little girl was. The mother gestured and moved her lips trying to form the words for the girl, but it did no good.

Finally, the mother, as a last resort, whispered the Scripture verse to her daughter: "I am the light of the world." Immediately the child's face lit up and a smile appeared on it as she said with supreme confidence: "My mother is the light of the world!" Of course, everybody smiled and some laughed aloud. But, on reflection that may not be far from wrong. A mother is, in many ways, the light of a child's world.

My father was a preacher but, quite honestly, my mother taught me most of what I know about God. I learned that God loves me from my mother's wise advice. She explained things in a way that I could understand them. It is easy for us to underestimate the value of the lessons a child receives from a loving mom in the informal setting of the home.

One night, when I was twelve, I woke up feeling that I had committed the unpardonable sin. When I was a child, I felt that to win God's love I had to be perfect. Needless to say I wasn't. With my salvation depending on me, or so I thought, I was upset that night. It was Mom who sat up with me and explained God's infinite mercy and grace to a frightened twelve-year-old. After explaining God's vast love for me, she asked a question that I have never forgotten. I have used it over and over again to help individuals who fear that they can't be forgiven: "Do you think that at twelve years of age you have exhausted God's infinite mercy?" That question brought me back to my senses. I learned that night that my salvation is never dependent on my deserving it. It's an act of God's grace and I accept the gift of salvation when I believe in Him. I am forever indebted to my mom for sitting up with me that night, explaining how good God is. It shaped my life and still shapes my ministry.

One of my heroes from history is G. Campbell Morgan. He pastored Westminster Chapel in London, England. He also traveled extensively with D. L. Moody in this country. He had four sons and they all became preachers. At a family reunion, a friend asked one of the sons, "Which Morgan is the greatest preacher?" The son glanced at his father and said, "Mother!" I understand what that young man meant.

If you are a mother, don't allow anyone to demean your importance. Tony Campolo is a professor of sociology and often mingles with highly educated individuals. He wrote of an experience he shared with his wife. He said, "I was once at a very sophisticated academic gathering at the University of Pennsylvania. I didn't want to be there, and I felt uncomfortable with the kinds of conversation that were going on. A woman colleague who taught sociology struck up a conversation with my wife and me. At one point she turned to my wife and asked, in a condescending fashion, 'And what is it that you do, my dear?' My wife, who is one of the most articulate people I know, shot back, 'I am socializing two *Homo sapiens* into the dominant values of the Judeo-Christian tradition in order that they might be the instruments for the transformation of the social order into the kind of eschatological utopia that God willed from the beginning of Creation!' Then my wife asked politely and sweetly, 'And what is it that you do?' The woman answered humbly, 'I...I...teach sociology.' "

Mothers, you are shaping the world by shaping your children and you certainly deserve a day. In fact, you deserve much more than a day and we honor you.

41–That's What Friends Are For

Mrs. Edwards, a guidance counselor, recalled a conversation she had with a young student. She wrote, "Cheri, a first grader, was having trouble adjusting to school. I called her into my office for a chat, confident that my many years of training as a guidance counselor had more than prepared me to handle the situation. 'Cheri,' I said, 'I want to be your friend. I will never tell your mommy or your daddy or your teacher anything we talk about if you don't want me to. I want you to know that you can always trust me.' With tearful eyes, she looked up and replied, 'Gee, Mrs. Edwards, you're just like my dog.'" In many cases a dog can be a man's (or a girl's) best friend.

It's possible for a show of friendliness to become a formality that is shallow at best. A priest saw Robert Schuller's TV program *Hour of Power* and was impressed by Schuller's practice of having everyone turn to greet the worshipers seated near him or her. The priest felt that his church was a bit stuffy and could use a little more friendliness. So, one Sunday he announced that the following week they were going to initiate this custom of greeting each other. At the close of this same service, a man turned around to the woman seated behind him and said, "Good morning." She looked at him with shock at his boldness and said, "I beg your pardon! That friendliness business doesn't start until next Sunday."

True friendship is much more meaningful than going through the motions. The Bible provides a perfect example of it. When the apostle Paul was writing his last letter, just before his execution in Rome, he described his situation to Timothy. He included in that letter a revealing statement: *"Only Luke is with me"* (2 Timothy 4:11). That statement hints at the close relationship between Luke and Paul. Early church tradition suggests that Luke was born a Greek in Antioch and became a physician before being converted. After his conversion, we know that he joined Paul, Silas and Timothy in Troas on Paul's second missionary journey. In the book of Acts Luke described being shipwrecked with

Paul on the island of Malta. The book of Acts ends with Paul being jailed in Rome with his friend Timothy nearby.

After Paul's death, early church tradition suggests that Luke went to Greece from Rome where he wrote his two-volume history of Jesus and the early church–the Gospel of Luke and the book of Acts. His second volume, the Acts of the Apostles, is mostly about Paul's missionary journeys. In four passages, Luke includes himself in the story, using the pronoun "we" to narrate various events.

One second century historical record explains that Luke had remained unmarried and died in Boetia at the age of 84. As with all tradition, some of our information about Luke is conjecture. One thing about Luke, though, is certain. Paul never had a better friend.

We live in such a competitive society that it's easy to overlook the importance of having a friend who isn't in your life to compete with you, but is there to help complete you. Some missionaries to the Philippines set up a croquet game in their front yard. Their *Agta Negrita* neighbors came to watch so the missionaries taught them to play.

At one point the missionaries explained that when you hit an opponent's ball with yours one of the options available to you is hitting the other person's ball as far as possible off the field of play. Given that opportunity, a young Filipino didn't understand why he would want to do that so he refused. As the match continued the players would go through the last wicket and then, surprisingly, go back to help the other players. It was a team effort. Finally, the last player finished. The missionaries watched as all the Filipinos shouted and cheered for the first time, "We won! We won!" That's the spirit of authentic friendship. They weren't competing against their friends, they wanted to help them win.

Dale Carnegie wrote *How to Win Friends and Influence People* and with it influenced an entire generation of

Americans. One of his helpful suggestions on making friends will work for anyone. He said, "You can make more friends in two months by becoming interested in other people than you can in two years by trying to get other people interested in you." I have repeatedly seen the shyest people overcome their timidity when they start talking about a topic that interests them.

Where Gwen and I live there are quite a few fishermen. If you can get a quiet fisherman talking about fishing he is hard to stop. Many friendships have begun with someone simply taking an interest in another person's vocation and hobbies.

That formula has always been effective. In Queen Victoria's time, a young woman had the good fortune of being escorted to dinner by William E. Gladstone, who was considered one of the most brilliant diplomats of the nineteenth century. On the following evening, the same young woman was escorted by Benjamin Disraeli, novelist, statesman and twice prime minister of Great Britain. When asked for her impression of these two great rivals, she replied, "After an evening with Gladstone, I thought he was the most brilliant man I'd ever met. After an evening with Disraeli, I thought myself to be the most fascinating woman in the world!" There is no question as to which evening she enjoyed the most.

The truth about friendship is that our friends make us feel better about ourselves. There is a striking example of that in the account of a graduate student who went to live for one year with the Navajo Indians of the Southwest. Part of the research for his doctoral dissertation included living in the Navajo community. An elderly grandmother of the family with whom he resided spoke no English at all, yet a very close friendship formed between the her and the student. Over the months he learned a few phrases of Navajo, and she picked up a little of the English language. When it was time for him to return to the campus and write his dissertation, the entire tribe held a going-away celebration. As he prepared to get into the pickup truck and leave the Navajo community for the last time, the grandmother came to tell him good-bye. With tears streaming from her eyes, she placed her hands on either side of his face, looked directly into his eyes and expressed one of the highest compliments that can be paid to friendship. She said, "I like me best when I'm with you."

We do feel better about ourselves when we are with real friends. Even when we are struggling, our friends bring out the best in us. Each of us needs a friend who will make us feel good about ourselves.

My regard for friendship was made clearer by the story of two young men who went into World War I together. They had been neighbors and friends all their lives. They played the same sports in school so they could be on the same athletic teams. They went into the army together and were assigned to the same unit. One day, after a particularly fierce firefight, their outfit returned to the trenches and discovered that one of the two friends was missing. He was still lying in no-man's-land between their position and the enemy.

His best friend asked the sergeant if he could go get his buddy. "You can go," said the officer, "but it's not worth it. Your friend is probably killed, and you will throw your own life away." But, the man went. Somehow, he managed to get to his friend, hoist him onto his shoulder, and bring him back to the trenches. The two of them tumbled in together and lay in the trench bottom. The officer looked at the would-be rescuer, and said, "I told you it wouldn't be worth it. Your friend is dead and you are wounded." "It was worth it, though, sir," he said. His commander responded, "What do you mean, 'worth it?' I tell you your friend is dead." "Yes, sir," the boy answered, "but it was worth it, because when I got to him he was still alive, and he said to me, 'Jim, I knew you'd come.' "

I want a friend who will be there when everyone else gives up on me. Even more than that, I want to be the kind of friend who is there for my friends. I want the friends in my life to be able to say to me, "I knew you'd come." That's what friends are for.

42—Don't Forget

Memorials mean different things to different people. I read about a man who was sporting a two-carat diamond. One of his friends noticed it and asked, "Where did you get that beautiful diamond?" The man responded, "This is a memorial stone. A friend of mine died leaving a will. In the will he named me the executor and provided that the executor should take $3,000 out of his estate and buy a stone to his memory. This is it!" What a clever, self-serving way to remember someone.

Sometimes a memorial can be misunderstood. One Sunday morning, the pastor noticed little Alex was staring up at a large plaque that hung in the foyer of the church. The plaque was covered with names, and small American flags were mounted on either side of it. The seven-year-old had been staring at the plaque for some time, so the pastor walked up, stood beside him and said quietly, "Good morning, Alex." "Good morning, Pastor," replied the young man, still focused on the plaque. He asked, "Pastor McGhee, what is this?" "Well, son, it's a memorial to all the men and women who died in the service." Soberly they stood together, staring at the large plaque. Little Alex's voice was barely audible when he finally managed to ask, "Which one, the 9 o'clock or the 10 o'clock service?"

Memorial Day weekend is a time to remember those who died in the service. Our American way of life has been preserved at the cost of many lives. We owe a huge debt to those who have given their lives to protect our freedom.

While we remember them this weekend, a Scripture comes to mind. David expressed an attitude that would be good for each of us to share: *"Praise the LORD, O my soul, and forget not all his benefits–who forgives all your sins and heals all your diseases"* (Psalm 103:2-3).

One of the failures of human nature is that we are prone to forget. You don't want to forget birthdays or anniversaries.

You certainly don't want to forget what God has done for us through Jesus.

The late dictator of Greece, General Metaxas, was once invited to try out a new seaplane. As a trained pilot who loved to fly, he decided to take the controls himself. He flew the plane extremely well until he was about to land the plane at an airport. His host spoke up and said, "Excuse me, Excellency, but it would be more suitable to come down on the sea as this is a seaplane." "But of course," laughed the General, "What am I thinking of!"

The General thereupon made a perfect landing on the water and turning to his host he remarked, "I must compliment you for drawing attention to the incredible blunder that I nearly made." Upon saying that, the general opened the door of the seaplane and stepped out into the sea.

Forgetting where we are can be embarrassing, but in the Bible, forgetting is much more serious. When Scripture says that God remembers it means that God is about to do something. Remembering is always connected to action. In the same way, Scripture connects forgetting with moral failure, not mental weakness. To forget is to fail to act. When David said, *"Forget not all his benefits"* he was encouraging us to appropriate what God had provided.

One of God's benefits that we are to receive is forgiveness of sin. He *"forgives all your sins,"* not just some of them. The Hebrew language is very graphic and this word *"sins"* is an interesting example of that. The word is *'avon*. It describes crooked, twisted and distorted behavior. But the root of it is even more expressive. Girdlestone, in his *Synonyms of the Old Testament*, explains the word this way: "A course of conduct that will in the end prove unprofitable to the doer. It presents the evil devices of man in their false, hollow and unreal aspect. By the use of this word the inspired writers put a stamp of nothingness or unreality on every departure from the law of God."

Literally, the word means emptiness or nothingness. That is what sin is. It is emptiness. It is trying to find fulfillment in things that don't fill us. It is looking for pleasure only to see the exhilaration of the experience evaporate.

One of the benefits we receive from God is forgiveness from all the things we have tried apart from God that left us empty and frustrated. Our twisted behavior was just an attempt to stop the ache on the inside. David found that in adultery with Bathsheba and the murder of her husband, Uriah, he was left in spiritual pain.

Many people have a story not unlike the *U2* song, "Still haven't found what I'm looking for." Thank God for forgiveness. Don't ever forget to appropriate that wonderful gift. There is no need for any of us to live empty lives.

To paraphrase Henry Drummond, a great Scottish preacher: "We all know who deserved to die. We all know Who *did* die. We know *we* were not wounded for our transgressions, we were not bruised for our iniquities. But, we know Who was. The Lord has not dealt with us according to our iniquities; but we know with Whom He has. We know Who bore our sins in His own body on the tree—One who had no sins of His own."

Every Friday night, until his death in 1973, an old man would walk to a broken pier on the eastern seacoast of Florida. He would walk slowly, and slightly bent, with a bucket of shrimp. Seagulls would flock to him and he would feed them. Friends would recognize the man, Captain Eddie Rickenbacker. Many years before, in October 1942, Captain Rickenbacker was on a mission in a B-17 to deliver an important message to General Douglas MacArthur in New Guinea. But, there was an unexpected detour which would hurl Captain Eddie into the most dangerous adventure of his life.

Somewhere over the South Pacific, the Flying Fortress became lost beyond the reach of radio. Fuel ran dangerously low, so the men ditched their plane in the ocean. For nearly a month Captain Eddie and his companions were stranded at sea. Eight days out, their rations were long gone or destroyed by the salt water. It would take a miracle to sustain them. One of the men led devotions and prayed for a miracle. Then they sang a hymn of praise.

Something landed on his head. He knew that it was a sea gull. The gull meant food—if he could catch it. Captain Eddie caught the gull. The men ate it. They used its insides for bait to catch fish. The survivors were sustained and their hopes renewed because a lone sea gull, uncharacteristically hundreds of miles from land, offered itself as a sacrifice.

Captain Eddie made it. And he never forgot. Because every Friday evening, about sunset...on a lonely stretch along the eastern Florida seacoast...you could see an old man walking...white-haired, bushy-eyebrowed, slightly bent. His bucket filled with shrimp was to feed the gulls.

"Forget not," David said. About 2,000 years ago, Jesus sacrificed His life to keep us alive. May we never forget.

43—Rejoice in the Lord

Grace Crews related an incident to which many of us can relate. "When I was working in a U.S. Senator's office, one of my responsibilities was to conduct tours for visitors. One day I had just finished a tour and was told that another unscheduled group would be arriving soon. I hurried to get lunch.

"A bit frazzled at the last-minute change in plans, I was trying to get my thoughts together when I looked up to see someone staring at me from across the room. That person looks familiar, I thought, glancing away. Again, I looked up and the unidentified woman's eyes met mine. Finally, the third time, I smiled, raised my hand, and waved. The woman smiled and waved back. I don't have time to be sociable, I realized, concentrating on my lunch. Then my mind snapped into focus—the woman who looked so familiar was my own reflection in the mirrored wall."

Many of us know what it is to get so caught up in the rush of life that we lose our sense of what's happening around us.

Lily Tomlin made an astute observation: "The trouble with the rat race is that even if you win you're still a rat."

Paul always ends his letters with practical issues. He touches what we believe but then relates our beliefs to how we live. One of the problems of the Philippians is still a problem—our mental attitudes and how they affect our lives.

When Paul wrote the Philippian church, he was in prison in Rome waiting to learn whether he would be acquitted or executed. With Nero on the throne, he had every reason to think he may die, though he was acquitted this time. While in prison and facing the prospect of execution he wrote amazing advice for all of us, *"Always be full of joy in the Lord. I say it again—rejoice!"* (Philippians 4:4—NLT). That is, for Paul, one of the keys to a satisfying life. We can live beyond the control of our circumstances if we learn to *"be full of joy in the Lord."*

Too often Christians have not manifested the kind of joy that draws people to faith in Christ. Oliver Wendell Holmes once said, "I might have entered the ministry if certain clergymen I knew had not looked and acted so much like undertakers."

Robert Louis Stevenson once entered in his diary, as if he was recording an extraordinary phenomenon, "I have been to Church today, and am not depressed."

It is hard for us to imagine that we can have joy in the middle of trying circumstances. Yet Paul uses the Imperative mood. It is a command to be full of joy and no one is excepted. That principle is carried over from the Old Testament. David was in a precarious position when he penned Psalm 63. He was in a cave, surrounded by Philistines, and was waiting for the stirring in the tops of the trees to indicate that God was moving ahead of him in battle. He wrote, *"Because your love is better than life, my lips will glorify you. I will praise you as long as I live, and in your name I will lift up my hands"* (verses 3-4).

Whether we are in prison or in a cave, whether we are enjoying God's blessing or struggling through a crisis, we can be full of joy in the Lord.

When Luke wrote his Gospel and described the birth of Jesus the recurring theme is joy. Jesus came into a world that was filled with political, religious and moral corruption. When He came, joy broke through the depressing circumstances that faced the human race.

Paul doesn't tell us to rejoice that we are in prison or to be full of joy because we are suffering. He tells us that our joy is in the Lord. In addition, we can always rejoice in Him. Christian joy is independent of things on earth because it has its source in the continual presence of God.

Our attitude is connected to another person and another place. Maybe you have observed this. At a sporting event, the crowd is watching a game but suddenly responds with a roar having nothing to do with the game they are watching. A score has gone up on the scoreboard showing that a team they don't like is losing. We are watching a game that is played out in our lives, but the scoreboard we can also see tells us that Jesus has won every battle. I may not be able to enjoy today's events, but I can rejoice in the big picture. Jesus has won!

Helmut Thielicke pastored in Berlin during World War II. His consistent faith and witness in spite of Hitler's ungodly rule gave him credibility to address Christians after the war. Many of us would do well to ponder these comments from the pen of Helmut Thielicke: "Should we not see that lines of laughter about the eyes are just as much marks of faith as are the line of care and seriousness? Is it only earnestness that is baptized? Is laughter pagan? We have already allowed too much that is good to be lost to the church and cast many pearls before swine. A church is in a bad way when it banishes laughter from the sanctuary and leaves it to the cabaret, the nightclub and the toastmasters."

Not even pastoring during Hitler's tyranny could dampen Thielicke's joy.

I hope that each of us will have days when joy comes readily. Reality is that we may also face difficult days. But, our circumstances do not determine whether or not we can be joyful. We rejoice in the Lord and no matter what is happening in our lives for the moment, He is still Lord. He stands above our troubles and we can draw our joy from Him.

The world is hungry for that kind of joy. Tony Campolo has that kind of contagious attitude. He wrote: "I seem to be particularly dangerous when I get on elevators. Our society teaches us to turn and face the doors and stand there quietly. Once when I was in the elevator of a New York skyscraper filled with very serious-faced businesspeople, I smiled and said, 'Lighten up. We're going to be traveling together for quite a while. Why don't we sing?' Incredibly, they did! I don't know whether they were intimidated by me or just wanted to have some fun, but businessmen with attaché cases in hand and businesswomen in their power suits joined me in singing, 'You Are My Sunshine.' When I got off at the seventieth floor, one man got off and walked down the hall with me, wearing a big smile on his face. I asked him, 'Are you going to the same meeting I'm going to?' 'Nah,' he said, 'I just wanted to finish the song.' "

Maybe there are people around us who want to hear a happy song in the face of the pressures of their days. Paul says that we can sing and be joyful no matter what is going on in our lives. That kind of joy is contagious.

44—Courage

There are many different qualities important to someone who wants to live a life of faith. Not the least of these traits is courage. Whether we are young or old, courage is an important part of the life of any believer.

One summer evening during a violent thunderstorm, a mother was tucking her small boy into bed. She was about to turn off the light when he asked with a tremor in his voice, "Mommy, will you sleep with me tonight?" The mother smiled and gave him a reassuring hug. "I can't dear," she said, "I have to sleep with your daddy." A long silence was broken at last by his shaky little voice: "The big sissy." Even little people have an instinct to identify courage.

I love sports. My wife, Gwen, thinks I would watch a Tiddly Winks Championship if there was such a thing and it was televised. I especially enjoy watching football. One football coach was describing a game his team had played against a far superior team. Not one of their running plays had gained any yardage in the contest and reporters asked him, after the game, why his team's running plays were such a failure. The coach answered, "We were tipping them off. They knew exactly who was going to carry the ball. Every time we broke from the huddle, two of our running backs were laughing and the other one was white as a sheet."

Paul addressed the issue of courage when he wrote the Corinthians, *"Be on your guard; stand firm in the faith; be men of courage; be strong"* (1 Corinthians 16:13). That is a powerful admonition. *"Be men* [and I might add, women] *of courage."* In the King James Version it is stated robustly, *"Quit you like men."* Women, of course, are not excluded from this idea of bravery. Some of the bravest people in history have been women who faced hardships and overcame them with fierce courage.

Setting gender aside, Paul's advice to the Corinthians still applies to each of us. Paul practiced what he preached. When he was writing the Philippian church from a prison cell, not knowing whether he would live or die, he included this thought: *"I eagerly expect and hope that I will in no way be ashamed, but will have sufficient courage so that now as always Christ will be exalted in my body, whether by life or by death"* (Philippians 1:20). Let's admit it. All of us are looking at either life or death and it takes courage to face either one.

One thing must be said about Christian faith. Jesus doesn't deceive us. He calls us to courage. Rather than His challenge turning us away from faith, though, it appeals to our higher instincts. The result is a body of believers who rise above every challenge and respond positively to any situation.

Not long ago at a high school, three military recruiters showed up to address some seniors. Graduation was only a few months away, and the military men were there for an obvious reason. They wanted to inform the graduating young men and women of the options and opportunities military service would provide.

The meeting was to last forty-five minutes. Each recruiter—representing Army, Navy, and Marine Corps—was to have fifteen minutes. The Army and Navy recruiters were carried away. When it came time for the Marine to speak, he had two minutes. So, he walked to the podium with two minutes remaining to make his pitch. He stood utterly silent for a full sixty seconds—half of his time. Then he said this: "I doubt whether there are two or three of you in this room who could even cut it in the Marine Corps. I want to see those two or three immediately in the dining hall when we are dismissed." He turned smartly and sat down.

When he arrived in the dining hall, a mob of students was waiting for him. They were ready to take on the challenge. Jesus is that kind of Recruiter. He invites all of us to come, but He doesn't conceal the fact that faith calls for courage.

The Lord who faced Gethsemane and proceeded to Calvary inspires us to face our fears and walk in faith.

When Martin Luther was facing the possibility of torture and martyrdom for his faith he proclaimed, "Here I stand, God help me, I can do no other." One of his most intense enemies was Duke George. Once when an assignment called for him to pass through Duke George's territory, and the death threat there, his friends tried to talk him into changing his plans. His response was typical of the bold, outspoken Luther, "I will go though it rain devils and Duke Georges for three days."

Christian courage doesn't always make headlines. There are moments of bravery often unnoticed except by a very few people. One such case involved a student from a public school in Arkansas. This seventh-grader did something that wasn't popular in his school. He took a New Testament to class with him, tucked inside his shirt.

One day three boys approached him, grabbed his New Testament and said, "You sissy. Religion is for sissies. Prayer is for sissies. Don't ever again bring this Bible back to school."

He handed his Bible back to the biggest one of the three and said, "Here, see if you've got enough courage to carry this around school just one day." He immediately won their admiration and made three new friends.

Courage brings rich rewards. A little boy and his brother were given the job of starting a country school's old-fashioned, pot-bellied coal stove before the start of classes each day. One morning the two boys poured kerosene on the hot coals and the stove blew sky high. Glenn would have escaped, but his brother had been left behind. Rushing back to help, Glenn suffered terrible burns, as did his brother. When others arrived, the building was engulfed in flames. They dragged him out of the school more dead than alive. His brother died, and Glenn's legs sustained severe damage.

While Glenn was in the hospital he overheard his doctor telling his mother that her son would die. He didn't want to die and made up his mind that he would fight to live. He then heard a doctor tell his mother that he would be a cripple because of the damage to his legs. The truth is Glenn's legs had no feeling in them. His mother massaged his legs each day after he came home from the hospital, but they were still numb. He wanted to walk but he was confined either to a bed or a wheelchair.

One day his mother left him in the yard in his wheelchair. He threw himself from it, dragged himself to the fence around their property and pulled himself along, stake to stake. He wore a smooth path in the yard beside the fence. Ultimately, he was able to stand and walk feebly. With persistent effort, he was able to, at last, run. He ran for the sheer joy of running.

Glenn entered Madison Square Garden in 1934, this young man who was not supposed to survive, who would surely never walk, who could never hope to run. In addition, this determined young man, Dr. Glenn Cunningham, ran the world's fastest mile.

In our world, it takes courage to identify with Jesus Christ. But, after all, courage is one of our strong suits. The person who will influence others is a person who walks through his life filled with courage. Whether facing life or death that person can say, with Paul, *"I eagerly expect and hope that I will in no way be ashamed, but will have sufficient courage so that now as always Christ will be exalted in my body, whether by life or by death"* (Philippians 1:20).

45—Get to Know God

Knowledge is important. That's why we spend so much time in classrooms where we learn to read, write and add numbers. That's why we train to become proficient in our professions. When I lift the hood of my vehicle, I don't have a clue as to what I'm seeing. I do trust that the mechanic knows the difference between the carburetor and the fan belt.

When I go to a doctor, I read the educational qualifications on the wall of his or her office. I'm relieved to know that my doctor has received a good education. My wife, Gwen, recently asked a surgeon if she had done a particular surgery Gwen was facing. The surgeon said that it was a good question. We were both gratified to learn that the doctor has lengthy experience in this particular operation. I don't want to be on an operating table and hear, just before being put to sleep, "Does anyone know where the appendix is?"

Knowledge is not only important, it's a good thing. Someone once sent John Wesley a note that said, "The Lord has told me to tell you that He doesn't need your book-learning, your Greek and your Hebrew." Wesley answered, "Thank you, sir. Your letter was superfluous, however, as I already knew the Lord has no need for my 'book-learning,' as you put it. However, although the Lord has not directed me to say so, on my own responsibility I would like to say to you that the Lord does not need your ignorance either."

It's important to learn from others and there's nothing wrong with second-hand knowledge. I encourage everyone to read books. A person who can read but doesn't has no advantage over a person who can't read. A world of knowledge is available to anyone who will read.

Paul, in 2 Timothy 4:13 (NLT), urged Timothy: *"When you come, be sure to bring the coat I left with Carpus at Troas. Also bring my books, and especially my papers."* Charles

Haddon Spurgeon had an insightful comment on that request. He said of the apostle, "He is inspired, yet he wants books! He has been preaching at least for thirty years, yet he wants books! He has seen the Lord, yet he wants books. He has had a wider experience than most men have, yet he wants books! He has been caught up into the third heaven, and has heard things which it is unlawful to utter, yet he wants books! He has written the major part of the New Testament, yet he wants books!"

Don't underestimate the power of "book-learning." When it comes to studying the Bible we have to admit that if someone had not studied Greek and Hebrew we wouldn't have an English Bible. Since the Old Testament was written in Hebrew and the New Testament was written in Greek, the work of expert translators has made the Bible available to us in English.

My reflection on knowledge was initiated by a Bible Study I lead on the Outer Banks. We were studying 2 Timothy and I came to a statement by the apostle Paul that struck me forcibly. He said, *"I know whom I have believed, and am convinced that he is able to guard what I have entrusted to him for that day"* (2 Timothy 1:12). It's clear that what convinced Paul of God's ability was the fact that Paul knew Him.

An interesting thing about the original language of the New Testament is that there are different words for "knowing." All the words are valid and we have experienced knowledge in the different ways. One of the words describes knowing as the result of gathering evidence and evaluating it. If someone I trust eats a piece of chocolate cake and tells me that it tastes good, I know that it does. I don't know because I tasted it, I know because I was given that information by someone else.

Paul used a different Greek word for "knowing." He used a word that means, "I see." It describes a knowing that comes from grasping the truth personally. Paul wasn't just reporting on what he had been told about God, he was reporting on what he personally knew about God.

When Paul said, *"I know whom I have believed"* he was describing knowledge based on his personal experience. I can know *about* God because someone I trust gives me information. I know God in Paul's sense of the word when I personally experience Him. Many people know about God but remain unconvinced of His ability. The solution for that problem is to know Him personally.

I have a joint bank account with my wife, Gwen. I don't worry about what she is doing with our resources because I know her. I don't just know about her, I know her. I trust her because I know what she is like. I am confident in her character because I have experienced her integrity. None of us would meet a stranger and set up a joint bank account with him or her just because of information we gathered from others. We would want to know that person for ourselves so we could be convinced of his or her trustworthiness.

It is our mission to introduce people to Jesus. We aren't making disciples for ourselves and we aren't asking anyone to be convinced just because we have experienced him. We are saying to everyone; get to know Jesus for yourself. If you know Him by personal experience, you will be convinced. Don't just know about Him. Many people know about Him. The ones changed by His power are the ones who meet Him in a way that leaves them saying, "I see. I get it now."

A certain old recluse lived deep in the mountains of Colorado. When he died, distant relatives came from the city to collect his valuables. Upon arriving, all they saw was an old shack with an outhouse beside it. Inside the shack, next to the rock fireplace, was an old cooking pot and his mining equipment. A cracked table with a three-legged chair stood guard by a tiny window, and a kerosene lamp served as the centerpiece for the table. In the dark corner of the little room was a dilapidated cot with a threadbare bedroll on it.

The relatives picked up some of the old relics and started to leave. As they were driving away, an old friend of the recluse, on his mule, flagged them down. "Do you mind if I help myself to what's left in my friend's cabin?" he asked. "Go right ahead," they replied. After all, they thought, what inside that shack would be worth anything?

The old friend entered the shack and walked directly over to the table. He reached under it and lifted one of the floorboards. He then proceeded to take out all the gold his friend had discovered over the past 53 years—enough to build a palace. The recluse died with only his friend knowing his true worth. As the friend looked out of the little window and watched the cloud of dust behind the relatives' car disappear, he said, "They shoulda got to know him better."

We will never know the treasure available in Him until we know Him. Paul's advice to all of us is, "Get to know Him better."

46–Take Time to Think

A newly retired couple cashed in their stocks and bonds to purchase one of the finest motor homes available on the market. One of the great features of their new vehicle was the cruise control. As they were traveling up the West Coast, the husband became tired and asked his wife to drive while he went in the back to take a nap. She was not familiar with cruise control, but tried it and discovered that it worked perfectly.

She happened to be driving on one of those stretches of highway that went mile after mile without a curve in the road. After an hour of driving, she got up to go to the bathroom. While she was in the bathroom and her husband was sleeping, the camper ran off the road and was totaled. Neither she nor her husband were seriously injured, though they were shaken.

When the Highway Patrol arrived at the scene to determine the cause of the accident the officers discovered that the wife thought cruise control was the same as automatic pilot. She had confidence that the motor home would steer itself. This is not only a true story, it's also an illustration of Christians who put their lives on cruise control and neglect worship, prayer and Bible study.

There are many blessings available to us in our culture, but there is also a danger. We can get so busy that we neglect the time it takes to think. It's easy to rush through prayer and Bible reading as though we are eager to get rid of an unwelcome visitor who is intruding on our day.

Paul wrote the Colossians and challenged them in Colossians 3:2 to *"set your minds on things above, not on earthly things."* That means that we are called to make a choice about our thinking. I tend to think about things in the here and now. My mind automatically focuses on issues and problems I'm facing in the present. I deal with deadlines that drive my decisions. Paul advised me to take some time and think about things above. He doesn't want any of us to run on cruise control, get careless and wreck our lives.

Sometimes God allows circumstances to come that cause us to reorder our priorities. Bill Hybels quoted a man who wrote about his time in the hospital: "I came to realize I no longer really cared for what the world chases after, such as how much money you have in the bank and how many cars are parked in the garage. As it says in Ecclesiastes, chasing after these things is like chasing the wind, anyway. Suddenly, the rat race became vanity to me, utter vanity. I felt naked before God. If I died, I would take none of the stuff with me. All that really mattered ultimately was my relationship with the Lord, my relationship with family and friends. If it weren't for the loss of my health, I could have wasted the rest of my life chasing achievements and acquiring more transitory things."

I have observed a major problem that comes along with a lack of reflection on things above. When I don't take time to think and meditate, listen to God and do what He tells me, I lose my sense of where I'm going. Life can become, for any of us, what it's like for a hamster on a wheel. It runs furiously but goes nowhere.

Never underestimate the power of quiet time with God. It produces vision and keeps us on track with His purposes. Bible reading is one of the ways I hear from Him and its results are not always seen immediately. I read about a place in the Southwest that would not support plant life. The soil was so salty that nothing would grow. One day a woman threw seeds out the back door and, to her surprise, they began to grow. The reason is simple. Month after month, she'd thrown dishwater out of that door. The continual soaking had rinsed the salt out of the soil, making it fit for life. That's what Bible reading does for one's mind.

Curtis Carlson, founder of the Carlson Companies and best known as the inventor of Gold Bond Stamps as well as being one of the wealthiest people in Minnesota, has spent his life building and expanding. When asked what personal qualities contributed to the building of his successful empire, Carlson responded, "I think my success is the result of my ability to see, to imagine how things can be. I'm not distracted by how things are."

When we spend time in prayer, meditation and reading God's Word, we enhance our ability to see, and as Carlson puts it, "to imagine how things can be." One of the prices we pay for the rat race, in which we neglect thinking on things above, is lack of vision.

There is tremendous power in seeing a picture of the future that shapes our lives. One of the blights of civilization last century was the reality of concentration camps in Hitler's Germany. While most victims of the torture of the camps did not survive, some did. When a study was done to determine why some lived through the ordeal, the story of Victor Frankl was noted.

He was a successful Viennese psychiatrist before the Nazis threw him into such a camp. "There is only one reason," he said in a speech after the war, "why I am here today. What kept me alive was you. Others gave up hope. I dreamed. I dreamed that someday I would be here, telling you how I, Victor Frankl, had survived the Nazi concentration camps. I've never been here before, I've never seen any of you before, I've never given this speech before. But in my dreams, in my dreams, I have stood before you and said these words a thousand times."

How can we dream the kinds of dreams that will pull us through challenges? By taking the time to meditate. When we meditate on things above God can fill our hearts with pictures of the future as He wants it to be.

A model for every dreamer is Walt Disney. On Saturdays, Disney took his daughters to a local park to ride the merry-go-round and play. While sitting on a bench eating snacks and watching his children enjoy their rides on the carousel, Disney imagined an elaborate family park filled with happy families. He put every detail into place. From the Pirates of the Caribbean to Main Street USA, Disneyland is the result of Disney's ability to create the future in his mind. This pioneer of family amusement had no similar facilities to draw ideas from. He relied on his imagination to design the original blueprint.

That wasn't enough. He planned a park in Florida that would be the ultimate in family entertainment. He died before that dream became a reality. Mike Vance tells about being at Disney World soon after its completion when someone said to him, "Isn't it too bad, Mike, that Walt Disney didn't live to see this." Vance replied, "Oh, he did see it, and that's why it's here!"

My prayer is that each of us will take time to meditate on things above, read God's Word and pray. God doesn't want us to see things the way they are, He wants us to see them the way He planned them to be.

47–The Value of Storms

Storms can make us or break us. Sometimes the storm is unexpected success. Charles Conn wrote an interesting account of the dangers of success: "When I lived in Atlanta, several years ago, I noticed in the Yellow Pages, in the listing of restaurants, an entry for a place called *Church of God Grill*. The peculiar name aroused my curiosity and I dialed the number. A man answered with a cheery, 'Hello! *Church of God Grill.*'

"I asked how his restaurant had been given such an unusual name, and he told me: 'Well, we had a little mission down here, and we started selling chicken dinners after church on Sunday to help pay the bills. Well, people liked the chicken, and we did such a good business, that eventually we cut back on the church service. After a while, we just closed down the church altogether and kept on serving the chicken dinners. We kept the name we started with, and that's *Church of God Grill.*' "

Talk about getting distracted from one's mission! And, the storm that threw them off course was success.

Whether our storms feature the dangers of success or the pain of tragedy, they don't have to break us. When we are thrown into situations that require total dependence on Jesus, we can develop stronger faith. Mark's Gospel describes a storm that threatened the disciples' lives while Jesus was in the boat with them. The incident developed as they were taking a boat across the Sea of Galilee. *"A furious squall came up, and the waves broke over the boat, so that it was nearly swamped. Jesus was in the stern, sleeping on a cushion. The disciples woke him and said to him, 'Teacher, don't you care if we drown?' "* (Mark 4:37-38).

While Jesus was sleeping, the disciples were making some interesting discoveries. They learned that they weren't as strong spiritually as they thought they were. When Jesus was awakened, He identified their weaknesses. *"He said to* his disciples, 'Why are you so afraid? Do you still have no faith?' "* (Mark 4:40). Each of us wants more faith. The way God supplies it is in allowing circumstances to come that will require us to lean on Him more completely. As we increase in faith doubts may surface. Don't despair! That can be the opportunity for greater understanding of how great God is.

I met Len Hawes in Adelaide, Australia in 1990. He had a healing ministry. He told me that he was praying for the sick in one service when a little boy, 9 years old, tugged on his pant leg. The little boy asked Len, "Does God heal?" "Yes," said Len. The boy continued, "Will He heal today?" "Yes," Len answered. Then the little guy asked his last question, "Will he heal me today?" Len told me that he looked at the boy carefully to see if some serious issue was visibly wrong with him. The boy appeared relatively normal so Len said, "Yes." Then the little boy surprised the healing evangelist with his disability: "I'm blind in one eye."

Len said that he had no awareness of strong faith, but just to be compassionate he took the boy aside and prayed quietly for God to heal the blind eye. The nine-year-old yelled, "I can see." Then Len yelled, "You're kidding!"

Even the best of us can struggle with faith when we are in the middle of a crisis. When Jesus asked, *"Why are you afraid,"* He put His finger on the enemy of our faith.

When we fear that the worst will happen, our own thoughts may help to bring it about. Someone once wrote, "Fear is the wrong use of imagination. It is anticipating the worst, not the best that can happen."

A salesman, driving on a lonely country road one dark and rainy night, had a flat. He opened the trunk—no lug wrench. The light from a farmhouse could be seen dimly up the road. He set out on foot through the driving rain. Surely, the farmer would have a lug wrench he could borrow, he thought.

Of course, it was late at night—the farmer would be asleep in his warm, dry bed. Maybe he wouldn't answer the door. And, even if he did, he'd be angry at being awakened in the middle of the night. The salesman, picking his way blindly in the dark, stumbled on. By now, his shoes and clothing were soaked. Even if the farmer did answer his knock, he would probably shout something like, "What's the big idea waking me up at this hour?" This thought made the salesman angry. What right did that farmer have to refuse him the loan of a lug wrench? After all, here he was stranded in the middle of nowhere, soaked to the skin. The farmer was a selfish clod—no doubt about that!

The salesman finally reached the house and banged loudly on the door. A light went on inside, and a window opened above. A voice called out, "Who is it?" His face white with anger, the salesman responded, "You know darn well who it is. It's me! And, you can keep your blasted lug wrench. I wouldn't borrow it now if you had the last one on earth!"

Fear can create a crazy scenario.

Gwen and I walked through a storm together. She had surgery to remove a cyst the size of a cantaloupe from her abdomen. We were grateful to the many who prayed for her. God did answer prayer. The cyst was benign and there were no traces of cancer in her system. When Gwen left the recovery room and arrived at her hospital room, I leaned over and told her what the surgeon told me, "The surgery was successful." Gwen said something to me she had not confessed before the operation. She whispered, "I'm glad it wasn't cancer. I was scared." I said, "Me, too." No matter how much we want to be heroes of faith, our miracles are still manifestations of His grace.

The enemy tries to use doubt to attack each of us. An Eastern bishop was accustomed to paying an annual visit to a small religious college. On one such visit, the bishop engaged in an after-dinner conversation with the college president. The religious leader offered the opinion that the millennium could not be long in coming since everything about nature had been discovered, and all possible inventions had been made. The college president disagreed, stating that he felt the next fifty years would bring amazing discoveries and inventions. In his opinion, human beings would be flying through the skies like birds within a relatively short time. "Nonsense!" shouted the bishop. "Flight is reserved for angels!" The bishop's name was Wright. He had two sons—Orville and Wilbur.

Even though we live in a secular environment that doesn't encourage faith, God meets us where we are. Whether we are fearful disciples or have a family member who throws doubts on our dreams God honors the faith we have. The writer of Hebrews pointed out a comforting truth for us as we wrestle with crises: *"Let us fix our eyes on Jesus, the author and perfecter of our faith"* (Hebrews 12:2). He is not only the Author of our faith; He is the One who works with us in our weakness to perfect it.

Here is great news. Jesus still calms storms for those of us who are not through growing in faith. Maybe all of us have times when we are like the father who brought his tormented son to Jesus in Mark 9:24, *"I do believe; help me overcome my unbelief!"*

I would never glorify unbelief. God can be trusted and He rewards faith. Doubt is not your friend or mine. But, I know this, too. My prayer has quite often been the same as that father's request, "Jesus, I do believe. Help me overcome my unbelief."

48–The Key to Everything

In C. S. Lewis's classic, *The Lion, the Witch and the Wardrobe*, children stumble into the land of Narnia. Narnia is an ice-cold land where it is always winter and Christmas never comes. The children are taken to the home of Mr. and Mrs. Beaver. The weather starts to change, the ice begins to melt, and Mr. Beaver says that Aslan is on the move. He is describing the might and majesty of Aslan, the lion who is a type of Jesus. After Mr. Beaver explains that Aslan is on the move, the young girl, Lucy, asks, "Is–is he safe?" Replies Mr. Beaver: "Safe? Who said anything about safe? 'Course he isn't safe. But he's good."

Those who follow Jesus will admit that Jesus leads them on an adventurous journey that is filled with excitement and risk. But, we have also found that He is good. That is why we can trust Him when we don't understand what is happening to us. We know that, behind all our crazy circumstances, God is there and He is good.

When I attended seminary the Cold War was still on the verge of heating up and the Soviet Union was a major threat to world peace. One of the seminary professors had family who lived in the Soviet Union and he made a statement that struck me as odd. He said that the favorite book of Christians behind the Iron Curtain was the book of Revelation.

I found that odd because I regarded the book of Revelation as one that is difficult to interpret. Many times I have been involved in discussions about the meaning of the book and I have found a wide range of speculation about it. I agreed with one of Charles Spurgeon's comments: "I know a minister whose shoe laces I am unworthy to unloose, whose preaching is often little better than a sacred miniature painting–I might almost say holy trifling. He is great upon the ten toes of the beast, the four faces of the cherubim, and the mystical meaning of badger's skins; but the sins of the businessmen, the temptations of the times, and the needs of the age, he scarcely ever touches upon.

Such preaching reminds me of a lion engaged in mouse-hunting."

It's not that I didn't value Revelation. It's the clearest picture we have of the end of the age. It's just that the clearest picture we have is portrayed with visions and images that are difficult to understand. Anyway, I agreed with Spurgeon that our focus should be on helping people face the challenges that confront them every day.

However, the Dr. Ewert's comment about Revelation sparked a fresh interest in the purpose of the book. The professor explained that Christians behind the Iron Curtain were comforted by the fact that the book showed the ultimate triumph of Jesus. Somehow, in the midst of John's visions and the many prophecy charts I had seen, I had missed that. We may disagree about whether the scorpions whose tails sting are tanks, military helicopters or demonic powers, but we can't disagree about the fact that when all the dust of conflict has settled and the smoke of battle is cleared Jesus is triumphant.

Two passages in Revelation capture the heart of the book. In the eleventh chapter the apostle John records, *"The seventh angel sounded his trumpet, and there were loud voices in heaven, which said: 'The kingdom of the world has become the kingdom of our Lord and of his Christ, and he will reign for ever and ever' "* (verse 15).

That is our hope and that is my philosophy about the future of the world and the human race. Jesus overcomes all the forces of evil and reigns forever. Nothing could be clearer than that.

The other statement is a summation of what I believe about Jesus. He says of Himself, *"I am the Living One; I was dead, and behold I am alive for ever and ever! And I hold the keys of death and Hades"* (Revelation 1:18).

The phrase that grabs my attention is, *"I hold the keys."* I am convinced that Jesus doesn't just hold the keys to death and Hades, He *is* the key to everything." If I were asked, "What is the point of the last book of the Bible?" I would answer with something like, "It shows that Jesus is the key to everything."

Because He has forgiven our sins, He is the key to the past. He is also the key to the present (*"I am the Living One"*) and the key to the future (*"I am alive for ever and ever"*).

Through His Resurrection Jesus is the key to life. He reminds us, *"I am the Living One."* Death is an enemy of each of us. Whether it is the death of a family member, a friend, or even a pet, death hurts. Because Jesus has defeated death, we can experience victory over the pain that accompanies it. Paul said, "Where, O death, is your sting?" (1 Corinthians 15:55). There are some tough chapters in our lives, but the Resurrection of Jesus shows us God's plan for the last chapter. Because He lives we, too, can live in the confidence that not even death can defeat us.

The truth of the Resurrection has historically brought victory to believers. An interesting picture of this occurred in Austria during Napoleon's invasion. His army had advanced to within six miles of Feldkirch, Austria. It looked as though Bonaparte's men would take Feldkirch without resistance. But, as Napoleon's army advanced toward their objective in the night, the Christians of Feldkirch gathered in a little church to pray for deliverance. The next day was Easter.

When morning came the bells of the village sounded out across the countryside. The tolling of the bells celebrated the Resurrection of Jesus. Napoleon's army, not realizing it was Easter Sunday, thought that in the night the Austrian army had moved into Feldkirch and that the bells were ringing in celebration. Napoleon ordered a retreat, and the battle at Feldkirch never took place. The Easter bells caused the enemy to retreat, and peace reigned in the

Austrian countryside. The truth of the Resurrection still puts the enemy to flight and brings peace.

The title of the last book in the Bible is "The Revelation of Jesus Christ." If it is a revelation of Jesus, what does He mean to us? What Jesus means to me is illustrated by a story that Bob Weber, past president of *Kiwanis International*, used to tell. He had spoken to a club in a small town and was spending the night with a farmer on the outskirts of the community. He had just relaxed on the front porch when a newsboy delivered the evening paper. The boy noted the sign *Puppies for Sale*.

The newsboy got off his bike and said to the farmer, "How much do you want for the pups, mister?" "Twenty-five dollars, son." The boy's face dropped. "Well, sir, could I at least see them anyway?" The farmer whistled, and in a moment the mother dog came bounding around the corner of the house tagged by four of the cute puppies, wagging their tails and yipping happily. At last, another pup came straggling around the house, dragging one hind leg. "What's the matter with that puppy, mister?" the boy asked. "Well, Son, that puppy is crippled. We took her to the vet and the doctor took an X-ray. The pup doesn't have a hip joint and that leg will never be right."

To the amazement of both men, the boy dropped the bike, reached for his collection bag and took out a fifty-cent piece. "Please, mister," the boy pleaded, "I want to buy that pup. I'll pay you fifty cents every week until the twenty-five dollars is paid. Honest I will, mister." The farmer replied, "But, Son, you don't seem to understand. That pup will never, never be able to run or jump. That pup is going to be a cripple forever. Why in the world would you want such a useless pup as that?"

The boy paused for a moment, then reached down and pulled up his pant leg, exposing that all-too-familiar iron brace and leather knee-strap holding a twisted leg. The boy answered, "Mister, that pup is going to need someone who understands him to help him in life!"

How can we describe the wonder of Jesus? The Ruler of the universe, the One who reigns forever, the Christ who defeated death, has come to us who were crippled and disfigured by sin. He understands us and can help us through life. The risen, living Christ has given us hope. Revelation says that He wins. Because of Him we, too, can win.

49—The Best News of Your Life

I searched out G. K. Chesterton because I learned that he had influenced C. S. Lewis, one of my heroes. Chesterton's intellect and powerful ability to reason, combined with an impressive sense of humor, made him a formidable defender of the Christian faith. One of the issues he addressed in his book, *Orthodoxy*, is the fact that all men are born in sin.

He wrote: "Modern masters of science are much impressed with the need of beginning all inquiry with a fact. The ancient masters of religion were quite equally impressed with that necessity. They began with the fact of sin—a fact as practical as potatoes. Whether or no man could be washed in miraculous waters, there was no doubt at any rate that he wanted washing. But certain religious leaders in London, not mere materialists, have begun in our day not to deny the highly disputable water, but to deny the indisputable dirt. Certain new theologians dispute original sin, which is the only part of Christian theology which can really be proved."

If we are honest with ourselves we know from our own experiences the reality of original sin. Selfishness, rebellion and brokenness are consequences of our separation from God. Our first decisions as infants were about our own comfort and the satisfaction of our individual needs. Maybe you have noticed that even our wonderful children, after they learn to say "Mama" and "Daddy," learn to say "Mine."

We not only begin life under the influence of sin, but we soon discover the fact of human weakness. There is evidence that even when people sin, they can often be incredibly inept. For example, eighteen-year-old Charles A. Merriweather broke into a home in Northwest Baltimore on the night of November 22-23, 1978, and ransacked the house. When he discovered that the woman who lived there had only $11.50 in cash, he asked her, "How do you pay your bills?" "By check," she replied. He ordered her to write out a check for $30. Then he changed his mind and upped it to $50. "Who shall I make it out to?" asked the woman, a 34-year-old government employee. "Charles A. Merriweather," said Charles A. Merriweather, adding, "It better not bounce or I'll be back." Charles A. Merriweather was arrested several hours later.

Another example of a foolish sinner is the incident that happened to Mrs. Hollis Sharpe. Mrs. Sharpe lived in Los Angeles and regularly took her miniature poodle, Jonathan, out for a walk so he could do his duty. As a responsible and considerate citizen, Mrs. Sharpe would carry a plastic bag to clean up after Jonathan.

On the night of November 13, 1974, Jonathan had finished his business and Mrs. Sharpe was walking home with the bag in her right hand. A mugger came up behind her, shoved her to the ground, grabbed her plastic bag, jumped into a car and sped away with the spoils of his crime.

Mrs. Sharpe suffered a broken arm, but didn't lose her sense of humor. "I only wish there had been more in the bag," she said.

When Paul wrote his letter to the Romans, he was addressing both our sins and our human weakness. What hope is there for us when we are born with sin influencing every decision we make? Paul answers that question with the best news of our lives.

Paul said to the Romans, *"I am not ashamed of the gospel, because it is the power of God for the salvation of everyone who believes"* (1:16). That's great news for all of us who are looking for salvation.

"Gospel" is a word that literally means "good news." Paul's summation of the good news in the book of Romans is that we have all sinned, but the death and resurrection of Jesus is an adequate remedy for that sin. He then explains that the Holy Spirit has been given to us to empower us to live a new life. To know that we are not bound by sin and limited to human weakness because of Jesus' life, death and resurrection is the best news in the world.

Paul explains that the "good news" is the power of God. "Power" is a translation of the Greek word *dynamis*. We derive our word "dynamite" from that word.

All of us have heard good news that didn't affect us. Somebody wins the lottery and is immediately wealthy. That may be good news for them but it doesn't help me pay for my groceries or gasoline. The good news about Jesus, though, is more than the words I hear about others—it is power that helps me. It produces results. It's not just a theory. God's inexhaustible and irresistible power brings me from sin to salvation. It brings me from human weakness to godly ability.

The only reason that the Soviet Union didn't beat us in the race to reach the moon was the fact that they didn't have a rocket powerful enough to get the job done. Without God, I can't reach beyond my weakness, but He has brought good news, His power is available to get me where He wants me to go.

In its July 2005 issue *Charisma* magazine told the story of Barry DuFae Myers, an African American. Myers worked for 15 years in 30 movies: among them *Passenger 57*, *Lethal Weapon 2* and *Lethal Weapon 3*. He got involved in the music industry producing and promoting "P. Diddy" Combs, Prince, Snoop Dog and Tupac Shakur. In 1993, he co-founded *Rip-It Records*, which earned more than $30 million in sales.

He didn't grow up believing in Jesus. His second cousin was Malcolm X and he was raised a Muslim. His partner, Louis Bell, Jr., who co-founded *Rip-It Records* with him accepted Christ in August 1997. He invited Barry to go to church with him. In October 1997, Barry received Jesus as his Savior. Myers says that his conversion was the result of three women who came to his studio, prayed with him and led him to Christ. "They were my mother, sister and a family friend." He was instantly delivered from cocaine. He also pulled the plug on *Rip-It Records* because he and Louis didn't approve of the music they were producing. He is now teaching at his local church in Florida.

The good news of Jesus is really what Paul said it is—it is *"the power of God for the salvation of everyone who believes."* For those of us who have felt the impact of sin and have done foolish things with our lives there's a way out. Believe the good news that Jesus can free us. It is the best news of our lives.

50—Regaining A Sense of Direction

Clarence Jordan, author of the "Cotton Patch" New Testament translation and founder of the interracial *Koinonia* farm in Americus, Georgia, was getting a red-carpet tour of another minister's church. With pride, the minister pointed to the rich, imported pews and luxurious decorations. As they stepped outside, darkness was falling, and a spotlight shone on a huge cross atop the steeple. "That cross alone cost us ten thousand dollars," the minister said with a satisfied smile. "You got cheated," said Jordan. "Times were when Christians could get them for free."

Over the years, the Cross has become the most prominent symbol of Christianity. It is the way we identify the significance of Jesus' life and death. He died in our place. It is amazing to think that the most wonderful Person who ever lived was crucified as a criminal, but that was why He came.

Cary Grant once told how he was walking along a street and met a fellow whose eyes locked onto him with excitement. The man said, "Wait a minute, you're ... you're—I know who you are; don't tell me—uh, Rock Hud— No, you're ..." Grant thought he'd help him, so he finished the man's sentence: "Cary Grant." And the fellow said, "No, that's not it! You're..."

There was Cary Grant indentifying himself with his own name, but the fellow had someone else in mind. The apostle John says of Jesus, *"He was in the world, and though the world was made through him, the world did not recognize him"* (John 1:10, NIV). And, even when Jesus identified who he was—the Son of God—the response was not a welcome recognition, but rather the Crucifixion.

There are some conclusions the Cross of Christ forces us to face. First, sin must be horrible. When I'm tempted to think sin doesn't matter much I remember the Cross. Our sins, yours and mine, put Jesus there. The best Man who ever lived, Who never did anything wrong, was executed for our misdeeds.

The second conclusion I reach is that God must love us very much. He could have abandoned each of us to our respective fates but He didn't. Paul wrote the Roman church and stated, *"You see, at just the right time, when we were still powerless, Christ died for the ungodly. Very rarely will anyone die for a righteous man, though for a good man someone might possibly dare to die. But God demonstrates his own love for us in this: While we were still sinners, Christ died for us"* (Romans 5:6-8). Jesus didn't die for us because we were good. We weren't. He died for us because He loved us even while we were rebelling against Him.

Maybe the best conclusion of all about the Cross is that salvation is free. When Jesus said, *"It is finished"* (John 19:30) He was telling the world that there is nothing left for us to pay. The word that is translated "It is finished" is one Greek word, *tetelestai*. It was commonly used by the Greeks of that day. It means, literally, "It has been and will forever remain finished."

This word was used in three specific ways in Jesus' day. If a promissory note were paid, the one holding the note wrote *tetelestai* across it. It meant that the debt was paid in full. The death of Jesus paid off everything we owed God. We never have to pay for our sins and mistakes if we believe that Jesus died for us.

When property was purchased, the transfer was not valid until the deed was dated and signed. When this was done, the clerk wrote *tetelestai* across it. On the Cross Jesus signed the deed that provided every blessing God promised us. We can receive the promises of God because Jesus signed the title to them with His death.

Another example of its use was when a father sent his son on a mission. The son was not to return until he had performed the last act of his assignment. When he did return successfully he used *tetelestai* to report to his father the effective completion of his task. Jesus was saying to His Father, "I did everything I came to do. The mission is accomplished."

The Cross is beautiful to believers. It marks the end of our struggle to find God. He found us. It marks the end of our attempts to bridge the gap that separated us from Him. He stretched across the chasm to reach us. That is why it is a symbol of Christianity. We see crosses on church spires, we wear crosses as jewelry. Some have crosses tattooed on their bodies. The Cross was the turning point of human history. We don't have to beat ourselves until we bleed to get His attention. He has taken note of us and has reached loving arms out to receive us. The Cross proves that.

It's hard for me to grasp the love of God that led Jesus to the Cross to take my place. A picture of that kind of love comes from Brazil. Maria lived in a village there. Her husband died when her daughter, Christina, was an infant. When Christina was approaching adulthood, she let her mother know that she wanted to go to Rio de Janeiro but her mother warned her against it. She knew that if Christina went to Rio the chances were that she would become a prostitute to survive.

One day Maria came home to find her daughter had left for Rio. Her heart was broken. She took a bus to the city, hoping to find her daughter before she ruined her life. On her way to the bus stop, she went to a drug store and entered a photo booth. She set aside the money she needed for the bus ticket and spent the rest on black and white photos of herself.

When Maria arrived in Rio, she feared the worst. She knew that her daughter had no way to make money and she knew that she would probably turn to prostitution to feed herself. So Maria went to all the places prostitutes gathered—bars, hotels, nightclubs—and taped the pictures of herself. She wrote a note on the back of each and taped them to bathroom mirrors, hotel bulletin boards and the insides of phone booths. Then she went home.

Sure enough, Christina became a sad, unhappy prostitute. Home looked good, but she was too proud to go back. One day she was coming down the staircase of a hotel lobby and saw a picture of her mother taped to a mirror. She pulled the picture off the mirror and turned it over. The note read: "Whatever you have done, whatever you have become, it doesn't matter. Please come home." She did.

The Cross is God's picture, posted where we can see it, and the message is still, "Whatever you have done, whatever you have become, it doesn't matter. Please come home." The message hasn't changed through the years. God is still inviting us to come home.

I need to come to the Cross regularly. Nancy Cheatham helped me understand why. She wrote: "My sister bought a new car that was loaded with high-tech options. The first time she drove the car in the rain, she turned a knob she thought would start the windshield wipers. Instead, a message flashed across the dash: 'Drive car in 360 degrees.' She had no idea what that meant, and so when she got home she read the car manual. She learned that while trying to turn on the windshield wipers she had inadvertently turned off the internal compass, and the car had lost its sense of direction. To correct the problem, the car had to be driven in a full circle, pointed north, and then the compass had to be reset."

It's important for us to come to the cross again and again. That's where our compasses are reset. That's where we regain our sense of direction. There we remember who God is and what He has done for us.

51—Love to the Limit

Part of the charm of the Lord's Church is its mixture of different ingredients. When complimented on her homemade biscuits, the cook at a popular Christian conference center told Dr. Harry Ironside, "Just consider what goes into the making of these biscuits. The flour itself doesn't taste good, neither does the baking powder, nor the shortening, nor the other ingredients. However, when I mix them all together and put them in the oven, they come out just right."

Each of us has his or her own idiosyncrasies, but when God brings us together, something beautiful is created. The combination of our different personalities makes a wonderful Church.

Still, our variety makes the formation of loving relationships such a challenge. The differences that make us a beautiful creation can also be obstacles to forming loving relationships. The apostle Peter wrote, *"Above all, love each other deeply, because love covers over a multitude of sins. Offer hospitality to one another without grumbling"* (1 Peter 4:8-9).

Peter puts his finger on some real hurdles we face when we begin to love each other. The expression "multitude of sins" shows that there are times when we will see each other's weaknesses and failures.

"Grumbling" speaks of an attitude that can creep into any of our lives. We love someone but the inconvenience that comes with commitment can lead us to give in to negative feelings.

Little Nan demonstrated our dilemma in her prayer: "Dear God, I bet it is very hard for you to love everybody in the whole world. There are only four people in our family and I can never do it." Maybe all of us can identify with Nan at one time or other. The ones we are closest to can sometimes be the most difficult to love.

There are some lessons about love that Peter wants us to learn. When he says, *"Love each other deeply"* he uses a Greek word that we translate "deeply." It means, literally, to stretch out. R. C. H. Lenski defines it as "stretched out, put to the full strain, exerted to the limit of its strength." Peter wants us to know that the love he is describing is stretched to the limit. Xenophon used the same word to describe a horse made to go at a full gallop.

There might be some people who find it easy to love everyone, but if we were honest, most of us would admit that we meet individuals who require us to "stretch." Peter is telling us that the love God wants to exhibit through us stretches us until we can reach everyone.

Another lesson Peter gives us explains how to love those who sin. Surely, each of us has met someone who loves to dig up our weaknesses and broadcast them. You may even have been a victim of exaggeration. Love doesn't do that. It covers sin.

That doesn't mean that love says sin is okay. It does mean that love doesn't abuse the discovery of sin in someone's life. Love doesn't approach people with suspicion, looking for skeletons in their closets and ready to leap on them with condemnation.

A man named John was driving home from work late one night when he spotted a hitchhiker. Feeling compassion for the lone traveler, he stopped his car to give the man a ride. As he rode, though, he became suspicious of his passenger. John had laid his coat on the seat between them and, while driving, reached over and quietly felt in his coat pocket for his wallet. It wasn't there!

Furious, he slammed on his brakes and said, "Hand over the wallet immediately!" The hitchhiker looked stunned, but handed over a wallet and got out of the car. John drove off burning with anger.

When John got home he rushed into the house to tell his wife what had happened. She interrupted him and said, "Before I forget, John, do you know that you left your wallet at home this morning?"

He had left a poor, confused hitchhiker by the side of the road, robbed by a driver who had been motivated by suspicion.

One more lesson about love. It doesn't complain. There is something about a "put upon" look that undermines the kindest actions.

A family invited their pastor to their home for a Sunday dinner. Wanting to impress the man of God with the family's spirituality, the mother asked the little girl to say the blessing. The girl responded, "I don't know what to say." The mother coached her with, "Just say what you've heard Mommy say." So, her daughter bowed her head and prayed, "Oh, God, why did I invite the preacher to dinner on a hot day like this."

We just can't hide complaining attitudes. They will surface and ruin our good deeds.

With all its challenges, Peter says that it's worth it for a believer to stretch love to its limit. As the recipient of so much love from so many people, I can say that it brings healing when it is delivered sincerely. People who have loved me to the limit have enriched my life. If you're like me, you've been loved when you really didn't deserve it. That makes it an awesome gift.

An obvious question comes to mind. How do I love like that? It all begins with the amazing love God has shown us. I wasn't born with selfless love. No one was. I can only pass on what I have received.

Gwen and I saw that clearly while we were speaking at a conference on St. Simons Island in Georgia. During a break in the conference schedule, we took a walk. As we walked through a field, we saw a girl who was walking a big dog. Suddenly the dog broke away from her and began running toward us with a decided limp. We were alarmed and a little frightened. It wasn't an "ankle biter," it was a good-sized dog. When the brown visitor finally reached us, it panted and wagged its tail. It seemed happy to see us.

The girl who had been walking the dog had been shouting at it to stop while she was running toward us. That had added to our anxiety. She seemed worried. She ran up, out of breath, and said, "I didn't know what he was going to do. He was dropped on our doorstep and had either been beaten badly or hit by a car. His rear leg is atrophied. A vet said that the injury had been untreated for about three months. When we first found him, he was suspicious and hostile. The SPCA representative would not even take him because he growled so viciously. We began feeding him and caring for him until he began to trust us. I just didn't know how he would react to you."

That is how it is with Jesus and us. He took us when we were wounded, mistreated and probably defensive. He loved us and cared for us until we became so healed that we could love to others. It isn't so hard to pass something along once Someone has given it to us.

52—Hope for the Hopeless

Our perspective on circumstances can definitely affect our attitudes. Whether we have a positive or negative attitude toward life depends not so much on our circumstances but on how we view them.

Becky Barnes describes an incident that shows the power of a positive perspective. At the elementary school where she teaches they had a problem with students throwing rocks. The principal made an announcement over the intercom warning students that anyone caught throwing rocks would be taken home by him personally. Later that day, during afternoon recess, one of the teachers caught a kindergartner throwing a rock. "Didn't you hear what the principal said this morning?!" the teacher said in disbelief. "Yeah," replied the proud lad, grinning from ear to ear. "I get to go home in the principal's car!"

Somerset Maugham, the English writer, once wrote a story about a janitor at St Peter's Church in London. One day a young vicar discovered that the janitor was illiterate and fired him. Jobless, the man invested his meager savings in a tiny shop, where he prospered, bought another, expanded, and ended up with a chain of stores worth several hundred thousand dollars. One day the man's banker said, "You've done well for an illiterate, but where would you be if you could read and write?" "Well," replied the man, "I'd be janitor of St. Peter's Church in Neville Square."

The prophet Jeremiah lived during a time of devastation for the nation Israel. The people had rebelled against God and worshiped idols until God punished them by sending them into exile. Nebuchadnezzar took the best of their population into captivity and destroyed their city, Jerusalem, and their temple.

At first, the exiles held out hope for a quick return to Jerusalem, but that didn't happen. Consequently, they began giving in to feelings of hopelessness and meaninglessness. They felt abandoned. Psalm 137 graphically describes their despondency: *"By the rivers of Babylon we sat and wept when we remembered Zion. There on the poplars we hung our harps, for there our captors asked us for songs, our tormentors demanded songs of joy; they said, 'Sing us one of the songs of Zion!' How can we sing the songs of the LORD while in a foreign land?"* (Psalm 137:1-4).

God instructed Jeremiah, still living in Jerusalem, to write a letter to the exiles. In that letter is one of the most encouraging Scriptures in the Bible. Jeremiah wrote, *" 'For I know the plans I have for you,' declares the LORD, 'plans to prosper you and not to harm you, plans to give you hope and a future' "* (Jeremiah 29:11).

This wasn't written to people who had gotten things right. This was written to people who had gotten it all wrong. They were in Babylon because of their own sins. That letter could be written to any of us who have made mistakes and feel we can't make it. This is a word for everyone who has hung his harp on a tree and sat down to cry. God's plans are *"to prosper you and not to harm you."*

Psychologist William Marston asked three thousand people, "What have you to live for?" He was shocked to discover that 94 percent were simply enduring the present while they waited for the future—waited for something to happen—waited for "next year"—waited for a "better time"—waited for "someone to die"—waited "for tomorrow." For some people hope is a wistful longing "for tomorrow" that comes from their desire to escape "today."

That is not what the Bible means by hope. In both the Old Testament Scriptures and the New Testament Scriptures hope is the confident expectation of something good. No matter what we are going through, we are eagerly anticipating a better day ahead.

That is what God wanted the exiles to know and that is what He wants us to know. His plans for us are to give us hope and a future.

On a cruise from Mexico to Hawaii in 1979, Los Angeles lawyer John Peckham and his wife, Dottie, put a note in a bottle and tossed it into the Pacific. Three years and nine thousand miles later, Vietnamese refugee Nguyen Van Hoa leaned down from a tiny, crowded boat and plucked the bottle from the South China Sea—amazed to find a name and address, a dollar for postage and the promise of a reward. "It gave me hope," said Hoa, who had escaped from a prison camp in Vietnam.

Safe in a United Nations refugee camp in Thailand, Hoa wrote the surprised Peckhams. For two years they corresponded; Hoa married and had a son. The Peckhams were able, at last, to sponsor Hoa and his young family as they immigrated to America. They found hope in a bottle.

We, too, have hope. God can take the most unpleasant experiences and turn them into a surprising and wonderful future.

A number of years ago, in a mental institution outside Boston, a young girl known as "Little Annie" was locked in the dungeon. She was considered hopelessly insane. Seeing no possibility of her recovery, the doctors in charge just locked Annie in the basement in a small cage.

About that time, an elderly nurse was nearing retirement. She felt there was hope for "Little Annie," so she started taking her lunch into the dungeon and eating outside "Little Annie's" cage. She felt perhaps she should communicate some love and hope to the little girl.

When the elderly nurse started visiting her, "Little Annie" gave no indication that she was even aware of her presence. One day, however, the elderly nurse brought some brownies to the dungeon and left them outside the cage. "Little Annie" gave no hint she knew they were there, but when the nurse returned the next day, the brownies were gone. From that time on, the nurse would bring brownies when she made her Thursday visit. Soon after, the doctors in the institution noticed a change was taking place. After a period of time they decided to move "Little Annie" upstairs. Finally, the day came when the "hopeless case" was told she could return home. But, "Little Annie" did not wish to leave. She chose to stay and try to help others.

Many years later, Queen Victoria of England asked Helen Keller, "How do you account for your remarkable accomplishments in life? How do you explain the fact that even though you were both blind and deaf, you were able to accomplish so much?" Without a moment's hesitation, Helen Keller said that had it not been for Anne Sullivan ("Little Annie"), the name of Helen Keller would have remained unknown.

Anne Sullivan, the hopeless little girl, changed the world. She found hope in a cage in the basement of an insane asylum and brought hope to a girl trapped in a world where she couldn't see or hear. That is the power of hope. It overcomes despair and desperation. It says to any "today," "I am anticipating tomorrow." God's plan for you and for me is to give us *"a hope and a future."*

53—Changing Your World

To celebrate an old man's seventy-fifth birthday, an aviation enthusiast offered to take him for a plane ride over the little West Virginia town where he had spent all his life. The old man accepted the offer. Back on the ground, after circling over the town for twenty minutes, his friend asked, "Were you scared, Uncle Dudley?" "No-o-o," was the hesitant reply. "But I never did put my full weight down."

It is easy for us to treat God that way. We will get on board but we won't put our full weight down. The only way to serve Jesus is with our complete trust in His goodness and a desire to fulfill His purpose for our lives. James Calvert displayed that kind of trust when he went as a missionary to the cannibals of the Fiji Islands. The captain of the ship warned him of the dangers before depositing him on one of the islands: "You will lose your life and the lives of those with you if you go among such savages." Calvert replied, "We died before we came here." Once we have surrendered our lives to Christ, we can trust Him completely with our destinies.

Scripture gives a message of hope to those who trust God. Psalm 9:10 says, *"Those who know your name will trust in you, for you, LORD, have never forsaken those who seek you."* Whether we are in a one-engine plane over a town in West Virginia or stepping onto an island to share the good news with cannibals, we can trust this fact—God will never forsake those who seek Him.

There is no question that life brings challenges to us and we face, more often than we realize, threats to our safety. To know that God is there and won't forsake us is a foundational truth that gives us strength.

I read about a strange little fish that lives in the Red Sea. The scientists among us call it a *Pardachirus marmoratus*. The rest of us know it as the *Moses sole*. It is similar to a flounder in appearance and its uniqueness is that it secretes a milky substance from the base of its dorsal and anal fins. This substance is known to repel sharks—it actually freezes the shark's jaw.

Dr. Eugenie Clark discovered this fact, and carried out much of the research on this fish. She once noticed that when she touched this fish a milky white liquid oozed out and made her fingers tingle. When she discovered this, she started testing the liquid with other types of fish. After many experiments, she decided to test it with sharks. She found a *Moses sole* that still had some liquid on it, tied it with string and lowered it into the water. She watched as a shark swam toward the fish, stopping abruptly in front of it looking as if its mouth were frozen. After a moment, the shark swam away from the fish. As a result, she performed more experiments with the fish confirming that the poisonous substance would "repel" sharks.

As Psalm 22:4 puts it: *"In you our fathers put their trust; they trusted and you delivered them."* Not only does trusting God mean that He won't abandon us, it means that He will stay around and deliver us.

When Gwen and I made our only missions trip to Africa we spent our time in the nation of Zambia. Our first stop was the town of Livingstone. There is a museum there commemorating David Livingstone's life and we visited it. David Livingstone was one of my heroes and a prime example of someone who trusted God when his life depended on it.

While traveling through Africa in the 1800s and opening up the Dark Continent to the light of the Gospel, Livingstone encountered a remote tribe in the Congo region. He had learned, and respected, the local custom of calling on the tribal chief before entering the village. Failure to comply with this custom could have cost him his life. Livingstone was required to wait outside the village with all his possessions lined up next to him. The chief, as a sign of acceptance, would take whatever he desired from among the missionary's possessions. To complete the exchange, the chief would give the guest something of his own. Then and only then would Livingstone be authorized to enter the village and share the gospel.

Livingstone had set out his Bible, writing pad, clothes, shoes, blanket—and his goat. Livingstone suffered from a weak stomach that required him to drink goat's milk on a daily basis. The local drinking water was often questionable, so this was his key to survival. Often Livingstone had asked God to heal his infirmity, but it seemed he was sentenced to drinking goat's milk every morning.

The chief emerged from his tent. Ornately attired in ivory and gold, the chief was followed closely by his advisors and priests. He surveyed the possessions of the missionary, while Livingstone silently prayed, "Lord let him take anything he wants except my goat!" The chief promptly walked over to the goat and pointed at it, and one of his advisors whisked the animal away! Livingstone stood stunned. A few moments later, the man who took his goat returned. In exchange, he handed Livingstone a stick and left. Livingstone was exasperated. "A stick?! Ridiculous! Here, he takes my life's sustenance, and in return I get an old stick!" A man standing close by, seeing Livingstone's confusion, quietly spoke. "Oh, no! That's not a stick. My friend, that is the chief's very own scepter. With it, you will gain entry to every tribe and village in the interior. You have been given safe passage and great authority as a gift from the king!" Then Livingstone realized what God had done. From that time forward, Livingstone spread God's Word to thousands and thousands of Africans. And, as a side note, Livingstone's stomach ailment was healed, too.

Many of us read the Psalms for encouragement as we face the challenges of our lives. They are honest prayers that express clearly the fears, frustrations and joy that each of us experience. The message throughout the Psalms is simple: Trust in God no matter what life is throwing at you.

Even God's most humble creatures can reap the benefits of trusting Him. A local parks commission was ordered to remove the trees from a street that was to be widened. As they were about to begin cutting down the trees, the foreman and his men saw a robin's nest in one of the trees and the mother robin sitting on the nest. They left that tree until later. Returning, they found the nest occupied by little wide-mouthed robins. Again, they left the tree. When they returned later they found the nest empty. The family had grown up and flown away. But, something at the bottom of the nest caught the eye of one of the workmen—a soiled little white card. When he separated it from the mud and sticks, he found that it was a small Sunday School card and on it were the words, "We trust in the Lord our God." The robins had built that message into their nest.

Maybe we could all build that message into the foundational structure of our lives: "We trust in the Lord our God." Psalm 9:10 says that He will never forsake us.

54—Living Life to the Fullest

I spent the early part of my life with an inadequate view of God. I tried to earn God's love. I wanted to live life to the fullest and thought that meant keeping the rules. Many people still live that way. I had to learn that He already loved me and that a good life was His free gift. Charles Swindoll, in his book, *The Grace Awakening*, tells of a couple in a very strict Christian college. This particular college maintained a list of rules. One requirement was that you not work on Sunday. A student caught his wife hanging out some clothes she had washed on Sunday afternoon and turned her in to the authorities. He gets a good grade for rule keeping but a failing grade for marriage.

A few years ago, I found a book entitled *You Can't Eat Peanuts in Church and Other Little Known Laws*. Trying to write a law that fits any situation leads to craziness. For example, in Gary, Indiana it is illegal to attend a theater within four hours of eating garlic. While that may not be a bad idea, it makes a lousy law.

In North Carolina, where I live, singing out of tune in church is illegal. If we still took that law seriously, the North Carolina jails would be filled. And, in Oregon there is a law that makes it illegal for a dead person to serve on a jury. I wouldn't think that law would be necessary.

Most of us have wrestled with the question, "How do I get the most out of life?" Maybe you have thought, as I have, "If I only had more money I would be happy." Money is wonderful. It gives us the ability to pay our bills and help others, but it alone won't make us happy. Howard Hughes was fabulously wealthy but died in bondage to phobias and, from the last photos of him, was physically depleted by starvation. He ended his life as a frail, broken multi-billionaire.

To find an example of a full life I don't have to look any farther than my dad. At his funeral, my brother-in-law, Mac, summed up Dad's life eloquently: "Wallace didn't need props to be happy." I will never forget that line. While many are looking for props to fill up the emptiness of their lives there are others who, like my dad, have found the secret of contentment.

Paul wrote a letter to the church at Ephesus and made clear how we can have a full life. *"May you experience the love of Christ... Then you will be filled with the fullness of life and power that comes from God"* (Ephesians 3:19 NLT). The key to living life to the fullest is experiencing the love of Christ.

Once we have experienced this amazing love we want to introduce His love to others. Really living means that we have found God's love and are helping others share it.

Julius Hickerson was a promising young doctor who could have made a respectable living by practicing medicine in the United States. Instead, he chose to go to Colombia as a missionary. He had been there for two years with little visible results when he was tragically killed in a plane crash while attempting to take medical supplies to a remote village.

When they searched the wreckage of the downed aircraft, some of the local Colombians found a Bible written in their own language. They began to read it. Soon some of them became Christians. These new believers started a church and went off to other villages to tell their neighbors the good news about Jesus. Sometime later, unaware of what had taken place, the Southern Baptists sent a missionary into that area. The missionary was surprised to find a thriving church in this remote region. He asked how this had happened without a missionary and one of the Colombians showed him a Bible. On the inside of the cover was the name *Julius Hickerson*! Someday in heaven, Julius will meet men and women who are there because of his sacrifice. That's living!

It is important that we experience God's love for us. Rule keeping doesn't bring us life. We can't earn God's love, He gives it to us. Nor can money buy a full life. Experiencing God's love is the answer to personal emptiness. As Paul says, *"Then you will be filled with the fullness of life and power that comes from God."* Isn't that our goal? We want to be filled with the fullness of life.

When the question comes to mind: "How can God loving me make a difference in my life?" just look at what God's love means. We were alienated from God without the resources we needed to reach Him when Jesus came to bring God and us together. Because of Jesus, I can know the love of God.

Without Jesus, we can't really enjoy the fullness of life God plans for us. Jim Petty pictured this by describing an incident from his youth:

"Once when I was a teenager, my father and I were standing in line to buy tickets for the circus. Finally, there was only one family between us and the ticket counter. There were eight children, all probably under the age of twelve. You could tell they didn't have a lot of money. Their clothes were not expensive but they were clean. The children were well-behaved, all of them standing in line, two-by-two behind their parents, holding hands. They were excitedly jabbering about the clowns, elephants and other acts they would see that night. One could sense they had never been to the circus before. It promised to be a highlight in their young lives.

"The father and mother were at the head of the pack standing proud as could be. The mother was holding her husband's hand, looking up at him as if to say, 'You're my knight in shining armor.' He was smiling and basking in pride. The ticket lady asked him how many tickets he wanted. He proudly responded, 'Please let me buy eight children's tickets and two adult tickets.'

"The lady quoted the price. The man's wife let go of his hand, her mouth dropped and the man's lip began to quiver. The father leaned a little closer and asked, 'How much did you say?' She repeated the price. He didn't have enough money. How was he supposed to tell his eight kids he didn't have enough money? Seeing what was going on, my dad put his hand in his pocket, pulled out a $20 bill and dropped it on the ground. (We were not wealthy in any sense of the word!) My father reached down, picked up the bill, tapped the man on the shoulder and said, 'Excuse me, sir, I think this is yours.'

"The man knew what was going on. He wasn't asking for a handout but certainly appreciated the help in a desperate, heartbreaking, embarrassing situation. He looked straight into my dad's eyes, took my dad's hand in both of his, squeezed tightly onto the $20 dollar bill and replied, 'Thank you, sir. This really means a lot to me and my family.' My father and I went back to the car and drove home."

That's the picture. We were in line but we couldn't get in. We weren't good enough and didn't have the resources to buy our way in. But, Jesus loved us enough to pay our way into God's presence. Living life to the fullest is being aware that Someone we didn't even know at the time was standing behind us ready to give us everything we need.

55—We Are God's Masterpieces

In *Fortune* magazine, executive consultant Richard Hagberg told this story: The head of one large company told him about an incident that occurred as he and his wife waited in line to get his driver's license renewed. He was frustrated at how long it was taking and grumbled to his wife, "Don't they know who I am?" She replied, "Yeah, you're a plumber's son who got lucky."

That just points out a truth we know instinctively. We can't take all the credit for any success we enjoy. Years ago, one of our congregation gave me a painting that portrayed a turtle on a fence post. You know it didn't get there by itself.

James Montgomery Boice made an interesting comment about the Christian life. He said, "When you become a Christian you may think that all your struggles are over, and you may be disappointed and even discouraged to learn that in one sense the struggle is only beginning. Before, you were unhappy but not schizophrenic. Now you are struggling."

I love that explanation. Christians sometimes feel schizophrenic because we have the Holy Spirit living in us and the devil on the outside tempting us. Thankfully, the apostle John told us, *"The one who is in you is greater than the one who is in the world"* (1 John 4:4).

Because we are in a continuing struggle, it is important that we know how to handle imperfection. If we are honest, we each could admit that there have been times when we've failed. That doesn't mean we are happy about our failures or are willing to settle for them. It means that we are human and are continually dependent on God and His strength.

There are two ways of responding to failure. Some people refuse to let others forget the mistakes they've made. James Hewett told a story that graphically portrays how some people respond to the imperfection of others. He described a father who was helping his six-year-old son put a model plane together. They were using one of those super adhesive glues. In less than three minutes, his son's right index finger was bonded to a shiny blue wing of his DC-10. The boy tried to free his finger. He tugged it, pulled it, waved it frantically; but he couldn't budge his finger free. Soon, they located a solvent that did the job and ended their little crisis.

Sometime later, the father visited a new family in their neighborhood. The father of the family introduced his children: "This is Pete. He's the clumsy one of the lot." "That's Kathy coming in with mud on her shoes. She's the sloppy one." "As always, Mike's last. He'll be late for his own funeral, I promise you." That dad did a thorough job of gluing his children to their faults and mistakes.

Hewett continued his point by explaining that people do it to us and to those we love all the time. They remind us of our failures, our errors, our sins, and they won't let us live them down. Like that little boy trying frantically to free his finger from the plane, there are people who try, sometimes desperately, to free themselves from their past. They would love a chance to begin again.

When we don't let people forget their past, when we don't forgive, we glue them to their mistakes and refuse to see them as more than something they have done. However, when we forgive, we gently pry the doer of the hurtful deed from the deed itself, and we say that the past is just that—past—over and done with. God does what we are unable to do or what those around us don't want to do or are unable to do for us.

When we accept his forgiveness, he separates us from our sins. The psalmist said, *"As far as the east is from the west, so far has he removed our transgressions from us"* (Psalm 103:12). That means as far as you can imagine, that offense will be wiped away, blotted out. The good news—the very good news—of the gospel is that we don't have to remain in bondage, glued to our sins. The healing power of God is ours for the asking, promising freedom and the loving embrace of a Father who forgets our past and clothes us for a new life.

Paul wrote the church in Ephesus and expressed an amazing truth. He explained, *"For we are God's masterpiece. He has created us anew in Christ Jesus, so that we can do the good things he planned for us long ago"* (Ephesians 2:10, NLT). The Greek word translated "masterpiece" is the word *poiema*. We see it in English as the word "poem." We are God's work of art.

No matter what imperfections we have seen in ourselves, God takes us as we are and shapes us into the masterpiece He had in mind from the beginning.

But, what if we have really made a mess of our lives? That doesn't matter.

Over a hundred years ago, in a Scottish seaside inn, a group of fishermen were relaxing after a long day at sea. As a waitress was walking past the fishermen's table with a pot of tea, one of the men made a sweeping gesture to describe the size of the fish he claimed to have caught. His hand collided with the teapot and sent it crashing against the whitewashed wall, where its contents left an irregular brown splotch.

Standing nearby, the innkeeper surveyed the damage. "That stain will never come out," he said in dismay. "The whole wall will have to be repainted." "Perhaps not." All eyes turned to the stranger who had just spoken. "What do you mean?" asked the innkeeper. "Let me work with the stain," said the stranger, standing up from his table in the corner. "If my work meets your approval, you won't need to repaint the wall."

The stranger picked up a box and went to the wall. Opening the box, he withdrew pencils, brushes, and some glass jars of linseed oil and pigment. He began to sketch lines around the stain and fill it in here and there with dabs of color and swashes of shading. Soon a picture began to emerge. The random splashes of tea had been turned into the image of a stag with a magnificent rack of antlers. At the bottom of the picture, the man inscribed his signature. Then he paid for his meal and left. The innkeeper was stunned when he examined the wall. "Do you know who that man was?" he said in amazement. "The signature reads 'E.H. Landseer!' "

Indeed, the well-known painter of wild life, Sir Edwin Landseer, had visited them. God wants to take the stains and disappointments of our lives and not merely erase them, but rather turn them into a thing of beauty.

Others may see our failures and try to glue us to them and label us by them for the rest of our lives. God takes us with our weaknesses and turns us into masterpieces that display His creative power.

56—It's All About Jesus

Let's face it. We all need help. Zig Ziglar used to tell of the woman who dashed out of her house as the garbage truck pulled away. She was wearing an old bathrobe and large curlers. Her face was covered with cream; she had on a chinstrap and sported a beat up pair of slippers. She yelled at the garbage man, "Am I too late for the garbage?" "No, ma'am," he replied, "hop right in."

As much as we are willing to admit our need for change, it still comes hard. Consider these crazy statements from our nation's history. Charles H. Duell, director of the U. S. Patent office in 1899 said, "Everything that can be invented has been invented." H. M. Warner, of Warner Brothers Pictures, said in 1927, "Who wants to hear actors talk?" Tris Speaker, an outstanding baseball player, said in 1927, "Babe Ruth made a big mistake when he gave up pitching." A Michigan banker advised Henry Ford's lawyer not to invest in the new automobile company: "The horse is here to stay, but the automobile is only a novelty." And, the classic: At a church conference in 1876 Bishop Wright told a college president that if God wanted men to fly He would have given them wings. That Bishop had two sons—Orville and Wilbur.

The key to changing is Jesus. Nothing is more important than knowing who Jesus is. Haddon Robinson tells about a pastor who was into telling stories to the children. He'd bring all the children up, and they'd sit on the floor, and he'd tell them a story. One day he said, "Boys and girls, I want to tell you a story about someone who likes to live in the woods, but sometimes we can see him in our yards. Anybody have any idea who I am talking about?" No takers.

He said, "I want to tell you about a creature that lives in the woods and sometimes in our yards, has a big bushy tail, and likes to eat nuts. Anybody have any idea what I'm talking about?" No takers.

He said, "I'm talking about a creature that lives in the woods, sometimes in our yards, big bushy tail, eats nuts, likes to climb trees, jumps from tree to tree—now, does anybody know what I'm talking about?"

One kid raised his hand to take the pastor out of his misery. The preacher asked the child, "Do you know what I'm thinking about?" The kid said, "Yeah. I know the answer should be Jesus, but it sounds like a squirrel to me."

Knowing Jesus and moving from religion to relationship is the key to the New Testament's message. The book of Hebrews addresses our reluctance to change and challenges us to relate to God in a new way, through Jesus Christ. It was written to individuals who wanted to return to the beauty of the Old Testament ritual. And, that ritual was beautiful and meaningful! It served an important purpose. It was the symbolism of those ceremonies that prepared the world for Jesus.

However, Jesus brought simplicity and some felt that they had lost something they wanted to recapture. The writer of Hebrews explained why it was important to move from the past and embrace Jesus. Yes, he says, we had angels in the Old Testament, but the Son is greater than angels are. We had a great leader in Moses, but Moses couldn't lead God's people into the Promised land. We had a mighty warrior, Joshua, but Joshua couldn't give Israel rest. There was a majestic priesthood, but the priests were imperfect and had to offer sacrifices for their own sins.

In the first chapter of Hebrews, the writer explains that we had prophets, but what they said was never complete. He wrote, *"In the past God spoke to our forefathers through the prophets at many times and in various ways, but in these last days he has spoken to us by his Son, whom he appointed heir of all things, and through whom he made the universe"* (Hebrews 1:1-2).

The prophets had an important message, but Jesus is God's final and complete revelation. The Old Testament ceremony was important. It was God's idea. Now Jesus has come. We still read the Old Testament and live by its principles because they came from God, but Jesus has brought a new dimension to our relationship with God. He said to His disciples, *"I no longer call you servants, because a servant does not know his master's business. Instead, I have called you friends, for everything that I learned from my Father I have made known to you"* (John 15:15).

I have many formal relationships. One of them is with the government. Every year, on April 15, I go through the same ceremony as many others. I send the government my taxes. It's a ritual I don't miss because the consequences are serious. However, I don't have a personal relationship with the government. I don't have "friends" in the IRS I can call for lunch and fellowship.

On the other hand, I have friends whose company I enjoy. They know me and I know them. We laugh together and, in times of crises, have cried together. I know how to reach them and have confidence that they will be there for me.

Jesus took us from the formal observation of rules and regulations to friendship with God. The Ten Commandments, for example, are valid. They let us know what God expects from us. The sad truth is that we broke them. Maybe not all of them but enough of them to be in trouble. Jesus came, kept everyone of them for me, and then died in my place so I could be free from the fear of punishment. Not only that, He calls me friend. That's the relationship He offers.

I love the Old Testament because it tells me what God is looking for. I love Jesus because He fulfilled everything God expects from me. Because of Jesus, I moved from religion and ritual to a vital relationship with God. I can call Him Friend.

The turning point of history is Jesus. To miss Him is to miss a relationship with God. Two unbelievers were on a train, discussing the life of Christ. One of them said, "I think an interesting story could be written about him." The other said, "And you are just the man to write it. Tear down the prevailing sentiment about his divinity, and paint him as a man—a man among men." That man was Ingersoll, the noted atheist. The other man wrote that book. As he studied the life of Christ, he realized that he was writing about more than a man. The author was Lew Wallace. The book was *Ben Hur*. And, while writing his famous book, Wallace was converted.

If you want to know God, get in touch with Jesus. He is God's final revelation to us. Mother Teresa said, "You will never know that Jesus is all you need until Jesus is all you've got." Well, Jesus is all we've got, but thankfully He's all we need.

57–Breaking the Pattern of Failure

Many of us have an instinctive fear of failure. We don't take risks because we're afraid to fail. Yet, every time we've made progress, failure was part of the formula. I failed the first time I tried to tie my shoes. I failed the first time I tried to print. I failed the first time I tried to feed myself. It's amazing the mess a child can make with a spoon and a plate full of vegetables.

Erma Bombeck failed at dieting and prayed this prayer: "Lord, if you can't make me thin, make my friends look fat."

When I left Bible College I pastored a small church in the Shenandoah Valley of Virginia. There were ten people in the church when I started. At the end of the first year, there were still ten people, but it was a different ten. I couldn't even keep the same ten people coming. I not only felt like a failure, I had ample evidence to prove that I was. I was so shattered that I went back to school wanting to become a teacher. The logic was sound. If I taught where students paid tuition, they would have to come to class.

Thankfully, while I was in seminary I worked under a wonderful pastor of a local church and found that teaching the Bible in a local church was not only satisfying–it was what I wanted to do for the rest of my life.

Later, when Gwen and I were pastoring in Virginia Beach God blessed the church with growth and a wonderful congregation of people. It was a story of His grace. I was invited to go to Charlottesville, Virginia and speak at a Full Gospel Businessmen's Fellowship dinner. I was excited about going for two reasons. First, my life story is a testimony to the goodness of God. I knew failure and was beginning to discover God's blessing. Second, I had attended the University of Virginia and it was, to me, like coming back to the scene of the crime and saying, "I made it."

A long time before that I had promised God that if I ever was asked to tell my story I would try to be honest. I would talk about my mistakes, my failures and His grace. I did that in Charlottesville. After my talk, the president of the chapter invited anyone who desired to come to the front for prayer. One man walked up to me and said, "I'd like you to pray for me." I told him I'd be happy to do that. Then he asked, "Do you know why I want you to pray for me?" I looked around at the leaders of the chapter who were praying for people and responded, "Yes, I would." Then he said something I've never forgotten: "I can relate to you. I'm a failure."

His response reaffirmed for me that failure is part of everyone's story—even Christians. Each of us comes to Jesus with our weaknesses and our baggage and He changes our lives. The apostle Paul frequently drew the contrast between his life as a persecutor and the grace of God that changed him.

In the ninth chapter of Mark's Gospel, an incident helped me understand failure and what I can do about it. A father had a tormented son and tried to find help. Jesus was coming down from the Mount of Transfiguration when a desperate man approached him. The man said to Jesus, *"Teacher, I brought you my son, who is possessed by a spirit that has robbed him of speech. Whenever it seizes him, it throws him to the ground. He foams at the mouth, gnashes his teeth and becomes rigid. I asked your disciples to drive out the spirit, but they could not"* (verses 17-18).

"They could not." I've been there. The disciples were faced with the public embarrassment of failure. I guess all of us have been there. We messed up and someone saw it.

Jesus' next words strike me as an amazing analysis of the situation. *" 'O unbelieving generation,' Jesus replied, 'how long shall I stay with you? How long shall I put up with you? Bring the boy to me.' "* I'll never forget the impact those words had on me. *"Unbelieving generation."* Jesus put His finger on the cause of His disciples' failure. They were affected by generational unbelief. We live in a world that doesn't believe and if we allow its attitudes to infiltrate our thinking it will produce failure every time.

Jesus identified the brokenness of a world that had lost its faith. There was failure at every point in this story. The religious teachers had boxed God in and limited Him. The suffering boy was overwhelmed and victimized. The father was disillusioned by the disciples and the disciples were powerless. The problem all around them was described by Jesus as their *"unbelieving generation."*

Doubt and cynicism have become part of our culture. If you tell a man that there are 581,678,934,341 stars in the universe, he'll believe you. But, if a sign says, "Wet Paint," he has to make a personal investigation. In school, we learn to burn it, smell it, measure it and taste it. The questioning, doubting mind has become our standard of intelligence.

Sadly, doubt creeps into the church. A poll was taken at a National Council of Churches Convention in Miami. Just over half of the registrants believed that Jesus is God. Twenty-five percent believed miracles are real. One-third said the devil does not exist and sixty-two percent of them were certain of life after death.

I am in agreement with C. S. Lewis. He wrote that Jesus turning the water into wine was not a problem for him. God does that with every grape harvest. Seeds are placed in dirt, rain falls on the ground, the sun shines and a grape harvest is produced. Jesus multiplying the loaves and fishes was not difficult for him to believe because God does that with every wheat harvest. Seeds are planted in the ground, the rain falls, the sun shines and there is a multiplication of wheat. The only difference in the Gospel stories is that God just speeded up the process.

There may be no simple solution to breaking the pattern of failure but Jesus certainly gave us a place to begin. He said, "Don't let the doubt and skepticism of the world around you erode your faith." I may demonstrate my inadequacy by a poor performance. But, that shouldn't mean that I doubt God's power to intervene and bring victory.

There is good news in Mark's story. Jesus heals the boy. He doesn't allow their failure to lead to their disgrace. He intervenes and then uses the occasion of their weakness to teach them how to succeed. When they ask, "Why couldn't we?" He explains that they were up against an opposing power that could only be defeated by prayer. They learned their lesson. The book of Acts makes it clear that they continually defeated the enemy in the days after the crucifixion and resurrection of Jesus.

In short, my failures don't make me a failure. They give Jesus an opportunity to train me for success. My responsibility is to believe. Maybe you have given up on yourself. Don't! Believe in Jesus no matter what the "generation" around you does. Never let cynicism and doubt undermine your faith.

58—Find Your Fastball

I have battled a tendency which some of you may have experienced. I have measured myself against other people, usually with a demoralizing effect on how I see myself. As a pastor, all I have to do is compare myself with David Yonggi Cho to feel inadequate. He is the founder and senior pastor of Yoido Full Gospel Church in Seoul, Korea. In 2007, the membership was 830,000. The church conducts seven services each Sunday. If I allowed his success to determine the value of what I am doing, I would be depressed.

As a preacher, all I have to do to be miserable is compare myself with Billy Graham who has preached to one-fifth of the world's population. That's enough to make any preacher give up.

We do great harm to ourselves by comparing ourselves with others. Paul's advice to the Corinthians is still sound. His comment on those who measure themselves against others points out the foolishness of using the wrong measuring sticks: *"[T]hey are only comparing themselves with each other, and measuring themselves by themselves. What foolishness!"* (2 Corinthians 10:12, NLT).

There are two problems with looking at others as the standard of our success. First, we are to look at Jesus. That keeps us from becoming arrogant. Focusing on Jesus gives us hope because He can empower us to be more successful than we could ever be on our own.

Second, we haven't been given the same set of gifts as anyone else. There is no one else in the world with our particular package of abilities. We are responsible for what we do with what we are given and not for what we do with what someone else has been given.

Speaking of the way God keeps some preachers from becoming too proud, George Goldtrap of Tennessee tells about a church he pastored. He said, "We took out the paper towel racks in one church where I preached and put in those electric hand dryers. The very next week someone put a little note on one of those things. It said, 'Punch this button for a brief recorded message from our preacher.' " Ouch!

The problem with many of us is that, instead of focusing on the gifts we have been given, we get sidetracked. Samuel Blizzard conducted a study of pastors that demonstrates the point. The pastors he surveyed overwhelmingly agreed that their primary responsibility was to communicate the truth of Scripture to others. Yet, preparing sermons was fifth on the list of how they actually spent their time. The shocking statistic is that the ministers he surveyed spent just over one percent of their time preparing their messages. Prayer did not even make the list.

Each of us faces distractions that keep us focusing on minor things. Some of that is because we are measuring ourselves by someone else's ability and trying to compete with them. God wants us to focus on what He has created us to do. When I see a skilled administrator and try to be as good at that as he or she is I will be frustrated. That person is working with tools I don't have. When I hear a singer hit all the notes on perfect pitch, I have to admit that even singing lessons wouldn't take me that far. Part of life's challenge for each of us is to determine what God has given us so we can make full use of the investment He has made in us.

How many people spend their time wishing they had what someone else has. A young girl was not what anyone would have called beautiful and she knew that. By the time she was thirty-eight years old she was scrubbing floors for a living. She would go to the movies and think, "If only I had her looks." She would hear people sing and think, "If only I had her voice." One day she read a book, *The Magic of Believing*. She stopped worrying about what she didn't have and looked for what she had.

She remembered that in high school they called her the funniest girl around. She started turning her liabilities into assets and was soon making over one million dollars per year. Phyllis Diller is not beautiful and has a scratchy voice, but she has developed a successful career.

Just a sample of her humor shows how she has taken her natural gift and turned it into success. She said, on one occasion, "Burt Reynolds once asked me out. I was in his room." She has used her God-given sense of humor to change her life.

I love sports. Growing up in Northern Virginia I was a fan of the Washington Senators before they moved to Minneapolis and became the Twins. Jim Kaat was one of my favorites, both because he was a great pitcher and also because he was a bold, outspoken Christian. I was fascinated by the story behind his success.

Leo Hauser, in *Five Steps to Success* reported that Jim Kaat traced his success back to spring training in 1966. The Twins had acquired a new pitching coach, Johnny Sain, who silently watched pitchers perform. Then, one by one, he called them in for a personal chat.

"Jim," said Sain, "I've been watching you pitch. Tell me, what are your four best pitches?" Kaat, knowing his pitching ability well, responded: "My best pitch is my fastball. Then comes my curve. My slider and changeup are third and fourth."

"What pitch do you spend the most time practicing?" asked Sain. "My slider and changeup" said Kaat. "If I can improve on those two pitches, I know I'll have a good season."

Sain looked at Kaat, pondered his comments, and then responded, "I see it a little differently, Jim, and want you to take a different approach. Work on your fastball. I know it's your favorite pitch so go out there in practice, warm-ups, and during games and concentrate on your fastball. Throw your fastball 80 to 90 percent of the time all year and you'll win a lot of ball games." That year Kaat won 26 games and was pitcher of the year in the American League.

That will work for any of us. Find your fastball and build on it.

Here's an important lesson from history. In 1858, a Sunday School teacher, Edward Kimball, led a Boston shoe clerk to give his life to Christ. That clerk, Dwight L. Moody, became an evangelist. In England in 1879, Moody conducted a crusade and awakened evangelistic zeal in the heart of Fredrick B. Meyer, the pastor of a small church. F. B. Meyer traveled to America and had great success on college campuses. During one crusade on an American college campus, he led a student, J. Wilbur Chapman, to Christ. Chapman began holding crusades in different cities until he couldn't meet the demand for his ministry. He found a former baseball player, Billy Sunday, and began using him in citywide crusades. Billy Sunday held a revival in Charlotte, North Carolina and a group of businessmen enthusiastically planned another crusade. They invited Mordecai Hamm to preach. During Hamm's revival, a young man named Billy Graham heard the gospel and yielded his life to Christ. Billy Graham has preached to one billion people, or one-fifth of the world's population.

Only eternity will reveal the tremendous impact of that one Sunday School teacher, Mr. Kimball, who invested his life in the lives of others. Whether I am called to be a Billy Graham or an Edward Kimball, success is taking what God has given me and using it to the best of my ability.

59—Reigning in Life

We start life with a serious handicap. We inherited a sin nature from Adam. Even if you have trouble admitting that you're a sinner, you can look around and admit that everyone else is. But, remember, they look at you and see your faults, too. Maybe the problem all of us face is understanding how our lives can be so messed up by what someone else did a long time ago.

For those who think, "What someone did years ago shouldn't affect me," there is an old story of a ship that was traveling across the Mediterranean. One of the passengers cut a hole under his bunk. Some of the sailors saw him and demanded to know what he was doing. "What difference does it make to you?" he asked. "The hole's under my own bunk."

We know it doesn't matter whose bunk the hole is under. The whole ship will sink. The Bible says that Adam drilled a hole under his own bunk and the entire human race sank with him.

My life has been greatly affected by things I didn't do. I was born an American citizen rather than a British citizen because some people I've never met made a decision in 1776. They signed the Declaration of Independence and what they did determined that I would be an American and not British.

I love football. There is often suspense at the end of a play when there is a yellow flag on the field. If the flag is for a personal foul, the entire team is penalized fifteen yards. The other players might have executed their assignments flawlessly, but that doesn't matter. The whole team is penalized. Adam committed a personal foul against his Creator a long time ago and the entire human race has been penalized.

It's difficult to admit, but it's true that we pass more to our children than our physical genes. They get our weaknesses as well. And, we got ours from Adam.

With that being the case, what hope do we have? The apostle Paul addresses that issue in his letter to the Roman church. He wrote, *"For if, by the trespass of the one man, death reigned through that one man, how much more will those who receive God's abundant provision of grace and of the gift of righteousness reign in life through the one man, Jesus Christ"* (Romans 5:17).

What a great promise! We can "reign in life" through Jesus Christ, even though we were born with the weakness and sin we inherited from Adam. It is because Jesus came that we can live healthy, triumphant lives.

Richard Armstrong in his book, *Make Your Life Worthwhile*, reports the story about a man in Wales who sought to win the affection of a certain woman for 42 years before she finally said, "Yes." The couple, both 74, recently became "Mr. and Mrs." For more than 40 years, the persistent, but rather shy man slipped a weekly love letter under his neighbor's door. But, she continually refused to speak and mend the spat that had separated them many years before.

After writing 2,184 love letters without ever getting a spoken or written answer, the single-minded old man eventually summoned up enough courage to present himself in person. He knocked on the door of the reluctant woman's house and asked for her hand. To his delight and surprise, she accepted.

Imagine God's dilemma. Repeatedly He tried to get His message of love through to His human creation with little response. Finally, when there was no other way, He wrapped up His message in a person, Jesus Christ.

There are three words for life in the original language of the New Testament. Each one has come into English in some form. From *bios,* we get the word biology. From *psyche,* we get psychology and from *Zoe* we get zoology. The New Testament writers use these words in very distinct ways. *Bios* represents our possessions—the things we accumulate in life. *Psyche* is very close to our concept of personality.

The third word, *zoe*, is the one Paul used in Romans 5:17. It refers to the life that comes from God. It alone can break the grip of death on humanity. It alone can bring us to our destinies. It is the result of being born again.

Because of Jesus, we can receive a life that transcends our natural personalities and is far more than the stuff we own. It is a quality of life that can only come from God. I get my *psyche* from my ancestors. I acquire *bios* while I am alive. But, I get *zoe* from God. Jesus makes "life" available to me by faith.

We live in a world that says, "You get what you deserve." God's grace tells us that we receive from God what we could never earn. Our standing before God is His gift to those who believe in His Son. It's hard for many of us to believe that God just gives us the power to "reign in life."

The emperor Napoleon was reviewing some troops upon the Place du Carrousel in Paris. In giving an order, he thoughtlessly dropped the bridle upon his horse's neck, which instantly set off in a gallop. The emperor was obliged to cling to the saddle. At this moment, a common soldier of the line jumped in front of the horse, grabbed the bridle, and handed it respectfully to the emperor. "Much obliged to you, captain," said Napoleon, in one word making the soldier a captain. The man asked, "Of what regiment, sir?" Napoleon replied, "Of my guards!" and galloped off.

The soldier then laid down his gun and, instead of returning to his comrades, approached the group of officers. "I am," said the soldier proudly, "a captain of the guard." One general mocked him. "Who made you a captain of the guards?" he challenged. "He just did," said the young soldier, pointing to the emperor, who was still in sight. "I ask your pardon, sir," said the general respectfully. "I was not aware of your recent promotion."

The great news of the gospel is that we, who were born with a truckload of sin and weaknesses, have been promoted by God's grace. Through Jesus we are no longer victims of the past, we reign in life. Not because we are good, but because Jesus was good and He has paid for our promotion with His death and resurrection. In a world where so many of us have felt victimized, may we grasp the truth that He has freed us from bondage to failure and has made each of us winners.

60—Strength for Tough Times

These are tough times for many of us. Economic instability and uncertainty about the future form the headlines of newspapers and magazines every day. I have a friend who stopped watching the news because it's so depressing.

Some people feel that it's so hopeless they might as well give up. Charles Shultz, in "Peanuts," expressed that option. One day Linus and Charlie Brown were walking along and chatting with one another. Linus said, "I don't like to face problems head on. I think the best way to solve problems is to avoid them. In fact, this is a distinct philosophy of mine. No problem is so big or so complicated that it can't be run away from!"

Others feel like there's no use fighting it, they are destined to fail. A fortune-teller studied the hand of a young man and said, "You will be poor and very unhappy until you are thirty-seven years old." The young man responded, "Well, after that, what will happen? Will I be rich and happy?" The fortune-teller said, "No, you'll still he poor, but you'll be used to it after that."

Maybe all of us can relate to Thomas Lane Butts' description of an animal act in his book, *Tigers in the Dark*. "Several years ago there was a well-known television circus show that developed a Bengal tiger act. Like the rest of the show, it was done "live" before a large audience. One evening, the tiger trainer went into the cage with several tigers to do a routine performance. The door was locked behind him. The spotlights highlighted the cage, the television cameras moved in close, and the audience watched in suspense as the trainer skillfully put the tigers through their paces.

"In the middle of the performance, the worst possible fate befell the act: the lights went out! For twenty or thirty long, dark seconds the trainer was locked in with the tigers. In the darkness they could see him, but he could not see them. A whip and a small kitchen chair seemed meager protection under the circumstances, but he survived, and when the lights came on, he calmly finished the performance.

"In an interview afterward, he was asked how he felt knowing that the tigers could see him but that he could not see them. He first admitted the chilling fear of the situation, but pointed out that the tigers did not know that he could not see them. He said, 'I just kept cracking my whip and talking to them until the lights came on. And they never knew I could not see them as well as they could see me.'

"This experience gives us a vivid parable of human life. At some point in our lives, all of us face the terrifying task of fighting tigers in the dark. Some face it constantly. Many people cope daily with internal problems that are capable of destroying them. They cannot visualize their problems or understand them, but their problems seem to have them zeroed in."

Haven't we all felt that at times we were working where we can't see the dangers lurking, but we know they are there? Where do we who have faith turn when the lights go out and we're cracking our whips in the dark? I have turned to a truth that remains steady no matter what the circumstances of the day may be. Jesus is alive!

After Jesus was crucified and buried two women named Mary went to the tomb of Jesus on the first day of the week. When they arrived, they didn't find Jesus but, instead, found an angel sitting on the stone that had been rolled away from the front of the tomb, sealing it. They were confused but the angel gave them the good news that still sustains us. *"The angel said to the women, 'Do not be afraid, for I know that you are looking for Jesus, who was crucified. He is not here; he has risen, just as he said. Come and see the place where he lay' "* (Matthew 28:5-6).

"Do not be afraid" is a good word any time. It is especially good when things have seemed out of control, like the crucifixion of Jesus. We have our orderly expectations of how things should be and something we don't expect can rattle our confidence. Our retirement is in jeopardy. We may lose our job. Gas prices put a seemingly unbearable burden on our budget. Unexpected illness with its fear and added expense comes at us in the dark. The message to every believer, still, is "Do not be afraid."

For the Allied Armies of World War II to break Hitler's power, there had to be an invasion to put them on the continent of Europe. When the Allies landed on the shores of Normandy that invasion paved the way for the capture of Berlin. From those sandy beaches, the armies moved to destroy the power of a ruthless madman. Two thousand years ago, life landed on our broken planet and it has been invading the realm of death ever since. That life came through Jesus. Heaven has invaded earth and, for everyone who believes, life has overcome death.

The good news for any of us, in any cultural climate is the same news the two Marys heard from an angel, *"He is not here; he has risen, just as he said."*

The fact that Jesus is alive means that I can see the present world from a different perspective. Problems seem real. In fact, they are real. But, I can remember that they are temporary, not permanent. When Jesus defeated death, He defeated the last enemy we would have to face. In light of that, I can live without fear. As I tell myself quite often, a hundred years from now this problem won't matter.

Peter was a 28-year-old seminary student, training for the ministry, when he learned that he had cancer. He felt frail, weak and was struggling to cope with his situation when his wife and some friends took him to a mountain lake to spend the day. The mountain and the lake were beautiful.

His wife went to make reservations for them to return and stay at a cabin. It was booked well in advance, and they would not be able to come back and stay there for a year. While she was making the reservations, he wandered down by the lake. His friend walked up and asked what he was thinking. "It's just not fair. This mountain, these forests and this lake have been here thousands of years. They will be here next year and I will not be. My wife is making reservations to come back here in one year and I will not be with her."

He did not come back with his wife the next year. He was alive and with her, but the mountain was not there. It was Mount Saint Helens. That year it blew up and the top of the mountain, the lake and the idyllic cabin were gone. We so often think that the things around us are permanent and we are temporary. That is not true! All the things around us are temporary and we are eternal.

In the midst of our temporary struggles and trials, God wants us to reach out and lay hold of an eternal truth. Because Jesus is alive, we too shall live.

61—Humility

A cartoon in *Leadership* magazine pictured a pastor standing behind his pulpit. He was saying, "My sermon today is on humility, and in my opinion, it's one of the finest pieces ever written."

Being humble is a challenge to anyone. Any success at all becomes a potential temptation to take the credit for ourselves. When H. A. Ironside, a former pastor of Moody Church in Chicago, was a young Christian he said that he was convicted about his lack of humility. He went to an elder in his church who gave him a remedy. He advised him to march through the business district of Chicago at lunchtime wearing a sandwich board, shouting the Scripture verses written on the sandwich board for all to hear.

Dr. Ironside said that he did that and later that day lost the benefit of the experience. He thought to himself, "I'll bet there's not another man in Chicago who would have done that."

Several of us recently attended the United Pastors Network Conference that was held at Pastor Dale O'Shields' church in Gaithersburg, Maryland. Ten thousand individuals attend Pastor O'Shields' church each week. He conducts five services each weekend in his immense facilities.

Each pastor who spoke led a church with no less than 5,000 in attendance. It was a setting in which most pastors would have been intimidated. We weren't. Even though the speakers had churches far larger than those of most of the pastors in attendance, the preachers who spoke mingled with the other pastors and did everything they could do to put all of us in attendance at ease. We felt as if they were on our side as they shared principles that sustained their personal relationships with God that had led to the success of their ministries. None of their presentations focused on the mechanics of church building. The pastors focused on the core values of their relationships with God and people.

They honored the spiritual fathers who had shaped their lives and they honored God.

As we listened, we learned about passion for God and passion for the people we serve. That is the remarkable thing—we didn't just listen, we learned. The gentleness and humility of those pastors was noteworthy. The morning after the conference, I woke up with a verse running through my head: *"Take my yoke upon you and learn from me, for I am gentle and humble in heart, and you will find rest for your souls"* (Matthew 11:29). The part of that verse that reverberated through my mind was *"learn from me, for I am gentle and humble in heart."* We learn from teachers who are gentle and humble.

The opposites of Jesus' attitude are harshness that isn't gentle and haughtiness that isn't humble. Jesus wanted us to know that one reason we learn from Him is His gentleness and humility. That is still a winning combination.

Lawrence Richards, in his book of word studies, describes the Greek word translated "gentle." He explains that it is the opposite of "an angry harshness that grows out of personal pride and a dominating selfishness." Jesus is the most unselfish person who ever lived. Everything He did was in honor of His Father and for our good. He wanted us to know that His attitude was a key reason for our learning from Him.

A music lover met Johannes Brahms, the great composer. He asked him, "Would you write some music of a great masterpiece and sign it so I will always have a memory of this moment?" Brahms scribbled the first bars of "The Blue Danube" by Johann Strauss. He wrote under the music, "Unfortunately not by me."

A truly humble man is hard to find, yet God delights to honor such selfless people. Booker T. Washington, the renowned black educator, was an outstanding example of this truth. Shortly after he took over the presidency of Tuskegee Institute in Alabama, he was walking in an exclusive section of town when a wealthy white woman stopped him. Not knowing the famous Mr. Washington by sight, she asked if he would like to earn a few dollars by chopping wood for her.

Because he had no pressing business at the moment, Professor Washington smiled, rolled up his sleeves, and proceeded to do the humble chore she had requested. When he was finished, he carried the logs into the house and stacked them by the fireplace.

A little girl recognized him and later revealed his identity to the woman. The next morning the embarrassed woman went to see Mr. Washington in his office at the Institute and apologized profusely.

"It's perfectly all right, Madam," he replied. "Occasionally I enjoy a little manual labor. Besides, it's always a delight to do something for a friend." She shook his hand warmly and assured him that his meek and gracious attitude had endeared him and his work to her heart. Not long afterward, she showed her admiration by persuading some wealthy acquaintances to join her in donating thousands of dollars to the Tuskegee Institute.

Each of us wants to influence others. There are many ways to do that, but the qualities that make others want to learn from us are the same qualities Jesus exhibited: gentleness and humility.

62–Who's Got Your Back?

A preacher, ending his sermon, announced that he would preach on Noah and his Ark on the following Sunday and gave the scriptural reference for the congregation to read ahead of time. A couple of boys noticed something interesting about the placement of the story of the flood in the preacher's pulpit Bible. They slipped into the church and glued two pages of the pulpit Bible together.

On the next Sunday, the preacher got up to read his text. "Noah took unto himself a wife," he began, "and she was"– he turned the page to continue–"three hundred cubits long, fifty wide and thirty high." He paused, scratched his head, turned the page back and read it silently. Then he looked up at the congregation and said, "I've been reading this old Bible for nigh onto fifty years, but there are some things in it that are hard to believe."

What is not hard to believe is that all of us will, at some time in our lives, face adversity. After Fred Astaire's first screen test the memo from the testing director of MGM, dated 1933, said, "Can't act! Slightly bald! Can dance a little!" After he became a star, Astaire kept that memo over the fireplace of his Beverly Hills home.

An expert said of the great football coach, Vince Lombardi: "He possesses minimal football knowledge. Lacks motivation." Vince Lombardi lacking motivation? We need another expert!

Walt Disney was fired by a newspaper editor for lack of ideas. Disney may have had some shortcomings–all of us do–but lack of ideas was not one of them.

Those are a few examples of the discouraging circumstances that threaten to undermine our dreams. Life can be tough. A pastor told of observing "Christian Education Day" at his church. One feature of the service was to have each college graduate name his or her Alma Mater along with the school's colors. One man stood up and the pastor knew he had never attended college. When asked to name his school, the man said, "The College of Hard Knocks, colors black and blue." That school is undoubtedly on many of our resumes.

The book of Nehemiah in the Old Testament tells the story of the rebuilding of Jerusalem after the devastation of Nebuchadnezzar's invasion and the exile of the population. The walls of Jerusalem had been torn down and the city was left in desolation. When Nehemiah came from Persia to manage the city's reconstruction, the local population rose up to resist him and hinder the project. When the walls were halfway up, in chapter 4, the pressure began to affect the workers and they wanted to give up the effort. Discouragement set in.

The book of Nehemiah points out some lasting truths. There will be a time when we are misunderstood. Somewhere criticism will be directed our way. We will face occasions when we are struggling with faith and someone will tell us we aren't going to make it. In other words, when we begin to make a difference in our world arrows of discouragement will be fired at us.

In Nehemiah 4, we are given ways to handle discouragement. Nehemiah never stopped working and he encouraged his weary workers with words of faith. *"After I looked things over, I stood up and said to the nobles, the officials and the rest of the people, 'Don't be afraid of them. Remember the Lord, who is great and awesome, and fight for your brothers, your sons and your daughters, your wives and your homes"* (Nehemiah 4:14). The speech worked. They finished the rebuilding of the ruined city.

One principle of Nehemiah's success strikes me as particularly appropriate in our world. He established a support system for those who were struggling with the discouragement of a half-finished project.

Before talking about the need for connecting with others, it is important to understand that each builder in the book of

Nehemiah was responsible for rebuilding a particular section of the wall. That points out that there are things I can do that no one else can do for me. There are duties that others perform that I could not do nearly as well, if at all. Part of the success of God's kingdom in my life lies in my willingness to accept my responsibility.

It is a fact that no one can do it all. God doesn't expect any one of us to do it all. But, He does want us to accomplish what He gives us the grace to do.

I enjoy watching football. When a team is lined up at the goal line and is trying to score a touchdown, one running back may get the ball. If he gets in the end zone, it isn't because of his effort alone. Someone gave him the ball and many guys blocked for him. It's a team effort with each player doing his part. That's the key to success whether we are rebuilding a city or reaching out so others will know how good God is.

The problem is that we can become so preoccupied with our responsibility that we forget it's a team effort. Verse 19 points out the problem Nehemiah faced, and that we face: *"We are widely separated from one another along the wall."* That's fine. Each of us has a specific duty and it is right to pay attention to what we are assigned.

Nehemiah's solution to the isolation is still appropriate. In verse 20, he tells the workers, *"Wherever you hear the sound of the trumpet, join us there. Our God will fight for us!"* In those times when we are the target of the enemy's attack let's sound the alarm. Don't be ashamed to call for help. Don't try to fight alone!

"I don't need anybody else" may be the American way but it's not God's way. None of us, when faced with a brother or sister in trouble, is right to think, "I'm trying to get my family to heaven. Take care of yourself."

There are two important lessons for us from Nehemiah 4. First, if you're in trouble sound the alarm. Second, if you hear someone else's alarm, get involved. Nehemiah puts it this way: *"Join us there."*

Nature provides a great example of what God wants for each of us. The rhinoceros is blessed with his own private warning system. Because his tough hide is infested with ticks, a bird about the size of a starling and belonging to the same family rides on his back while it feeds on the insects. Whenever danger threatens, the tickbird voices an alarm to alert the rhinoceros which itself has very poor eyesight.

I need others who will be there for me when I face an overload of trouble. All of us have blind spots and value those who protect us from dangers we might not even see. We weren't meant to live isolated, lonely lives. God intends each of us to be part of a community in which someone has our back.

63—Guidance by Surprises

Sometimes God is working out something in our lives that we cannot see. Circumstances often do not conform to our plans. When Gwen and I moved from Maryland in the late 1970's we had several options from which we planned to choose. None of them materialized. Instead, we went to Virginia Beach and enjoyed a long stint of ministry and made a great number of wonderful friends.

We left Virginia Beach and moved to Australia, thinking we would spend the rest of our lives there. We loved the two years in the Sydney area, preaching regularly at Penrith Christian Life Centre and holding services in every Australian state.

We then moved back to the United States and were involved in the ministry of The Life Church, supporting Pastors David and Jo Ann Baird. We continue to be involved in the ministry of that great church. Then, through circumstances we did not manipulate, we came to the Outer Banks of North Carolina, where we still live.

Looking back over those moves reminds Gwen and me that God has often led us by surprising us. Most of us can relate to those times when we started in one direction and God redirected us to another. Frequently it turns out that we were in the dark about our eventual destination.

James Whistler, whose famous painting is "Whistler's Mother," started out to be a soldier. He failed at West Point because he could not pass chemistry. "If silicon had been a gas," he used to say, "I should have been a major-general."

There is an account of the Apostle Paul's life in Acts 16 that has helped me understand the ways of God. God wanted a church in Europe, but Paul's focus was on Asia Minor. Paul and Silas were taking one step at a time. They trusted the Lord's guidance—and He led them to Philippi in Greece. However, the guidance came piecemeal and there were problems that could have discouraged them before they reached their ultimate destination.

Paul's frustrated attempts to go to Ephesus and Bithynia were recorded by Luke: *"Paul and his companions traveled throughout the region of Phrygia and Galatia, having been kept by the Holy Spirit from preaching the word in the province of Asia. When they came to the border of Mysia, they tried to enter Bithynia, but the Spirit of Jesus would not allow them to"* (Acts 16:6-7).

Paul would eventually go to the province of Asia where he would launch a revival in Ephesus, but not yet. Bithynia was a natural choice because it was the richest province in Asia Minor (now Turkey). The picture is interesting. Paul was headed west and tried to turn south toward Ephesus. The Holy Spirit said "No." So, he tried to turn north to Bithynia. The Holy Spirit said "No" to that as well.

So what do we do when we can't go north or south? We do what Paul did. We keep moving.

When Paul arrived at Troas, he could no longer continue. He had to stop at the edge of the Aegean Sea. There Paul was ready for one of the most important decisions of his ministry. He was sent to Europe! Harry Emerson Fosdick described Paul as having taken advantage of "the leftovers of a broken plan."

Paul wanted Ephesus or Bithynia and instead ended up at Troas.

How many of us started in one direction and, when reviewing our journey, realize that God had another destination in mind? Phillips Brooks, an Episcopalian pastor, wrote my favorite Christmas Carol, *O Little Town of Bethlehem.* He gave lectures on preaching that have blessed generations of preachers.

His success as a Boston pastor was remarkable. While serving a church there he received a letter: "Dear Mr.

Brooks: I am a tailor in a little shop near your Church. Whenever I have the opportunity I always go to hear you preach. Each time I hear you preach I seem to forget all about you, for you make me think of God."

But, Phillips Brooks didn't plan to be a preacher. He wanted to be a teacher. In his attempt to have a teaching career, he failed miserably. He was devastated. His father wrote a friend of Phillips during that time: "Phillips will not see anyone now, but after he is over the feeling of mortification, he will come and see you."

Adoniram Judson wanted to go to India as a missionary. When he arrived there, the East India Company would not let him land. He tried for one year to change their minds, but the door was still closed. Instead, he went to Burma and changed that nation.

When Joseph was a teenager he had two dreams that suggested he would inherit the family farm. Instead, he was betrayed by his brothers and languished in an Egyptian prison. Ultimately, God's providence brought him to his destiny. He became the Prime Minister of the greatest nations on the face of the earth.

He looked back and saw God's hand in the strange journey he had taken. He said to his repentant brothers, *"And now, do not be distressed and do not be angry with yourselves for selling me here, because it was to save lives that **God sent me** ahead of you.... But **God sent me** ahead of you to preserve for you a remnant on earth and to save your lives by a great deliverance"* (Genesis 45:5, 7).

We can all learn a lesson from Paul. Instead of playing the "what if" game ("What if I had gone to Bithynia") His imagination was touched by the possibilities that awaited him.

While waiting for direction in Troas he had a vision of a man from Macedonia who said, *"Come over to Macedonia and help us"* (Acts 16:9). That is where God wanted Paul.

Because of the "Not yet" leadings of the Holy Spirit and the vision from God the gospel went to Philippi and would reach into Europe. It was a significant moment in the history of Christianity.

Helen Roseveare put it this way: "As I came home from church one evening, I was struggling to recognize God's guidance for my life. Suddenly, I drove into dense fog and could see nothing. Poking my head out the window, I noticed a tiny light from the road ahead. As I inched my car forward, it blinked out and another set of oncoming headlights took its place some yards ahead. I crawled along, following just the short distance I could see—one light after another—until the fog cleared. Then I realized that this is how God guides me. He shows me how far I need to go at any given moment. And, step-by-step, I move from one light to the next. Confident of God's guidance, I let go of the need to see his complete plan."

Wherever we are in our spiritual journey, let us seize our opportunities God has given us and see the fulfillment of His plans. He may lead us by surprising us but, don't be mistaken, He leads!

64—Our Ministry Begins

My friends and I used to laugh at a man who was never able to take a position. His philosophy was, "Some of my friends are for it, some of my friends are against it and I'm with my friends." After having laughed at his indecision, that's where I am today. I have friends who voted for the Republicans, friends who voted for the Democrats and they're all still my friends.

After each election in our nation, you may have noticed that Messiah was not on the ballot. However strongly we may have felt about any election, Jesus was Lord before we voted and He is still Lord. We never elect a Deliverer, we elect a President who faces enormous challenges. Maybe all the candidates we considered were extraordinary individuals. Ultimately, we select one to lead us.

We as believers have a unique and important responsibility after an election. Two Scriptures stand out for me. The first is Matthew 5:13– *"You are the salt of the earth."* Salt may not seem as important to us as it was to the culture in which Jesus said those words. But in Jesus' day salt was a primary preservative. Without refrigeration food would spoil quickly. Salt was used to make sure there was no spoilage. We were not left in the world to remain in saltshakers. God placed believers in society to act as a preservative against moral decay.

Pollsters said that young evangelicals, who were under thirty years of age and voted in our last Presidential election, gave their top three moral concerns: Poverty, global warming and Darfur (the horrendous genocide in that country). To those moral issues we add abortion. It is important for every believer to accept the responsibility for being the "salt of the earth."

Salt makes us thirsty. They say you can't eat just one potato chip. Well, after eating all those salty potato chips we need a thirst quencher. Maybe one of the greatest challenges believers face in any society is the challenge of making people thirsty for God. One of my disappointments as a Christian is the people I meet who haven't been drawn to Jesus by believers, but have been driven away from Him by condemnation and self-righteousness. We are on earth to make those who don't know Jesus thirsty for a relationship with Him.

Isn't that what Jesus did? A few years ago, I saw a question that shook me deeply: Sinners liked Jesus, why don't they like us? A new President has been elected and America still needs a Savior. His name is Jesus and our responsibility is to be the "salt" that creates a thirst for Him in our communities.

In 1985, a forty-foot, forty-five ton whale, affectionately named Humphrey, made a wrong turn during his migration along the California coast. The wayward mammal became a national celebrity when he turned into San Francisco Bay, swam under the Golden Gate Bridge, and managed to navigate seventy miles upriver. For more than three weeks, Humphrey defied all efforts to get him back to salt water. Finally, marine biologists decided to see if they could lure him with the recorded sounds of feeding humpbacks. It worked. Humphrey responded to the "happy humpbacks" and followed "them" back to the Pacific. Lonely, frustrated and lost people just might follow the sound of happy, feeding Christians to the source of life and joy—Jesus.

The second Scripture that I find to be important touches on our post-election responsibility as Christians. In fact, our real ministry begins after an election. Paul wrote Timothy and said, *"I urge, then, first of all, that requests, prayers, intercession and thanksgiving be made for everyone—for kings and all those in authority, that we may live peaceful and quiet lives in all godliness and holiness. This is good, and pleases God our Savior, who wants all men to be saved and to come to a knowledge of the truth"* (1 Timothy 2:1-4).

It is our political leaders who have the responsibility for maintaining a climate favorable to peace, quiet, godliness and holiness. The good news of salvation can be proclaimed in that atmosphere. As Paul explained, we pray for our leaders because they can serve God's purpose in proclaiming the good news about Jesus: *"This is good, and pleases God our Savior, who wants all men to be saved and to come to a knowledge of the truth."*

In my zeal for politics, God doesn't want me to lose sight of my goal. I am here to help others know Jesus. Anyone who becomes President of the United States faces difficult decisions and staggering challenges. I don't envy him or her. The Bible does tell me to pray for that leader because political decisions influence the culture in which I live and in which the Church ministers. All of us who believe are to pray that America will see peace and quiet, godliness and holiness. That will, largely, be affected by what the President and other leaders do. Our prayers will make a difference.

A desperate need for any President is wisdom. Over the next four years, it is important for our political leaders to make decisions based on right priorities. Charles Swindoll tells a story from the tragedy of the Titanic that draws attention to what is important. When the Titanic was sinking a frightened woman found her place in a lifeboat that was about to be lowered into the raging North Atlantic. She suddenly thought of something she needed, so she asked permission to return to her stateroom before they lowered the lifeboat. She was granted three minutes or they would have to leave without her.

She jumped out of the boat and ran across the deck that was already slanted at a dangerous angle. She raced through the gambling room where all the money had rolled to one side and was ankle deep. She came to her stateroom and quickly pushed aside her diamond rings and expensive bracelets and necklaces as she reached to the shelf above her bed and grabbed three small oranges. She quickly found her way back to the lifeboat and got in.

Now that seems incredible because thirty minutes earlier she would not have chosen a crate of oranges over even the smallest diamond. But, the sinking of the famous ship had transformed all her previous values. Instantaneously, priceless things had become worthless. Worthless things had become priceless. And, in that moment she preferred three small oranges to a crate of diamonds.

May God help our President know what is important so he can make wise choices for our country! His assignment now is clear. He is now the President of our wonderful country and will be the leader of our government. Our assignment as believers is just as clear. We are to pray for him. If we do our job, we can help him do his. As Paul said, *"This is good, and pleases God our Savior."*

65–Enjoy the Ride

A few years ago Gwen and I were riding through South Australia with a pastor, Ian Zerna, and his wife, Yvonne. As we drove by a field near a farmhouse, we saw a sheep that had been killed. Ian stopped the car and notified the owner. A dog on the loose had killed the sheep and once a dog tastes blood, they told me, it would now be a danger to the other sheep. Ian explained that no one who saw a slain sheep would fail to notify the owner. Sheep are defenseless and it takes an entire community to look after them.

In his informative analysis of Psalm 23, *A Shepherd Looks at Psalm* 23, Philip Keller described his life as a shepherd. He told of a neighbor who was careless in tending his flock: "In memory I can still see one of the sheep ranches in our district which was operated by a tenant sheepman. He ought never to have been allowed to keep sheep. His stock were always thin, weak and riddled with disease and parasites. Again and again they would come and stand at the fence staring blankly through the woven wire at the green lush pastures which my flock enjoyed. Had they been able to speak I am sure they would have said, 'Oh, to be set free from this awful owner!' This is a picture which has never left my memory. It is a picture of pathetic people the world over who have not known what it is to belong to the Good Shepherd...who suffer instead under sin and Satan."

Like sheep, we need protection from our vicious enemy, the devil. All we need to do is look around at our world and we see the destruction and violence he causes. I wouldn't want to step out of my front door in the morning without knowing that Someone was watching over me.

In the tenth chapter of John's Gospel Jesus described Himself as the Shepherd who takes care of His sheep. He drew a contrast between His plans for us and the devil's plans with a wonderful statement many of us struggle to grasp. It is huge! *"The thief does not come except to steal, and to kill, and to destroy. I have come that they may have life, and that they may have it more abundantly"* (John 10:10 NKJV).

We can agree that the devil is a thief who steals, kills and destroys. This statement follows chapter nine in which a blind man is healed and immediately the religious hierarchy does everything it can do to break him down, finally throwing him out of the synagogue. Jesus is saying that religion can be harmful to your health.

The encouraging part of Jesus' words point to His willingness to do more than take us to heaven. He wants to enrich our life on earth.

Former professional golfer Doug Sanders once said, "I'm working as hard as I can to get my life and my cash to run out at the same time. If I can just die after lunch Tuesday, everything will be perfect."

We might be surprised at the number of people who see life as a limited period of time with ever decreasing resources. To those who think that way Jesus tells us that if we believe in Him we will receive more than mere existence, we will inherit abundant life. Another version translates John 10:10 this way: "*I have come that they may have life, and have it to the full"* (NIV). The Greek word behind both translations speaks of both quantity and quality of life. We aren't just to pass the time, we are to live life to the fullest.

Jimmy Brown described a trip to the carnival when he was twelve years old. His dad took him and a friend to a carnival. His father purchased an armband for each of them and they walked through the gates. As Jimmy described the day, "We were awestruck at all of the blinking lights, the throng of people, the voices disappearing into the night air, and, most of all, the numerous rides. We heard the shrieks of joy from those who were riding on the various rides in the carnival that night. Their faces were lit up much like the bright lights and you could see grins so wide that it seemed their faces would split open from their excitement.

"As I watched them, I could imagine the feeling of lightness in their stomachs as they were rocked to and fro. I could almost feel the breath being suddenly thrust out of their lungs as they lurched from side to side. It looked like so much fun! We walked on. Everyone that we approached seemed to be enjoying himself or herself greatly. Each ride that we came to looked more exciting than the previous one. The people aboard seemed to be having the time of their lives. The whole scene looked so inviting! And, yet, we had no money. My dad had paid for the armbands and told us we were on our own. Without any money, we were left to watch the others enjoy themselves.

"The more we saw everyone else having a great time, the more we wished we were able to purchase tickets in order that we might ride the rides. We were standing around, miserable, wishing my father would come and get us out of that place, when we heard him say to us, 'Hey, you two. What are you doing?' 'We are just watching these people on the rides,' I replied. 'Why aren't you riding any of them,' my father asked. 'We don't have any money to buy tickets,' I continued. 'Son, don't you know that the rides are included in the price that I already paid. Your armband gets you access to all of the rides.'

"We were stunned. We had no idea that we could have been enjoying the carnival to its fullest extent by just taking advantage of what my father had given us."

Too many times, we have been like Jimmy and his friend at the carnival. We see others happy, blessed and enjoying life. While they are filled with joy, we wonder why God doesn't show up and enable us to enjoy the good life. We reach into our pockets and find no resources with which to buy the tickets to all the fun rides.

Then we read a verse like John 10:10. Jesus didn't die just to take us to heaven, but to give us His blessing here on earth. That doesn't mean everything always goes my way. The "devourer" is still roaming around stealing, killing and destroying. But, it does mean that I am connected to the King of the universe who came to give me an abundant life. It means that I will not run out of resources after lunch next Tuesday.

As Jimmy Brown put it, "Many Christians walk around with a brightly colored spiritual armband on, never realizing that it gives them access to all of the blessings that Jesus Christ offers. They're at the carnival but they're not riding any rides…. Don't be satisfied to simply wear your armband…get on the ride!"

66–Keep Moving On

Perry Comer was preaching on spiritual growth and gave an example from plant life. He was making the point that sometimes we grow in the shadows of life. He pointed out that roses must be planted in the sun, but fuchsias thrive in the shade. After the service, he said that a woman approached him. "Your sermon did me so much good," she said. Before he had time to gloat too much, however, she added: "I always wondered what was wrong with my fuchsias."

In Isaiah, the prophet addressed people who had pretty well made a mess of things. In chapter 53, he explained that the Messiah would come and die for the sins of the people. Jesus did that when He died on the cross for us. In chapter 55, he promised Israel that after they went in bondage to Babylon God would forgive their sins and bring them back from captivity.

I am particularly encouraged by chapter 54. Isaiah described the broken nation by the picture of a childless woman. It looked like the future was permanently marred by what they had done and that there would be no hope for a fulfilled life. When they may have given up on their future because of their failure he encouraged them with these words: *" 'Sing, O barren woman, you who never bore a child; burst into song, shout for joy, you who were never in labor; because more are the children of the desolate woman than of her who has a husband,' says the LORD. 'Enlarge the place of your tent, stretch your tent curtains wide, do not hold back; lengthen your cords, strengthen your stakes' "* (Isaiah 54:1-2).

"Enlarge the place of your tent" is a challenging thing to say to a barren woman. How many of us think we don't qualify for God's blessing because we have made too many mistakes? Isaiah's words aren't only for Israel then, but they are for us now. No matter what we have done or where we have been, God is able to restore us and bless us if we'll only allow Him.

That does require us to make changes and prepare for His blessing. Change is a hard word for most people. Psychologists tell us that change is one of our basic fears. I like the title of a book I saw in a bookstore, *If It Ain't Broke, Break It*. Don't settle for where you've been. Get ready to expand the borders of your life.

Vance Havner once explained God's process with us by referring to the medicine cabinet. Sometimes your medicine bottle has on it, "Shake well before using." That is what God has to do with some of His people. He has to shake them well before they are ever useable.

I never liked soft shell crabs before moving to the Outer Banks. I wouldn't even try them. They looked like bugs that had been run over by a car and then deep-fried. I was in a social situation, though, when not eating them would've been rude, so I swallowed hard and dug in. I was hooked. They are a delicacy!

The intriguing thing about soft shell crabs is that they don't remain that way. They need the shell to protect them from being torn apart, yet when they grow, the old shell must be abandoned. If they did not abandon it, the old shell would soon become their prison—and finally their casket. During that terribly vulnerable period when their shells are soft, the transition must be scary. Hungry schools of fish are ready to make them a part of their food chain. Hungry residents of the Outer Banks are waiting for a feast. For a while at least, that old shell must look good.

We are not so different from crabs. To change and grow, we must sometimes shed our shells—a structure, a framework we've depended on. If we want to grow, we have to learn to give up the old, confining restrictions of our past.

One thing we have all learned is that we can't move forward while we are chained to our history. Fear can restrict us and keep us from growing. John Ortberg gives excellent advice: "There is no limit to his presence. There is no place where we can go, no activity we can engage in, where he is not watching over us. 'When you pass through the waters, I will be with you.' But, fear tries to convince us it is not so. Fear has created more practicing heretics than bad theology ever has, for it makes us live as though we serve a limited, finite, partially present, semi-competent God."

The problem with so many of us is that we see Jesus, but find it hard to grasp who He really is. It's difficult for us to believe that anyone could love us as much as He does and forgive us as freely as He forgives.

Cary Grant once told how he was walking along a street and met a fellow whose eyes locked onto him with excitement. The man said, "Wait a minute, you're...you're—I know who you are; don't tell me—uh, Rock Hud—No, you're..." Grant thought he'd help him, so he finished the man's sentence: "Cary Grant." And the fellow said, "No, that's not it! You're..." There was Cary Grant indentifying himself with his own name, but the fellow had someone else in mind.

We have a God who can look at us when we are barren and promise a better day ahead. The barren woman in Isaiah 54 is told to expand the borders of her residence because she is about to have a large family. God says to us, even when we have failed, begin to make changes to accommodate blessing. He wants us to stop living in the restrictions of who we used to be and what we used to do. In spite of our circumstances and in spite of ourselves He wants to enrich our lives.

Some people never recover from their past experiences. Rebecca Thompson fell twice from the Fremont Canyon Bridge. In some ways, she died both times. The first fall broke her heart; the second fall broke her neck. When she was 18 years old she and her 11-year-old sister, Amy, were abducted from Casper, Wyoming. Two men drove the 40 miles to Freemont Canyon Bridge, 112 feet above the

North Platte River. They beat and raped her. She convinced them not to do the same to Amy. They threw them both off the bridge. Amy was killed. Rebecca bounced off a ledge, landed in deep water, and survived.

In September 1992, 19 years later, she returned to the bridge with her boyfriend and two-year old-daughter. She sat and wept, retelling the story. The boyfriend took the daughter back to the car and, on the way, heard the splash as her body hit the water. Why did she jump? Anger? Guilt at having survived? Fear? The day she took her life, the two men were up for parole. Perhaps she couldn't bear the thought that they might come back. Her present and future were ruined because she couldn't find a way to cope with the trauma of her yesterday.

God wants to help us move beyond barrenness and enjoy blessing. Gwen saw a photo on the internet that pictures what Jesus has done for us. In a hospital, twins were lying in the same crib. They were born prematurely and one was very weak. The nurse violated regulations and put them in the same crib. The strong one had its arm around the weak one. When the strong one embraced the weak one, it immediately became stronger with improved vital signs.

Maybe we have been weak and barely surviving. Jesus came as a baby to put His arm around us and make us strong.

67—Thanksgiving

A few years ago, the *Peanuts* cartoon pictured Charlie Brown bringing out Snoopy's dinner on Thanksgiving Day. But, it was just his usual dog food in a bowl. Snoopy took one look at the dog food and said, "This isn't fair. The rest of the world is eating turkey with all the trimmings, and all I get is dog food. Because I'm a dog, all I get is dog food." He stood there and stared at his dog food for a moment, and said, "I guess it could be worse. I could be a turkey."

When we look around and see the plight others are facing it isn't hard to realize that we have many reasons to be thankful. My wife, Gwen, has had a difficult year physically. She went through major surgery in July, but we are thankful that she went *through* it. We certainly prayed and asked God to protect her and he did. While she was asleep in the operating room and we were in the waiting room, God stayed with her.

My mother had surgery for cancer several years before she went to heaven. As they wheeled her to the operating room one of the attendants remarked about how calm she seemed. She responded, "I'm not afraid. I'll either wake up here or in heaven and either one is fine with me." No matter what happens in the present our future is assured. Thanksgiving week is a good time for us to reflect on our blessings and say "Thank you."

Just a simple "Thank you" can mean a great deal to any of us. A company had a campaign among its workers to encourage ideas that would improve their business. The winner of the cash award was an employee who made the suggestion: "Have our representatives say 'Thank you.' "

The psalmist taught us how to approach God: *"Let us come before him with thanksgiving. Let us sing him psalms of praise. For the LORD is a great God, the great King above all gods"* (Psalm 95:2-3, NLT). My life may have its challenges but I can give thanks because "the Lord is a great God."

It is more than a polite gesture to come before God with thanksgiving. It is recognition of all that He has done for us. It is an expression of faith in what He is going to do.

My parents taught me always to say "Thank you." When someone did something for me Mom or Dad would prompt me with, "What do you say?" I would respond with "Thank you." The psalmist is encouraging us in the same way. He tells us that when we come into God's presence we begin our prayers with "Thank you."

Alexander Whyte, the Scottish preacher who pastored in Edinburgh, always began his prayers with an expression of gratitude. One cold, miserable day his people wondered what he would say. He prayed, "We thank Thee, O Lord, that it is not always like this."

We all face adversity from time to time. That's no reason to stop giving thanks. God promises to make even our difficulties work in our favor. *"And we know that in all things God works for the good of those who love him, who have been called according to his purpose"* (Romans 8:28).

There is an infinite supply of hope in those words "in all things." God guarantees that in my mistakes, in the times when others mishandle my life and in my decisions, He is working for my good. I am aware of what's happening in my life. I know what state of health I'm in and how much money I have in the bank. I know what condition the economy is in and whether I have a job or not. Paul, in Romans, advises me to look behind those circumstances and see God working for my good in the shadows of my life.

There is a strange memorial in the Alabama town of Enterprise. There they have erected a monument to an insect, honoring the Mexican boll weevil.

In 1895, the boll weevil began to destroy the major crop of the county, cotton. In desperation to survive, the farmers had to diversify, and by 1919, the county's peanut crop was bringing in far more income than cotton had produced during its most prosperous days. In that year of blessing a fountain and monument were built. The inscription reads: "In profound appreciation of the boll weevil and what it has done as the herald of prosperity this monument was erected by the citizens of Enterprise, Coffee County, Alabama." Out of a time of struggle and crisis had come new growth and success. Out of adversity had come blessing.

I know how to ask for things when times are tough. There's nothing wrong with that and over and over again the Bible tells us not to hesitate to ask. The trouble I have is remembering to thank Him for the last blessing before asking Him for the next one.

It's like the roofer who slips and is sliding down the slope of the roof. He calls out in a panic, "Help me, Jesus." Just then his pants catch on a nail, he is saved, and he says, "Never mind, Jesus, the nail's got me now."

On the island of St. Croix in the Virgin Islands there are two Thanksgiving days. In addition to the usual one we celebrate, they have a Hurricane Thanksgiving Day on October 25. It marks the end of the hurricane season.

First, Supplication Day, July 25, begins the hurricane season. On Supplication Day, all citizens of St. Croix are urged to pray that their little island will be spared the ravages of hurricanes. Not content with that, they appoint a day at the end of the season to thank God that their prayers were answered. They call that day "Hurricane Thanksgiving Day."

Most of us have a good many supplication days but too few thanksgiving days. It would be good for all of us if we made a practice of saying "Thank you" to God for what He has already done for us.

68—Faith That Grows With Time

Growing old is a challenge for anyone. As someone wisely remarked, "It's not a bad thing when you consider the alternative."

Jeanne Calment is the oldest living human whose age can be verified. On her 120th birthday, she was asked to describe her vision for the future. "Very brief," she said.

A friend of mine, knowing my age, sent me a story that I didn't think was so funny. A man was telling his neighbor, "I just bought a new hearing aid. It cost me four thousand dollars, but it's state of the art. It's perfect." "Really," answered the neighbor. "What kind is it?" "Twelve thirty."

With all the challenges of aging, there's a story in the Bible that inspires faith in us no matter how old or young we are. Even when I was much younger, Caleb was one of my heroes. Part of his story is told in the fourteenth chapter of Joshua. When Israel refused to enter the Promised Land, only two spies who had explored Canaan were confident of ultimate victory: Joshua and Caleb. Forty-five years later, after the nation had wandered in the wilderness for forty years, Israel again came to the land God had promised them. This time Joshua led them across the Jordan River and they began to conquer the Holy Land.

At that time, Caleb came to Joshua with a faith-filled request: *"Now then, just as the LORD promised, he has kept me alive for forty-five years since the time he said this to Moses, while Israel moved about in the desert. So here I am today, eighty-five years old! I am still as strong today as the day Moses sent me out; I'm just as vigorous to go out to battle now as I was then. Now give me this hill country that the LORD promised me that day. You yourself heard then that the Anakites were there and their cities were large and fortified, but, the LORD helping me, I will drive them out just as he said"* (Joshua 14:10-12).

Caleb did not underestimate the enemy, he knew about the giants and walled cities. He just placed great confidence in the presence of God. He believed that God would keep the promise He had made.

Among the remarkable qualities of Caleb's faith was his willingness to remain unaffected by the negative attitudes around him.

Some people are so negative! I read about a farmer who had a brilliant dog and a neighbor who was absolutely negative. If it was raining, the farmer would say to his neighbor, "Boy, look at it rain, God's cleaning things up." "Yeah, but if it keeps up it's gonna flood," the neighbor would respond. Then the sun would come out and the neighbor would say, "If it keeps that up, it's gonna just scorch the crops."

The farmer thought, "What am I gonna do to win this guy?" So, he trained his dog to walk on water. He didn't tell his neighbor, he just took him duck hunting. They shot at some ducks successfully and the man said to his dog, "Go get 'em." The dog walked to them on the water, picked them up and hopped back in the boat. The farmer said, "What do you think of that?" The neighbor said, "He can't swim, can he?"

Faith often means standing apart from the crowd. Sometimes we find ourselves in the minority when we trust God. A little farming town was undergoing a severe drought. Crops had withered, cattle had died and the villagers faced ruin. The people gathered at the local church to pray for rain. They spent the afternoon in prayer. While they were praying, the wind changed, there was a clap of thunder and everyone ran to the door of the church.

Sure enough, it was raining. They danced, hugged each other and shouted for joy. Then all the eyes turned to a seven-year-old girl who was standing, smiling and watching the rain—from under her umbrella. They had all gathered to pray for rain, but only one little girl had brought her umbrella.

When the twelve spies had returned from checking out Canaan forty-five years earlier they presented a minority report that was filled with unbelief. They concluded that God's people had no chance of possessing the land God had promised. Joshua and Caleb were the only ones on the committee who disagreed.

Clovis Chappell, a Methodist pastor, summarized the majority report this way: "Whereas we have spied out the land of promise. And whereas we have discovered certain facts about the land that God Himself did not know, To wit: That it is inhabited by giants; And whereas we have come to realize that God was mistaken in thinking that we could ever possess it, And whereas we have learned that He overrated both His power and ours; Be it resolved that we give up the task as a wild dream and turn our faces back to Egypt."

True faith always challenges us to see God more clearly than we see our obstacles. It means that we are willing to trust God when everyone around us is filled with fear.

Because faith involves risk, God will frequently act to push us into decisions of faith. He will intervene to overcome our reluctance to trust Him.

Danny Cox, a former jet pilot turned business leader, told his readers in *Seize the Day* that when jet fighters were first invented, they "flew much faster than their propeller predecessors. So pilot ejection became a more sophisticated process. Theoretically of course, all a pilot needed to do was push a button, clear the plane, then roll forward out of the seat so the parachute would open." Even though the parachute was behind him and located between him and the back of his seat, it was easy at those speeds to free himself when he jumped.

But, there was a problem that popped up during testing. Some pilots, instead of letting go, would keep a grip on the seat. The parachute would remain trapped between the seat and the pilot's back. The engineers went back to the drawing board and came up with a solution.

Cox writes: "The new design called for a two-inch webbed strap. One end attached to the front edge of the seat, under the pilot. The other end attached to an electronic take up reel behind the headrest. Two seconds after ejection, the electronic take-up reel would immediately take up the slack, and force the pilot forward out of his seat, thus freeing the parachute."

Bottom line? Jet fighter pilots needed that device to launch them out of their chairs. A former military pilot in Williamsburg, Virginia told me that the official name of the device is "Seat Separator." He also explained that the common name for the instrument is "Butt Kicker."

Faith requires courage, but sometimes we, too, want to hang on to our securities. Caleb didn't need a "Butt Kicker." He'd been waiting for his opportunity. For those of us who are reluctant to let go, God may use a "Butt Kicker" but that's the key to us realizing our dreams.

69—Let's Walk on Water

Maybe God is trying to tell me something. Some good things that happen to me are the result of my planning and decision-making. Many of my blessings, though, are divine coincidences. Several years ago, I was browsing in a Christian bookstore and saw a book, *If You Want to Walk on Water You've Got to Get Out of the Boat*, by John Ortberg. I may have been the only person on the planet who didn't know who John Ortberg was. But, I didn't. Now I'm a fan and have read every book he's written, but I bought that book purely for the title.

I wasn't looking for the book but the title grabbed me. Like so many others, I want to cling to my security blanket. Here was a book that helped me climb out of the boat and begin the adventure that changed my life. If you've read the fourteenth chapter of Matthew you know that Peter sank when he started walking on the water toward Jesus. You would also have read that Jesus pulled him to his feet again and Peter walked *on the water* with Jesus back to the boat.

The unexpected book-thing happened again. Gwen and I were in Long Island ministering with some dear friends of ours, Roger and Gill Blackmore. Roger is always ahead of me in knowing what's going on in the Kingdom of God. He is well-read and up to date. He has given me more than one book that has shaped my thinking. Before we left Long Island to return home, he gave us a book, *Wild Goose Chase*, by Mark Batterson.

It's another life-changing volume. Apparently, the early Celts called the Holy Spirit the "Wild Goose." The book is a challenge to leave the safety and security of one's comfort zone and enjoy the adventure available only to those willing to take a chance on God. I didn't seek out either of these books but God, in His providential way, put them in my path.

I have all the qualifications necessary to be the President of the local "Don't Take Chances, You Could Get Hurt" club. I like security. If God would have asked my opinion, I would have suggested that He put all the resources I would ever need in the bank, under my name, so I could reassure myself regularly that they were all there. Instead, He told me (all of us, actually) to ask for our daily bread.

I am on the adventure of chasing the "Wild Goose." That is what my heart really wants. I want to find out where He's going and what He's doing. But everyone should be warned: it's risky business.

Gwen and I live on the Outer Banks of North Carolina. Individuals who didn't grow up in church and have wandered into every poison patch there is surround us. I want to reach them with the love of God. That, in itself, is a recipe for adventure.

Here are some conclusions (in Batterson's own words) you will reach from learning to chase the "Wild Goose":

> "Quit living as if the purpose of life is to arrive safely at death."
> "Go after a dream that is destined to fail without divine intervention."
> "Don't let fear dictate your decisions."

The two books are similar in explaining that following Jesus can be the most exciting venture of our lives. John Ortberg told a story in *If You Want to Walk on Water....* that amazed me. He wrote:

"Doug Coe has a ministry in Washington, D.C. that mostly involves people in politics and government. An insurance salesman named Bob became a Christian and sought out Doug to be mentored in his newfound faith. As Bob learned about prayer, he decided to start praying for something. He told Doug he would begin to pray for Africa. 'That's kind of a broad target. Why don't you narrow it down to one country,' Doug suggested. 'All right. I'll pray for Kenya.' 'Do you know anything about Kenya?' Doug asked. 'No.' 'Have you ever been to Kenya?' 'No.'

"So Doug issued a challenge. He told Bob to pray for Kenya every day for six months and if nothing remarkable happened, he would give Bob $500. If Bob didn't pray for Kenya every day the challenge was off.

"Bob began to pray and for a long time nothing happened. Then one night he was at a dinner in Washington. As the people around the table explained what they did for a living, a woman explained that she ran the largest orphanage in Kenya. Bob pounded her relentlessly with questions. 'You've been to Kenya before?' she asked. 'No,' Bob responded. 'You know someone in Kenya?' 'No.' 'Then how do you happen to be so curious?' she asked.

"Bob explained that someone had challenged him to pray for Kenya. She invited Bob to visit Kenya and tour the orphanage, which he did. He was appalled by the poverty he saw and when he came home wrote large pharmaceutical companies. He reminded them that they would throw away large amounts of medical supplies each year that were unsold. Why not give them to the orphanage? Many of them did. The orphanage received more than a million dollars worth of medical supplies.

"The lady called Bob and said, 'Bob, this is amazing! We have had the most phenomenal gifts because of him letters you wrote. We would like to fly you back over and have a big party. Will you come?' The president of Kenya came to the celebration, because it was the largest orphanage in the country. He offered to take Bob on a tour of Nairobi. In the course of the tour, they passed a prison and Bob asked about the prisoners. 'They're political prisoners,' the president explained. 'That's a bad idea,' Bob said brightly. 'You should let them out.'

"Some time later Bob received a call from the State Department. 'Is this Bob?' 'Yes.' 'Were you recently in Kenya?' 'Yes.' 'Did you make any statements to the president about political prisoners?' 'Yes.' Bob told them what he had said. The State Department official explained that the president had freed the political prisoners. The U. S. government had tried for years to accomplish this without effect and had called to say thank you.

"Several months later, the president of Kenya made a phone call to Bob. He was going to rearrange his government and select a new cabinet. Would Bob be willing to fly over and pray for him for three days while he worked on this very important task? Bob flew to Nairobi and prayed for three days that God would give wisdom to the president of Kenya. All this happened because one man got out of the boat."

Here's the challenge. Why don't we do what Bob did and pray for the place God puts on our hearts? I can't promise you $500, but I don't have to. Watch what God will do in answer to our prayers. In six months, we may change the world.

70—Wise Men Still Seek Him

A Sunday School teacher wanted to teach the real meaning of Christmas to her class, so she told them the story of Jesus' birth from the Bible and taught them some Christmas carols. Then she asked the children to draw pictures that showed an event from the Christmas story.

One child drew the manger scene. There was a woman, a baby and a very fat man. When the teacher asked the child to explain the picture the explanation was simple and logical: "It's Mary, baby Jesus and Round John Virgin." Obviously, the child was paying attention when the teacher taught them to sing "'Round yon virgin, mother and child."

In his best-selling book, *The Jesus I Never Knew*, Philip Yancey contrasts the humility that characterized Jesus' royal visit to planet earth with the prestigious image associated with world rulers today: "Queen Elizabeth visited the United States, and reporters delighted in spelling out the logistics involved: her four thousand pounds of luggage included two outfits for every occasion, a mourning outfit in case someone died, 40 pints of plasma, and white kid-leather toilet seat covers. She brought along her own hairdresser, two valets, and a host of other attendants. A brief visit of royalty to a foreign country can easily cost 20 million dollars. In meek contrast, God's visit to earth took place in an animal shelter with no attendants present and nowhere to lay the newborn king but a feed trough."

The simplicity of Jesus' birth is one of the striking features of the story. Another remarkable part of the account in the Gospels is the cast of characters involved.

The most important person in the world, from a human perspective, was not present. Caesar Augustus, having been adopted by Julius Caesar, was the head of the Roman Empire. Augustus was busy devising new taxes to raise money for counteracting a small rebellion on the Northern frontier of the Roman Empire. He was worrying with a crisis in the empire's economy. Those things would have been more important to him than the birth of a peasant child in faraway Bethlehem.

King Herod was prevented from finding Jesus because of his evil intentions. He was so insecure and jealous for his position that he killed all the baby boys in Bethlehem in his attempt to destroy Jesus.

It's enough to say that not everyone was thrilled at the birth of Christ. Augustus was too busy to notice and Herod was too threatened to want Jesus to live.

Thankfully, that isn't the entire story surrounding the first Christmas. Shepherds received a personal invitation from heaven to find the baby and worship Him. Simeon, worshiping in the temple, saw the baby and knew that salvation had come to Israel.

One of my favorite Christmas bumper stickers, "Wise men still seek Him," reminds us of the remarkable story of the Magi who journeyed from Persia to find the baby. How they came to Bethlehem is one of the remarkable Christmas stories.

Tablets found in Persia, dating from the days of Jesus' birth, showed that Persian philosophers were expecting a great king to be born in the West. According to those records justice, righteousness, peace and joy would mark his reign. They even had a name for him, *Sosiosh*. Interestingly, the Persians were the only people of that day, besides the Jews, who believed in one God.

The men were astronomers and philosophers. The star that led them to the manger was certainly supernatural. For the star to identify a specific location showed that God intervened to guide the magi to Christ.

There are, however, some scientific facts that explain how God got their notice in the first place. In May 29, 7 B.C., Jupiter and Saturn were in conjunction and looked like a large star. On September 27, 7 B.C., Jupiter and Saturn lined up again. Again, on December 5, 7 B.C. it happened. Finally, a fourth time, in April, 6 B.C. Jupiter, Saturn and now Mars as well lined up to form a bright light in the sky. We know that the Persian astronomers believed the number four was significant so we can be sure that God had their full attention.

Those events do not explain the miraculous star, but they show the lengths to which God went to get the attention of the wise men.

The magi were Gentiles and pagans. We would probably not have invited them to see the Baby, but God did. They were intelligent men who were seeking the truth. Even though they were tainted by superstition, they were sincere seekers. God saw their hearts and turned heaven upside down to guide them to the Savior.

Some who will worship this Christmas are like the wise men. Without the privilege of growing up in church, they were hungry for the truth and God has led them to discover Jesus. Some are like the shepherds, who were surprised when the announcement came to them that a Savior had been born. Out of the city's social life, watching sheep, God sent them a special invitation. Some are like Simeon who held the baby in the Temple and saw the realization of all he had wanted. A faithful worshiper he had held on to the promises he knew from Scripture.

A woman missionary in the South Pacific Islands was explaining to a group of children the custom and significance of giving gifts at Christmas. "Giving gifts," she said, "expresses love and reminds us of the perfect gift of love we received from God: Jesus." Later that week, a young native boy came to the missionary's side and said, "I love you and want you to have this." He pulled from a straw basket the most beautiful shell the missionary had ever seen. As she admired its beauty, she recognized it as a special shell only found on the far side of the island, a half-day's walk from the village. When confronted by this, the boy smiled and said, "Long walk part of gift!" Christmas is God walking from heaven to earth to give us the gift of salvation.

A couple of thousand years ago God made the long walk from heaven to the manger. No matter what our background may be, the only proper response to Christmas is worship.

71—The Human Side of a Miracle

When a child was asked to draw a picture that showed one of the events of Christmas he drew an airplane. In the cockpit were two men, a woman and a baby. When asked to explain why he drew an airplane he replied, "It's Jesus' flight to Egypt." He continued by identifying the figures: "That's baby Jesus, His mother Mary, Joseph and, of course, Pontius the Pilot."

When we consider the individuals involved in the story of that first Christmas, it is clear that one of God's amazing wonders is His willingness to use ordinary people to accomplish His purposes. What we often do not see is that when God uses us it means that we sometimes press through our responsibilities without a sense of anything wonderful happening at all.

When Jonah was swallowed by a great fish he wasn't thinking, "What a wonderful miracle this is going to be." He cried out in Jonah 2:1-5 *"From inside the fish Jonah prayed to the LORD his God. He said: 'In my distress I called to the LORD, and he answered me. From the depths of the grave I called for help, and you listened to my cry. You hurled me into the deep, into the very heart of the seas, and the currents swirled about me; all your waves and breakers swept over me. I said, "I have been banished from your sight; yet I will look again toward your holy temple." The engulfing waters threatened me, the deep surrounded me; seaweed was wrapped around my head.' "*

Often when we are in the process of seeing a miracle all we know is that seaweed is wrapped around our heads.

Consider the experience of the young couple God used to bring Jesus into the world. Mary and Joseph faced misunderstanding connected to the birth of Jesus for the rest of their lives. In the Gospel of John Jesus was being taunted by His enemies who slandered Him with the words, *"We are not illegitimate children"* (John 8:41). That was a reflection on Jesus' parentage. Joseph and Mary gave up their reputations to see the miracle of Jesus' birth.

Mary was about to experience the miracle that changed the world. It wasn't that easy, though. Most mothers would agree that a 100-mile trip, taking three days, with a donkey as transportation is not the way to spend the final days of a pregnancy. I suspect that the glamour and excitement of the angel's words nine months before had worn off as Mary made the long trip to Bethlehem.

When we lived in Virginia Beach and Gwen was pregnant with one of our daughters she would go to the beach and dig a hole in the sand just so she could lie on her stomach.

Mary was a remarkable, lovely woman who models for all of us the unconditional obedience God wants.

God also worked through a godly man, Joseph. The Christmas story makes it clear that even before he knew what God was doing with Mary, Joseph was willing to shield her from humiliation.

When we read the Christmas story we are reminded that there are times when God's miracle involves our trying, tiring efforts. Miracles don't always consider our comfort. For the life of us, we can't hear the angels singing, and it is hard to remember exactly what Gabriel said. It can be extremely bumpy traveling mile after mile on the back of a donkey.

If Mary was like most pregnant women, Joseph had his share of pressure on that trip as well. When Gwen was pregnant, she would wake me up to tell me she couldn't sleep because she wanted me to share the joys of her pregnancy.

The outcome of a miracle, of course, is always worth whatever it takes. The angels' announcement to the shepherds was a joyful pronouncement: *"I bring you good news of great joy that will be for all the people. Today in the town of David a Savior has been born to you; he is Christ the Lord"* (Luke 2:10).

If God uses ordinary people like Joseph and Mary, we must also remember that God can use life's ordinary circumstances. Caesar Augustus was used, without his knowing it, to bring about the great event.

How did God use Augustus in his master plan? There was a rebellion on the Northern front of the Roman Empire, in Gaul. Money was needed to finance the military campaign. Augustus instituted a tax to finance that war. In order to comply with Augustus' order everyone in the empire had to go back to his hometown to register. Joseph and Mary had no choice but to go to Bethlehem. Circumstances forced them to make the difficult journey.

God moved the world to fulfill His plan. Micah, the prophet had said, *"But you, Bethlehem Ephrathah, though you are small among the clans of Judah, out of you will come for me one who will be ruler over Israel, whose origins are from of old, from ancient times"* (5:2). Joseph did not say to Mary, "Look, you are about due and Micah said the baby is to be born in Bethlehem."

God's promise as to the location of Jesus' birth was so powerful that He orchestrated the events of the entire empire to get Joseph and Mary where they were supposed to be. Every citizen of every village in the Mediterranean area was affected just to bring God's Word to fulfillment. We can trust God to do whatever it takes to fulfill in our tomorrows what He has promised today.

Benjamin Reaves tells about a small boy whose mother died when he was just a child. His father planned a picnic and the little boy, who had never been on a picnic, was excited. Several times that night the boy, too excited to sleep, awakened his father. The father sent the boy back to bed each time. Finally, the boy came one more time and the father, on the verge of exasperation, asked, "What's the matter now?" The boy said, "Daddy, I just want to thank you for tomorrow."

Maybe we're going through the discomfort that precedes a miracle. Maybe we feel like we've been riding 100 miles on the back of a donkey. But, God is in charge of our circumstances and is planning to keep His promise. We can always say, "Thank you, God, for tomorrow."

72–A Fresh Start

There is something about every January 1 that is inspiring. By 12:01 AM, January 1 of each year most of us have not made any mistakes. We have probably kept all of our resolutions up to that point and the year is full of promise. It is a measure of God's grace that He is willing to give each of us a fresh start.

One of the facts of Israel's deliverance from Egypt has always seemed remarkable to me. Their first celebration of Passover was not the first month of their calendar year, yet God told them that the month of Passover would be the "new" first month of their year. *"The LORD said to Moses and Aaron in Egypt, 'This month is to be for you the first month, the first month of your year' "* (Exodus 12:1-2). One of the things God is telling us is that the time of our deliverance is when life begins for us.

The apostle John says the same thing in his Gospel when he quotes Jesus' words to Nicodemus: *"You should not be surprised at my saying, 'You must be born again' "* (John 3:7). Each of us has a history that includes bad decisions, moral mistakes and faulty judgment. That is a heavy burden for any of us to carry. God was giving all of us hope when He explained to Israel that the month of their deliverance would be the "new" first month of their year. We can be encouraged by the fact that spiritual rebirth begins a new life.

We are not trapped in our past, but are free to live without condemnation because God has intervened in our lives. Whether we are like Israel, leaving behind old bondages, or are "born again" and have a new nature, God has provided for us to start over.

There is no better time to celebrate that fact than January 1. I am not a product of my history; I am a product of God's grace.

In John 3 Nicodemus came to Jesus at night. He had many things in his favor. He was sincere and was a committed religious leader. But, there comes a time when religion alone is not enough. We can scarcely imagine the difficulties Nicodemus had to overcome. He would stand apart from his peers for the rest of his life. While they would conspire to execute Jesus, he would take the risk of helping to bury the Son of God.

We aren't told everything Nicodemus was thinking but he had certainly come to realize the limitations of religion. He knew about Jesus' teaching and Jesus' miracles so it is fair to assume that he was thinking, "Jesus heals the sick. He comforts the despairing. He has overcome every obstacle He has faced. Maybe He can help me."

Something that had obviously captured his attention was the "miraculous signs" Jesus performed. The preceding passage makes that clear: *"Now while he was in Jerusalem at the Passover Feast, many people saw the miraculous signs he was doing and believed in his name"* (John 2:23). Nicodemus was ready to step beyond religion into a relationship with Jesus because he needed what Jesus offered: the miraculous power that can change a life.

While "born again" is a common term in our culture now, it is important to know what it means. It means that we receive a new nature. It means that we have left our old life with its sins behind. It means we now have access to our heavenly Father.

When I was growing up, I could raid my family's refrigerator. If I had done that in a neighbor's house, I would have served time in reform school. My special privilege had everything to do with the fact that I was an Odum.

Maybe we should take advantage of being born again, act at home in God's presence, and help ourselves to the promises He has made us. Religion shuts me out of God's presence unless I keep the religious rules. Being born again means that I can come to Him any time with any need. He is my Father.

Nicodemus had religion but was going to leave his meeting with Jesus as a man of faith. Religion can be complicated. The Archbishop of Canterbury, prior to a confirmation service, was instructing the young boys on what to call him—"Say, 'My Lord' or 'Your Grace.' " During the service he asked one of the boys how old he was. The boy was flustered and replied, "My God, I'm ten." How many of us have been "flustered" trying to be religious. We won't be "flustered" when we trust Jesus. Being born again means that we are now part of His family.

My mother's father started life when he was in his sixties. He had not even been particularly religious. Still, late in life he had a Nicodemus-like encounter with Jesus. At Granddad's funeral, his pastor recounted an incident in the hospital when my grandfather was dying. He saw Granddad's lips moving and assumed he wanted to say something. He leaned over and heard my grandfather softly singing "Amazing Grace." That's one of the reasons the song is so special to me. What a miracle that late in life Granddad had the chance to start over.

The author of that song, John Newton, had been a slave trader but had become a believer and a pastor in Olney, England. One Sunday in 1772 he was preaching from 1 Chronicles 17:16-17 about David's prayer: *"Then King David went in and sat before the LORD, and he said: 'Who am I, O LORD God, and what is my family, that you have brought me this far? And as if this were not enough in your sight, O God, you have spoken about the future of the house of your servant. You have looked on me as though I were the most exalted of men, O LORD God.' "*

He explained to his congregation how David had come to such a point in his life. David, who had who had committed adultery with Bathsheba and had killed her husband, Uriah, seemed so unworthy of the honor God was giving him. Yet

David praised God because he recognized the care God had shown him. David was a man who knew God's grace.

At the close of his sermon, John Newton read a poem, which expressed his own testimony. My grandfather sang it and many of us have as well. The first line is the story of God's amazing grace: "Amazing grace how sweet the sound that saved a wretch like me."

God graces us every twelve months with the hope of a guilt-free new year. When during this next year anyone finds deliverance he or she can start over, no matter what month it is. As Exodus says: *"This month is to be for you the first month, the first month of your year."*

An encounter with Jesus is totally life-changing, whatever that life has been. John Newton spoke of that new life in his own epitaph, which he authored: "John Newton, Clerk, once an infidel and libertine, a servant of slaves in Africa, was, by the rich mercy of our Lord and Saviour Jesus Christ, preserved, restored, pardoned, and appointed to preach the faith he had long labored to destroy."

May this be a year in which we all experience God's grace and we all find ourselves "preserved, restored, pardoned."

73—Don't Let Anyone Steal Your Dreams

I grew up in church. From the time I was young I heard these words: *"Now to him who is able to do immeasurably more than all we ask or imagine, according to his power that is at work within us, to him be glory in the church and in Christ Jesus throughout all generations, for ever and ever! Amen"* (Ephesians 3:20-21). It took years before I really began to understand the reality of this Scripture.

The Greeks had a way of emphasizing the meaning of a word. They would tack prepositions onto root words in order to strengthen them. "Immeasurably more" is one of those words. It combines "abundance," "out of that measure" and "beyond all that"—all three ideas. It means that God is able in abundance, out of that measure of abundance and still beyond all that. There is no way to measure His power.

The only limitation is our asking and imagining. Paul was noted for his bold prayers. He prayed them because he was confident that prayer tapped into God's immeasurable ability.

I learned a lesson about asking and imagining one Saturday night. I was nervous about my sermon for the next day. I had seen the sermon notes and was worried about the people who would come to church expecting something good. I went through the usual negotiations with God. "If you help me tomorrow I promise I will study harder and pray more next week." I finally arrived at the place most pastors can relate to: "God, save this sermon for the sake of the people. They don't deserve this."

When I say God spoke to me, I don't mean from the upper corner of the room. I am talking about a thought that I knew didn't originate with me. The thought was, "I want to save your city; I want to bring healing to nations. I want to restore broken homes and you can't do any better than, 'Save this sermon?'"

God wasn't rebuking my prayer so much as He was rebuking the small vision behind it. Jack Hayford pointed out years ago, in one of his sermons, that we are too prone to screen our prayers. He said that if we are afraid we will catch God in a weak moment and get something He doesn't want us to have, we can relax. We won't get it. He advised us to ask for what we want and trust God to act wisely and in our interest.

The power that produces supernatural results is already working in the believer. We have Divine resources that most of us have hardly explored. God is challenging us to large imaginations that lead to large requests so He can display His glory to the world.

An Eastern bishop was accustomed to paying an annual visit to a small religious college. On one such visit, the bishop engaged in an after-dinner conversation with the college president. The religious leader offered the opinion that the millennium could not be long in coming since everything about nature had been discovered, and all possible inventions had been made. The college president disagreed, stating that he felt the next fifty years would bring amazing discoveries and inventions. In his opinion, human beings would be flying through the skies like birds within a relatively short time. "Nonsense!" shouted the bishop. "Flight is reserved for angels!" The bishop's name was Wright. He had two sons—Orville and Wilbur. They flew the first airplane.

We live very near the Wright Brothers Memorial, erected to celebrate that first flight. On the monument is inscribed the words: "Conceived by genius, achieved by dauntless resolution and unconquerable faith."

God can do the wonderful things He wants to do if He can find believers who will display unconquerable faith.

There was a study done of World War II concentration camp survivors. What were the common characteristics of those who did not succumb to disease and starvation in the camps? Victor Frankl was a living answer to that question. He was a successful Viennese psychiatrist before the Nazis threw him into a concentration camp.

He survived and afterward gave the reason in a speech. "There is only one reason," he said, "why I am here today. What kept me alive was you. Others gave up hope. I dreamed. I dreamed that someday I would be here, telling you how I, Victor Frankl, had survived the Nazi concentration camps. I've never been here before, I've never seen any of you before, I've never given this speech before. But in my dreams, in my dreams, I have stood before you and said these words a thousand times."

It is important that we understand the value of our dreams and protect them from anyone who would steal them from us.

Monty Roberts owns a horse ranch in San Ysidro. The book *The Horse Whisperer* is his story. His father was an itinerant horse trainer. When he was a senior in high school, he was asked to write a paper describing what he wanted to be and do when he grew up. That night he wrote a seven-page paper describing his goal of someday owning a horse ranch, showing the location of all the buildings, the stables and the track. Then he drew a detailed floor plan for a 4,000 square-foot house that would sit on the 200-acre dream ranch. He put a great deal of his heart into the project and the next day he handed it in to his teacher.

Two days later, he received his paper back. On the front page was a large red "F" with a note that read, "See me after class." Roberts went to see the teacher after class and asked, "Why did I receive an 'F'?"

The teacher said, "This is an unrealistic dream for a young boy like you. You have no money. You come from an itinerant family. You have no resources. Owning a horse ranch requires a lot of money. You have to buy the land. You have to pay for the original breeding stock and later you'll have to pay large stud fees. There's no way you'll ever do it." Then the teacher added, "If you will rewrite this paper with a more realistic goal, I will reconsider your grade."

Monty Roberts went home and thought about it long and hard. He asked his father what he should do and his father told him it was his decision to make. Finally, after a week, Roberts turned in the same paper, making no changes at all. He told his teacher, "You can keep the 'F' and I'll keep my dream."

He tells this story in his dream house on his dream ranch. His teacher later confessed, "I was a dream-stealer."

The world is full of people without vision who are dream stealers. Don't let anyone steal your dream.

74—Love One Another

Last words are important, especially when you know they are going to be last words. I was driving my family once on a mountain road when I came around a curve to find another car in my lane, driving straight toward us. I uttered the profound words, "Good grief! Great day in the morning!" Thankfully, those weren't my last words. I hope to do better when my time really comes.

Jesus gave His last words the night before He died as He met with His disciples. Knowing what faced Him that night and the next day, He focused on the issues that were important to Him. He was explaining to them the things that really matter. Among His words is this instruction: *"A new command I give you: Love one another. As I have loved you, so you must love one another. By this all men will know that you are my disciples, if you love one another"* (John 13:34-35).

For many of us, we want to love in general but find it difficult to love specifically. Someone said it this way, "To dwell above with saints we love, that will be glory. To dwell below with saints we know, that's another story."

The reality of love is that we can't love God and not love our brothers and sisters. The Apostle John, who recorded Jesus' words in John 13, wrote in one of his letters: *"If anyone says, 'I love God,' yet hates his brother, he is a liar. For anyone who does not love his brother, whom he has seen, cannot love God, whom he has not seen"* (1 John 4:20).

In a boiler room, it's impossible to look into the boiler to see how much water it contains. However, running up beside it is a tiny glass tube that serves as a gauge. The level of water in the gauge shows the level of water in the boiler. How do you know you love God? You believe you love Him, but you want to know. Look at the gauge. Your love for your brother is the measure of your love for God.

Loving our brothers and sisters is more than going to the same church they attend. Charles Swindoll, in his book *Dropping Your Guard*, says that relationships are important. "No one says, 'Our family is a family because it eats together.' We do that in restaurants and school cafeterias. Unguarded, open relationships within the Body of Christ are just as important as the dispensing of Scriptural truth."

Bruce Larson wrote a book entitled, *There's a Lot More to Health Than Not Being Sick*. In it, he told of a story he had read. A woman, on the advice of her doctor, had gone to see a pastor to talk about joining his church. She had recently had a facelift and when her doctor dismissed her, he gave her this advice: "My dear, I have done an extraordinary job on your face, as you can see in the mirror. I have charged you a great deal of money and you were happy to pay it. But, I want to give you some free advice. Find a group of people who love God and who will love you enough to help you deal with all the negative emotions inside of you. If you don't you'll be back in my office in a very short time with your face in far worse shape than before."

Is there a risk involved in loving? Without question. When I was younger, there was a popular song on the radio—"Love Hurts." All of us who have loved have been hurt. Friendships that we thought would last forever have fallen apart. For some, marriages meant to last "until death do us part" ended in pain and divorce. We want to guard our emotions so we pull back into our protective shells hoping never to be hurt again. And, that causes something precious in us to die.

No one ever said it better than C. S. Lewis did: "To love at all is to be vulnerable. Love anything, and your heart will certainly be wrung and possibly be broken. If you want to make sure of keeping it intact, you must give your heart to no one, not even to an animal. Wrap it carefully round with hobbies and little luxuries; avoid all entanglements; lock it up safe in the casket or coffin of your selfishness. But, in that casket—safe, dark, motionless, airless—it will change. It will not be broken; it will become unbreakable, impenetrable, irredeemable.... The only place outside Heaven where you can be perfectly safe from all the dangers of love...is Hell."

With all its risks, Jesus still asks us to love each other. He even gives us the standard: *"As I have loved you, so you must love one another."* How has He loved us? Unconditionally.

Stephen Brown, a prominent preacher, eloquently described a homemaker who was washing dishes in the kitchen sink one day after the children had left for school. She looked at one particular plate. She stared at it for a long time and asked over and over again, "How many times have I washed this plate? How many times have I dried it? How many times will I wash it and dry it again?" She then set down the plate, took off her apron, packed a few of her belongings, and left.

That night she called home to tell her husband that she was all right, but that she just could not come home again. From time to time, over the next several weeks, she would call just to see how her husband and children were doing. But, she would never tell them where she was, nor agree to come home.

The husband hired a detective to search for her, and after picking up a few leads, the detective tracked her down. She was in another state, living in a small apartment over a luncheonette where she had a job as a waitress.

Her husband set out immediately to bring her home. When he found the place she was staying, he knocked on the door of her upstairs apartment. She opened the door, saw him, and did not say a word. She went into the bedroom, packed her belongings, and finally followed him out to the car. Then, in silence, he drove her back home.

Several hours later when the two of them were alone he finally spoke, and he asked her, "Why didn't you come home before? Over the phone I begged you to return. Why didn't you come?" The wife answered, "I heard your words, but it wasn't until you came for me that I realized how much you cared and how important I was to you."

It can be said that though the prophets of the Hebrew Bible may have tried to tell us about God's love, we never really got the message until Jesus showed up and found us.

That is Jesus' love for us. We didn't deserve it, but He loved us anyway. If we show that kind of love to others, we can change the world.

75—Never Give Up

An old song says, "We don't know where we're going, but we're on our way." The Bible reminds us that we are going somewhere. We, as believers, have an eternal destiny.

The book of Hebrews was written to those who were being tempted to go back to their old religious forms. They revered angels, Moses, Joshua, the priesthood and the sacrifices. They missed the pageantry of the Old Testament. The writer of Hebrews tells them, "Don't go back to ritual without Jesus, no matter how attractive the ceremony looks to you. Jesus is the One we have been waiting for."

A good question would be, "If I can't go back, how can I go forward?" The answer is in the twelfth chapter of Hebrews: *"Therefore, since we are surrounded by such a great cloud of witnesses, let us throw off everything that hinders and the sin that so easily entangles, and let us run with perseverance the race marked out for us. Let us fix our eyes on Jesus, the author and perfecter of our faith, who for the joy set before him endured the cross, scorning its shame, and sat down at the right hand of the throne of God."* (Hebrews 12:1-2).

The spiritual life is compared to a foot race. I think most of us would admit that we try harder when others are cheering us on. The writer of Hebrews tells us that a great audience surrounds us. The picture is of a race taking place in a large stadium. While we are running, we are not alone, even if we think we are. We are surrounded by *"a great cloud"* of witnesses.

Gwen and I were living in Sydney, Australia when the 2000 Olympic Games were held there. One of the most remarkable sights during those games was a preliminary contest in a swimming event—the men's 100-meter freestyle.

One of the contestants was Eric Moussambani of Equatorial Guinea, a 22-year-old African had only learned to swim the previous January. Eric had only practiced in a 20-meter pool without lane markers and had never raced more than 50 meters. This race would be twice that distance. He was in the completion by special invitation of the International Olympic Committee, under a program that permits poorer countries to participate even though their athletes don't meet customary standards. When the other two swimmers in his meet were disqualified because of false starts, Moussambani was forced to swim alone.

Eric Moussambani was, to use the words of an Associated Press story about his race, "charmingly inept." He never put his head under the water's surface and flailed wildly to stay afloat. With ten meters left to the wall, he virtually came to a stop. Some spectators thought he might drown! Even though his time was over a minute slower than what qualified for the next level of competition, the capacity crowd at the Olympic Aquatic Center stood to their feet and cheered the swimmer on.

After what seemed like an eternity, the young African reached the wall and hung on for dear life. When he had caught his breath and regained his composure, the French-speaking Moussambani said through an interpreter, "I want to send hugs and kisses to the crowd. It was their cheering that kept me going."

For many of us, in those times when we have almost come to a stop and are exhausted and gasping for breath, it's the encouragement of those around us that keeps us going. More people are cheering us on than we realize. We can't give up.

Running can be exhausting. It requires effort, but effort alone isn't enough. To run successfully also calls for discipline. As the writer of Hebrews explains, in order to run well we have to put aside weights and hindrances. Some of us have been more exhausted in our life of faith than we need to be because we have tried carrying unnecessary baggage while we run. We are living for Jesus, but have trouble giving up anger, lust, envy, bitterness and an assortment of those attitudes and actions that so readily attach themselves to us. It's hard to run while carrying baggage.

A passenger flying from Zurich to Beirut, Joseph Pasatour, complained to a flight attendant that he was suffocating. The plane landed at Athens and he was taken to a hospital where he died. When they examined him, they discovered he was a smuggler. He wore a corset in which he had concealed 1500 watches. The doctors determined that the smuggled merchandise restricted his breathing until he suffocated at the plane's high altitude.

Here is good advice: *"Let us throw off everything that hinders and the sin that so easily entangles."* It will keep us from suffocating.

While running it is important to keep our eyes focused. John Guest wrote in *Leadership* magazine about the danger that accompanies losing our focus. He told of a farmer who went out to gather eggs. As the farmer walked across the farmyard toward the hen house, he noticed the pump was leaking. So, he stopped to fix it. It needed a new washer, so he set off to the barn to get one. But, on the way he saw that the hayloft needed straightening, so he went off to fetch the pitchfork. Hanging next to the pitchfork was a broom with a broken handle. "I must make a note to myself to buy a new broom handle the next time I go to town," he thought. The farmer never gathered the eggs.

How do we focus successfully? The writer of Hebrews says, *"Let us fix our eyes on Jesus."*

In the 1968 Olympic games in Mexico City, Mamo Waldi of Ethiopia won the marathon, a grueling 26-mile, 385-yard race. About one hour after he had crossed the finish line sirens and whistles drew everyone's attention to the stadium's entrance. A single competitor, wearing the colors of Tanzania, came limping into the stadium. His name was

John Steven Aquari. He was the last man to finish the marathon in 1968. His leg was bandaged and bloody. He had taken a bad fall early in the race. Now, it was all he could do to limp his way around the track.

The crowd stood and applauded as he completed that last lap. When he finally crossed the finish line, someone asked the question that was on everyone's mind. "You are badly injured. Why didn't you quit? Why didn't you give up?" Aquari, with quiet dignity said, "My country did not send me seven thousand miles to start this race. My country sent me to finish."

We have started this life of faith and we will finish it. We will never give up! We were able to begin because of God's grace and that same grace will sustain us until we cross the finish line. Finish strong!

76-The Turning Point of Life

Frustrated expectations can shake up our world. That is exactly what happened to the disciples in the eighth and ninth chapters of Mark's Gospel. Jesus rocked their world when He explained what the immediate future held for them. *"He then began to teach them that the Son of Man must suffer many things and be rejected by the elders, chief priests and teachers of the law, and that he must be killed and after three days rise again"* (Mark 8:31).

That wasn't what they had in mind when they signed up to follow Jesus. They thought He would bring in the Kingdom of God and overthrow the Roman government. They didn't realize that He would place Himself at the mercy of Israel's religious leaders and would allow the Romans to take His life.

It is easy for us to look back at them and wonder why they didn't understand what He was saying. Jesus never mentioned His death without, at the same time, mentioning His resurrection. The disciples consistently heard what He said about His death but seemed to miss what He said about His resurrection.

We can be guilty of missing some of, or misunderstanding all of, what we hear. Becky Barnes, a schoolteacher from Arizona, wrote: "At the elementary school where I teach, we recently had a problem with students throwing rocks. The principal made an announcement over the intercom warning students that anyone caught throwing rocks would be taken home by him personally. Later that day, during afternoon recess, a teacher admonished a kindergartner for throwing a rock. 'Didn't you hear what the principal said this morning?!' the teacher said in disbelief. 'Yeah,' replied the proud lad, grinning from ear to ear. 'I get to go home in the principal's car!' "

It's fair to say that the kindergartner missed the point. Well, the disciples missed the point, too. That's one of the reasons for Jesus taking Peter, James and John up on the

Mount of Transfiguration where He had a appointment with His Father and two visitors–Moses and Elijah.

There, in the presence of His three disciples, Jesus was transfigured and had a conversation with Moses and Elijah. His divinity broke through His humanity and they never forgot that moment. More than fifty years later John would write, *"The Word became flesh and made his dwelling among us. We have seen his glory, the glory of the One and Only, who came from the Father, full of grace and truth"* (John 1:14). And, more than thirty-five years later Peter would write, *"We were eyewitnesses of his majesty.... We ourselves heard this voice that came from heaven when we were with him on the sacred mountain"* (2 Peter 1:16, 18).

One of the lessons the disciples learned on the mountain with Jesus was the importance of hearing what Jesus has to say in a world of competing voices and ideas. Jesus' two visitors were main figures in Israel's history.

Moses was the lawgiver who had led Israel out of Egypt. He authored the first five books of the Old Testament. Every Jewish leader claimed allegiance to him, even those who opposed Jesus.

Elijah was the outspoken prophet associated with national revival. He had called down fire from heaven and called the nation to turn from idolatry to serve the living God.

It is easy to understand why Peter would be distracted at the presence of those imposing visitors. In his excitement (and ignorance) he suggested that three tabernacles be constructed, one honoring Elijah, one honoring Moses and one honoring Jesus.

At this point God interrupted Peter with a corrective word: *"While he was still speaking, a bright cloud enveloped them, and a voice from the cloud said, 'This is my Son, whom I love; with him I am well pleased. Listen to him!'"* (Matthew 17:5).

Suddenly Moses and Elijah were gone and only Jesus remained. He was to be the focus. God wants no one to supplant Jesus. There is nothing as important to any of us as listening to Jesus.

Sometimes we hear Him in unexpected ways. Gwen and I attended a conference several years ago at which Bob Mumford was speaking. He told of a man who went to a meeting to hear a certain speaker. At that conference, the man sat behind a large woman who kept him from seeing the speaker clearly. That irritated him. Even worse, the woman kept saying, "Yes, Lord" and kept him from hearing everything the speaker was saying. Unable to see or hear, he was complaining to the Lord. The Lord spoke to him and said, "The message for you is not coming from the platform, it's coming from that lady—'Yes, Lord.' "

There are many voices clamoring for our attention. God's word to Peter, James and John is His word to us: *"This is my Son, whom I love; with him I am well pleased. Listen to him!"*

They were focusing on the past—Moses and Elijah. God wanted them to hear about the future. Jesus was divine and His death would lead to His resurrection and our ultimate triumph. God didn't want them to walk through the tragedy of the coming week without understanding that beyond the pain there would be glory. When we are in difficult situations, it is important to hear Jesus. His words will sustain us because He sees the glory on the other side of our crises.

Two soldiers bailed out of a plane in World War II. One was an American soldier who had spent time in Scotland. The other was a Scottish chaplain. At the POW camp, the Germans had built a fence separating the Americans and the British. But, each day the two men would meet at the fence and exchange a greeting.

Unknown to the guards, the Americans had a little homemade radio and were able to get news from the outside. Every day the American POW would share some news with the Scottish chaplain, speaking Gaelic because the Germans didn't understand it.

One day, news came over the radio that the German High Command had surrendered and the war was over. The American took the news to his friend, then stood and watched him disappear into the British barracks. A moment later, a roar of celebration came from the barracks. Life in that camp was transformed. Men who had been in bondage walked around singing and shouting.

When the German guards finally heard the news three days later, they fled into the dark, leaving the gates unlocked. The next morning, the British and American POWs walked out as free men. Yet they had truly been set free three days earlier by the news that the war was over.

When Jesus was transfigured, after explaining His death and resurrection, He gave a preview of the victory that would come to every believer. The enemy is still around but he has been defeated. Jesus is alive and has already won. That's why we can, right now, celebrate our victory.

77—God's Surprise

Jesus told stories that helped his listeners learn the truth. Among the interesting stories Jesus used to convey spiritual truth is the description of a man plowing a field and uncovering a great treasure. *"The Kingdom of Heaven is like a treasure that a man discovered hidden in a field. In his excitement, he hid it again and sold everything he owned to get enough money to buy the field—and to get the treasure, too!"* (Matthew 13:44).

It sounds like a farfetched story, but things like this have happened before. At the end of the 18th century, Charles IV of Spain was convinced that no one would be able to stop the progress of Napoleon. He had acquired a priceless collection of antique clocks and was the guardian of the Spanish crown jewels. In anticipation of Napoleon's victory, he asked a trusted servant to hide the priceless clocks in a wall of one of the 365 rooms of the palace. He also requested that he conceal the crown jewels in another wall of one of the 365 rooms. The servant did that.

Believing that one day the Spanish monarch would regain the throne, the servant marked the rooms by removing a portion of the draperies in each one. Napoleon did overthrow Spain and placed his brother, Joseph, on the throne. But, in 1814, with the defeat of Napoleon, Ferdinand VII, son of Charles IV, was restored to the throne of Spain.

His first act was to look for the treasures hidden by his father. They discovered that Napoleon Joseph had been something of an interior decorator. He had replaced all the draperies. Ferdinand had a choice, tear down the palace or let the treasures go. He forgot about the priceless clocks and crown jewels. This story was written off as a meaningless legend until a few decades ago. A plumber, doing repair work on some pipes in a wall, discovered the antique clock collection. Someday, someone will discover the crown jewels as well. Just as in Jesus' story of the treasure hidden in a field, there is priceless treasure awaiting discovery in the walls of the old palace.

What Jesus was expressing in this little story is that some people find the joy of a relationship with God seemingly by accident. It isn't an accident from God's perspective, but it can seem to be from ours.

The discovery in this parable was made in the day's routine. The farmer didn't wake up in the morning with angels singing at his bedside. When he went into the field to work, the clouds above him were not formed in the shape of a horseshoe. He went through his ordinary routine on a very ordinary day.

As he plowed, scraping together the meager existence that one can expect on one denarius per day, he hit something with his plow, a ceramic jar, and in it saw gold coins. That story is not surprising to those who heard Jesus tell it. A missionary to Syria in the late 1800s, W. M. Thompson, said that this was a common occurrence.

This was the chance of a lifetime, equivalent perhaps to winning the lottery. Unexpected treasure can change a person's life.

Troubles had been mounting up for this Midwest couple. First, they lost their jobs. Then the septic tank in their back yard caved in. This new problem reflected the way things were going for them—right down the drain.

When the husband began digging around the tank, though, the story changed. His shovel uncovered a gold coin. Eagerly, he forgot the sanitation issue and started digging with his hands. To his astonishment, he found 75 gold pieces. Suddenly, the couple's misfortune had become a fortune, for they now owned a coin collection worth from $200,000 to $1.5 million. Apparently, they had unearthed the cache of some rich prospectors of the 1849 gold rush era.

In the same way, many believers have been surprised by their discovery of Jesus. They may have been going through their routine day, pursuing their normal, boring activities, when suddenly Jesus was there. The shepherds of Bethlehem were surprised by the angels announcing the birth of Jesus. They were in the fields keeping sheep at the time. Paul the apostle was heading for Damascus to do his dirty work of persecuting Christians when he suddenly had an encounter with Jesus.

It is essential for all of us that we discover Jesus. We know what it is to work and sweat through our daily schedule. How awesome when, in the midst of the ordinary circumstances of life, we suddenly discover the treasure that changes our lives.

Sir Wilfred Grenfell, a famous British surgeon, walked past a D. L. Moody meeting in London. He went in out of curiosity and was about to leave during a man's lengthy prayer. Moody, though, stood and said, "Let us sing a hymn while our brother finishes his prayer." Impressed by Moody's approach to the long, boring prayer, he stayed for the rest of the meeting and gave his heart to Jesus. He hadn't been looking for Jesus. He found Him on an ordinary day in what may have seemed to be a coincidence.

The farmer in Jesus' story acted immediately. He didn't pause to think about what it might cost him. He *"sold everything he owned to get enough money to buy the field—and to get the treasure, too!"* Being a disciple of Jesus Christ is worth anything it may cost us.

What is valuable to us? A relationship with Jesus is worth far more than anything that could possibly come to mind.

Some people may think it costs too much to follow Jesus. We know that He is the treasure that makes all our other valuables pale in comparison. When we find Him, there is only one response: Give up everything else to have a relationship with Him.

78–The Life Worth Seeking

People find a relationship with Jesus Christ in many different ways. C. S. Lewis described his conversion in the book, *Surprised by Joy*. "You must picture me alone in that room in Magdalen, night after night, feeling, whenever my mind lifted even for a second from my work, the steady unrelenting approach of Him whom I so earnestly desired not to meet. That which I greatly feared had at last come upon me. In the trinity term of 1929 I gave in, and admitted that God was God, and knelt and prayed: perhaps, that night, the most dejected and reluctant convert in all England."

Others find Christ because they have desperately been looking for truth. In the first church Gwen and I pastored the first convert didn't come to Christ because we sought him out. He walked into one of our midweek services and came to the front after the service where he knelt, without an invitation, and received Jesus as his Savior. He was seeking the truth.

Jesus told a story that described the experience of those who are seeking the truth. *"Again, the kingdom of heaven is like a merchant looking for fine pearls. When he found one of great value, he went away and sold everything he had and bought it"* (Matthew 13:45-46).

As in all the parables Jesus told, there is a natural story around which He builds His message. He described a pearl merchant who was in the international market looking for exquisite pearls. He is described, in the original language of the story, as an *emporos*. That means that he wasn't the manager of a local jewelry store, but was a world traveler engaged in international business.

Maybe you are thinking, as I once thought, why didn't Jesus speak about diamonds? To my surprise, diamonds have only been valued for a little more than 100 years. Pearls have been prized since Jesus' day.

The Egyptians were the first to value pearls. Cleopatra had two pearls worth $4,000,000. The Romans learned to value them from the Egyptians and Julius Caesar gave his mother a pearl worth $350,000.

This merchant knew pearls. One day he would have sat in front of a local supplier as the other man spread out a collection of pearls. There, in the assorted pearls before him, he would have seen a pearl so outstanding that he would willingly give up everything else he possessed to have it. He was looking at the pearl he had been seeking all his life.

Usually when we picture someone sacrificing everything for one thing we imagine an agonizing scene in which a man carefully considers the value of the one thing he wants and weighs it against the value of everything he has. The story Jesus told leaves no room for that process. The businessman knows immediately that he must possess this pearl no matter what it costs him.

This story is not farfetched. New York socialite Mary C. Plant, in 1917, traded her Fifth Avenue mansion for a million dollar string of pearls. She loved pearls that much.

The problem facing all of us is that there are many pearls of some value to which we are exposed. They aren't bad things, in fact they have can be good things. Our problem is that we can make them the things we most value and because of them can miss the most important prize in life, a relationship with Jesus.

Some of us would have to admit that we have been driven by a variety of motivations. We want to be successful in our professions. We want to have the security of enough money. It may be that we are seeking love from another person or just want to be respected. There is nothing wrong with any of those things when we place them in their proper order, but not one of them can compare with the value of knowing Jesus.

Education is both wonderful and necessary. But, we can be so driven that we understand one college professor-turned-pastor who described what life can become. He said that there is the danger of "seeking one degree after another until you are dying by degrees."

We all have bills and know how important money is. But, making things what we value most in life can warp our behavior. There is the story of a young man who was infatuated with material things. He bought a BMW and was test-driving it at high speeds on a winding mountain road. He lost control of the car and was headed toward a steep drop off. At the last moment, he opened the car door and leaped to safety.

As his car plunged down the mountainside, consumed by flames, he wept aloud: "Oh no, my BMW, my BMW!"

An emergency worker arrived on the scene and noticed that the man had lost his left arm when he leaped from his automobile. He asked the grief-stricken man, "How could you cry over your BMW when you just lost your left arm?"

The man looked at his stump and began wailing, "Oh no, my Rolex watch!"

In his simple story, Jesus was telling us that there may be many things in our lives with value, but the one thing that supersedes all of them is knowing Him.

A young couple wanted to impress the important people in their community so they decided to attend all the parties and gatherings possible. In order to enhance their image they went to an older family friend and asked if they could borrow her very expensive string of pearls. The owner was reluctant but agreed to lend them.

Sadly, on the first night the young woman wore the pearls they were stolen. The couple was disconsolate. They decided to replace them rather than admit that they had lost them. They flew to another city and described them to a jeweler who copied the string of pearls as best he could. Then they took the replacement to the woman who had lent the necklace to them. But, they had to mortgage their house and incur a debt that it would take a lifetime to repay.

As the older woman was dying, the now-middle-aged woman went to her and confessed that they had never returned the real pearls, only an expensive replacement. "You fools," said the dying woman, "no one ever loans the real things. Those were imitation pearls. You've wasted your life."

Jesus was saying to all of us, in His simple story, "Don't waste your life on imitation pearls." A relationship with Him is worth any sacrifice we make because nothing can compare with the value of knowing Him.

79—A New Nature

A man named Russell Edward Herman left trillions of dollars to thousands of people he'd never met. What was the catch? Russell Edward Herman didn't have trillions of dollars. He was just a simple, poor carpenter.

While the wild, wild will of the late Russell Herman never paid off for his "beneficiaries," it certainly enlivened conversations. Take the tiny Ohio River town of Cave-In-Rock, for example. Herman bequeathed $2.41 billion to them. Cave-In-Rock's mayor, Albert Kaegi had this to say, "It's an odd thing to happen, isn't it?" While the will would never pay off, the mayor had no trouble imagining uses for the willed imaginary monies.

Russell Edward Herman had great intentions, but he lacked the resources needed to make them a reality. The greatness of God, however, stands in sharp contrast. God not only has made great and precious promises, He has the ability to follow through on every single one of them.

Sometime back, the Associated Press carried this dispatch: "Glasgow, Ky.—Leslie Puckett, after struggling to start his car, lifted the hood and discovered that someone had stolen the motor." Just having the key to the ignition means nothing if there is no engine to power the car forward.

The apostle Peter, in his second letter, gave us one of the most encouraging words in the New Testament: *"His divine power has given us everything we need for life and godliness through our knowledge of him who called us by his own glory and goodness. Through these he has given us his very great and precious promises, so that through them you may participate in the divine nature and escape the corruption in the world caused by evil desires"* (2 Peter 1:3-4).

God's power backs up the promises God makes. God is no Russell Edward Herman. God has the power to make His promises come true.

You may wonder how we can possibly measure the power of God. On May 18, 1980, Mount St. Helens, in the Cascade Range of Washington, exploded with what is probably the most visible indication of the power of nature that the modern world has ever seen. At 8:32 AM the explosion ripped 1,300 feet off the mountain with a force of ten million tons of TNT, or roughly equal to five hundred Hiroshimas. Sixty people were killed, most by a blast of 300-degree heat traveling at two hundred miles an hour. Some were killed as far as sixteen miles away. The blast also leveled150-foot-tall Douglas firs as far as seventeen miles away. A total of 3.2 billion board-feet of lumber was destroyed, enough to build 200,000 three-bedroom homes. Yet all that explosive energy is nothing compared to the power of God.

So what does God's power do for us? It gives us a brand new nature. Of course, we are not divine. My behavior too often gives me away for me to claim divinity. However, because of what Jesus has done for me I can now participate in His divine nature. Peter explains that through God's promises we *"may participate in the divine nature."* That makes all the difference in the world for us.

Imagine what participating in a new nature means. For example, one's nature determines one's appetite. It is the nature of sheep to eat grass. One of our cats ate a fly the other week. One of the few things that differentiate me from a cat is the fact that I've never wanted to eat a fly. Participating in the divine nature means that our new nature has created for us a new appetite. We love the Bible. We are nourished by prayer. That doesn't come from our old nature. It is a product of the change Jesus makes in us.

Nature determines which environment will be comfortable for us. Squirrels climb trees and fish swim in the water. Our church is located one block from the ocean so we hold our baptismal services at the beach. During one of those services, there was a storm off the coast but we decided to baptize anyway. I was walking out to get past the breakers in order to baptize our new converts when I was upended repeatedly by the waves. I was fully immersed five times before Matt, our associate pastor, and myself baptized the first believer. I found out that the ocean is fun to play in but it isn't my natural environment.

When we become participants in God's divine nature, we develop an instinct for a new environment. Worship satisfies something deep inside us and we live to be in God's presence.

We aren't born with that nature. Imagine the grace that finds us in our old natures, broken and wounded, and brings us into the wonderful family of God. It is God's amazing grace that allows us to participate in God's divine nature. It is His love and mercy that changes us.

A picture of what Jesus has done for us comes out of World War II. Bert Frizen was an infantryman on the front lines in Europe. American forces had advanced in the face of intermittent shelling and small-arms fire throughout the morning hours, but now all was quiet. His patrol reached the edge of a wooded area with an open field before them.

Unknown to the Americans, a battery of Germans waited in a hedgerow about two hundred yards across the field. Bert was one of two scouts who moved out into the clearing. Once he was halfway across the field, the remainder of his battalion followed.

Suddenly the Germans opened fire, and machine gun fire ripped into both of Bert's legs. The American battalion withdrew into the woods for protection, while a rapid exchange of fire continued. Bert lay helpless in a small stream as shots volleyed overhead. There seemed to be no way out. To make matters worse, he now noticed that a

German soldier was crawling toward him. Death appeared imminent; he closed his eyes and waited.

To his surprise, a considerable period passed without the expected attack, so he ventured to open his eyes again. He was startled to see the German kneeling at his side, smiling. He then noticed that the shooting had stopped. Troops from both sides of the battlefield watched anxiously. Without any verbal exchange, this mysterious German reached down to lift Bert in his arms and proceeded to carry him to the safety of Bert's comrades. Having accomplished his self-appointed mission, and still without speaking a word, the German soldier turned and walked back across the field to his own troop. No one dared break the silence of this sacred moment.

Moments later the cease-fire ended, but not before all those present had witnessed how one man risked everything for his enemy. Bert's life was saved through the compassion of a man whom he considered his enemy.

This courageous act pictures what Jesus did for us. He found us weak and wounded and carried us to safety. The good news we have for the world is that Jesus isn't our enemy, He is our Savior. And, if we allow Him to do it, He will change us so that we can participate in His divine nature.

80–Do You Want to Get Well?

I recently learned some facts from nature that identified the limitations some animals face. For example, if you put a buzzard in a pen that is six feet by eight feet and open at the top, the bird, in spite of its ability to fly, will be an absolute prisoner. The reason is that a buzzard always begins a flight from the ground with a run of ten to twelve feet. Without space to run it will not even attempt to fly but will remain a prisoner for life in a small jail with no top.

A bumblebee, if dropped into an open glass tumbler, will remain there until it dies, unless it is released. It never sees the means of escape at the top, but persists in trying to find some way out through the sides near the bottom. It will attempt to find a way out where none exists until it destroys itself.

Even in the animal kingdom, limitations can rob a creature of its ability. The same can happen to us. The apostle John records an interesting story in his Gospel. A man was lying helpless when Jesus walked into his life. *"Now there is in Jerusalem near the Sheep Gate a pool, which in Aramaic is called Bethesda and which is surrounded by five covered colonnades. Here a great number of disabled people used to lie–the blind, the lame, the paralyzed.... One who was there had been an invalid for thirty-eight years. When Jesus saw him lying there and learned that he had been in this condition for a long time, he asked him, 'Do you want to get well?' "* (John 5:2, 3, 5, 6).

Faith recognizes obstacles but it also recognizes God's power. There comes a time in all our lives when we come face to face with our limitations and cannot go on without God's help. The obstacles we face are too much for us to overcome in our own strength. That was the condition of the disabled man Jesus met in the fifth chapter of John.

One the challenges confronting any of us is our personal history. We bring our past with us when we meet Jesus. For many of us it is a lifelong story of rejection, failure and disappointment. Maybe we have had our good times, but we also bear the scars of the rough days behind us. That is one reason why faith is so difficult. Our past often makes it hard to believe.

I often think our world resembles this company of hurting people crowded around the pool of Bethesda. All of them were handicapped in some way. And, the man John described didn't have the strength to help himself.

The Scripture comes to mind, *"When we were still powerless, Christ died for the ungodly"* (Romans 5:6). *"Powerless"* in Romans 5:6 is the same word translated *"disabled"* in John 5:3. When we found it impossible to do anything for ourselves, Christ died for us.

The most devastating condition of this crippled man wasn't his helplessness. Jesus was there to overcome his weakness. It was his hopelessness: *"I have no one to help me."* Maybe his friends had given up long ago. Now they just dumped him beside the pool each day and left him to fend for himself. Thirty-eight years—they had given up, too.

Over the past thirty-eight years, there had been opportunities for healing, but each time it had been every man for himself. We can still visit the pool of Bethesda and the notable characteristic of it is that the steps down to the water are extremely steep—too steep for a crippled man to negotiate.

The name "Bethesda" means "house of mercy" but for this poor man it was the "house of disappointment." He described the frustration of trying to negotiate the steps in his own strength: *"While I am trying to get in."* He waited year after year for a miracle that never came. The problem with the pool of Bethesda was that the one who needed help the most was the one least likely to get it.

The entire story takes a dramatic turn when Jesus shows up. *"One who was there had been an invalid for thirty-eight years. When Jesus saw him...."* The condition of the man had been unchanged for thirty-eight years. When Jesus saw him, the miracle took place. That is the good news of the gospel. Jesus still sees us in our helplessness.

At first glance, the question Jesus asked seems almost pointless: *"Do you want to get well?"* What kind of question is that to ask an invalid? But, it is the right question. Jesus knew that He had the power to heal the man. He wanted to restore the man's dying hope. For thirty-eight years, the man had been unsuccessful. Jesus was coaxing him to hope again.

Jesus wanted to reawaken the man's desire, because the years had left this poor man paralyzed in his thinking as well as in his body. His hope had become weaker with every frustrated attempt to find healing. Mind you, there was some hope, because he was still at the pool. But, he didn't expect much.

Jesus saw the apathy on the man's face. The man had learned through the years to cope, to settle for the way things were. Jesus wanted to fan the flicker of desire that was left until the man could dream once more. Jesus was awakening the man's expectancy.

What followed can happen only because of Jesus. Jesus said to him, *"Get up! Pick up your mat and walk"* (5:8). As the Bible shows us repeatedly, when Jesus asked someone to do the impossible the power to accomplish it was provided.

When the miracle happened, there was no question as to who was responsible. Jesus enables the weakest among us to be well again. For us to take credit for the change would be to act like the woodpecker that was pecking away at a huge tree. Suddenly a bolt of lightning struck the tree and split it from top to bottom. The woodpecker flew off in a flash. Minutes later, he returned with several other woodpeckers. Pointing to the tree, he said proudly, "There it is. Look at what I did!"

Jesus loves to get glory by intervening in the lives of helpless people. John Henry Jowett told about a small village in England where an elderly woman died. She had lived with limited resources. She was not wealthy. She was uneducated and unsophisticated. In spite of her limitations, she engaged in a lifetime of serving others. When she died, they chiseled on her tombstone the words, "She did what she couldn't."

"Do you want to get well?" I don't care what your history is. I don't care how weak you are or how many times you've tried to get up only to fall down again. Jesus is the power source who can make your life effective. There have been obstacles in your life and mine. We may have been almost hopeless, but there is a mighty God who can overcome our obstacles and make us whole. His name is Jesus. He sees you and me and He is challenging us to dream again.

81–Hope for the Rejected

Life has its share of pain. Difficult circumstances, beyond our control, can make us suffer emotional pain. In 1858, the Illinois legislature–using an obscure statute–sent Stephen A. Douglas to the U.S. Senate instead of Abraham Lincoln, although Lincoln had won the popular vote. When a sympathetic friend asked Lincoln how he felt, he said, "Like the boy who stubbed his toe: I am too big to cry and too badly hurt to laugh."

Everyone wants to be loved. The only problem is that when we are open to be loved we are vulnerable and can be seriously hurt. One of the sad human-interest stories in the Bible is the account of Leah, Jacob's first wife. She was his first wife, but she wasn't his first choice. Jacob loved Leah's younger sister, Rachel.

Jacob's life is an interesting narrative. He had tricked his brother, Esau, out of the family birthright and had lied to his father to get the paternal blessing. His mother, Rebekah, sent him to her brother's house so Esau wouldn't get revenge on him after his father's death. For the next twenty years, Jacob worked for Uncle Laban. For seven of those years he was earning the hand of Laban's daughter, Rachel. On the morning after the wedding, Jacob discovered that Laban had given him Leah instead of Rachel and so he worked seven more years for Rachel.

The saddest part of the story is the pain Leah felt. Though she was his wife, Jacob didn't love her. His heart had been captured by Rachel. In Jacob's defense, he never intended to marry Leah. He thought he was marrying Rachel. Laban, the father of both girls, did Leah no favors. Now she was stuck in a loveless marriage and was trying to win Jacob's love by having sons. *"Leah became pregnant and gave birth to a son. She named him Reuben, for she said, 'It is because the LORD has seen my misery. Surely my husband will love me now' "* (Genesis 29:32). It is impossible to read those words without feeling compassion for Leah, who was trapped in circumstances beyond her control. *"Surely my husband will love me now"* is a glimpse into the soul of a wounded, rejected woman.

Rejection is painful. It seems that there is no way to work ourselves out of it. We can't do enough to win the love of some people. Leah lived a frustrating life of trying, but failing, to win the love that she wanted. With the birth of her second son, Simeon, she revealed the deep-seated pain she felt: *"Because the LORD heard that I am not loved, he gave me this one too"* (Genesis 29:33). She was not only unloved, but she knew it.

We have all experienced rejection in some ways. Someone we love doesn't return our love and there's nothing we can do about it. It hurts! In reading this account of Leah, it is hard to see the "good news" in it. The good news is hard to find in these verses. Leah didn't find Jacob's heart suddenly changed toward her. The good news is fully revealed in the life of Jesus. He demonstrates that God has accepted us. Jesus is the only One who can ultimately heal the pain of rejection.

For those of us who know how much it hurts to be caught in a painful situation we didn't create, the good news is that God loves us even if some others don't. That is seen in the life of Jesus. Jesus attracted people who were hurting because Jesus loves hurting people.

In his Gospel, Luke described a picture that showed the heart of Jesus: *"Now the tax collectors and 'sinners' were all gathering around to hear him. But the Pharisees and the teachers of the law muttered, 'This man welcomes sinners and eats with them' "* (Luke 15:1-2). Crowding around Jesus were the hurting, and rejected members of society. Standing aside criticizing Him were the religious leaders. The motley crew that was rejected by the religious elite was welcomed and loved by Jesus.

Leah's story reveals that she knew that only God could help a person who lived with rejection. Each time she had a child she talked to God about it. She even named one of her sons Judah, "Praise." It isn't reading too much into the story to see that her relationship with Jacob was not ideal, but her relationship with God was healthy. She found that God was Someone she could talk to honestly. She also trusted Him with the secrets of her heart and found his provision (He gave her six sons and one daughter) to be her source of hope.

What can anyone say to a person who is hurting? There really is only one message: God loves you. He doesn't reject anyone, even tax collectors and "sinners." That is how each of us was able to become part of His family. He simply loves us and, if we believe in Him, will break the pattern of rejection in our lives.

One day a beautiful, but very troubled, little girl came through the door of a Day Nursery. From the very beginning, the nursery worker became captivated by this child who had so little and needed so much. The little four-year-old was suffering from decisions she didn't make. She was born in prison after her mom had used marijuana, crack and cocaine her entire pregnancy.

The little girl was nonverbal and had very little control over her emotions or her behavior. It was clear that the girl's progress would be a mighty battle. Whenever somebody approached her, she became violent for long periods and ended up in a fetal position on the floor. The nursery worker found herself praying for the tormented little girl day in and day out.

As months rolled on, a relationship developed between the woman and the child whose mother wasn't able to care for her. The woman and the little girl worked through the challenges they faced, sometimes taking one step forward and four steps back. Daily, they sat in the big rocking chair in the Day Nursery office, swaying back and forth and back and forth. During those rocking sessions the compassionate attendant would sing "Jesus Loves Me." The four-year-old always settled down and became very still at the melody. Though she never spoke, peace seemed to fill her face as she listened to the song.

One day after a very long battle the woman held her special little girl to calm her fears and pain. In silence, they rocked back and forth and back and forth and back and forth. Then the girl looked up with tear-filled eyes and spoke for the first time ever. She said, "Sing to me about that Man who loves me."

All of us have suffered from life. All of us have been misunderstood and, probably, rejected. The good news is that there is a Man who loves us. His name is Jesus and He not only welcomes us, but He heals all our wounds.

82–Forgiveness

How do I put to rest my old mistakes and failures? The answer is by receiving the forgiveness that is available through Jesus. Forgiveness is an interesting concept. We need it if we are going to live in peace. Our memories can be like computer hard drives. Once we hit "save" the information is there. What if I told you that Jesus has access to the "delete" key and can get rid of our collection of sins? It's true. The "delete" key works.

My wife, Gwen, once wrote a book for Michael Cameron. He gave her handwritten notes and she formed them into a book. She kept what she had written in my computer. While taking a shortcut (I'm not the world's most patient person) I erased her entire book. I learned two things. First, that Gwen loves me more than I realized. She didn't leave me. Second, I discovered that it is possible to erase something from a computer hard drive. Some of you who know computers will think, "It was still there and you could have recovered it." Trust me when I tell you that it wasn't there at all. It was gone forever.

A wonderful aspect of Christianity, that is shared by no other religion, is the truth that God completely forgives sin. Hosea 14:4 says, *"I will heal their waywardness and love them freely."* Ephesians 4:32 encourages us, *"Be kind and compassionate to one another, forgiving each other, just as in Christ God forgave you."* The amazing promise in Hebrews is, *"Their sins and lawless acts I will remember no more"* (10:17).

There is a universal hunger for forgiveness. Ernest Hemingway wrote a story about a father and his teenage son. In his story, the relationship had become somewhat strained, and the teenage son ran away from home. The boy's father began a journey in search of that rebellious son. Finally, in Madrid, Spain, in a last desperate attempt to find the boy, the father put an ad in the local newspaper. The ad read: "Dear Paco, Meet me in front of the newspaper office at noon. All is forgiven. I love you. Your father." The next day, in front of the newspaper office, eight hundred Pacos showed up. They were all seeking forgiveness. They were all seeking the love of their fathers.

> When the Moravian missionaries first went to the Indians of Northern Canada, they could not find a word in the Indian language for forgiveness, so they invented one. They put several words together to make a new word: *issumagijoujungnainermik*. It is a formidable looking assembly of letters, but an expression that has a beautiful connotation for those who understand it. It means: Not-being-able-to-think-about-it-anymore.

The idea that God, who knows everything, cannot remember our sins may sound unbelievable. Yet, that's what the Bible says. An incident from the life of Clara Barton helped me understand that truth. Clara Barton was the compassionate woman who founded the American Red Cross. Someone once reminded her of an especially unkind act that had been done to her years before. Miss Barton couldn't seem to recall it. When her friend pressed her by asking, "Don't you remember it?" Barton responded, "I distinctly remember forgetting that incident." With God, forgetting our sins has nothing to do with memory loss. It is an act that reflects a decision He has made.

A Greek word that is translated "forgiveness" in the New Testament is *aphiemi*. The word literally means, "to send away." It is used in several different ways in Scripture. In Matthew 8:15 it describes a fever "leaving" a woman Jesus healed: *"He touched her hand and the fever **left** her, and she got up and began to wait on him."*

In 1 Corinthians 7:12-13 it is translated "divorce." When Jesus forgives us, He separates us from our sins and we are free from the guilt of them forever. We are actually divorced from our old ways.

In the seventh chapter of Luke, Jesus was at the house of Simon the Pharisee when a sinner (probably a prostitute) wept over His feet and wiped them with her hair. Jesus said to Simon, who was appalled at the display of affection: *"I tell you, her many sins have been **forgiven**—for she loved much"* (Luke 7:47). Jesus used the word *aphiemi*.

The Vietnam-era Pulitzer Prize-winning photo of 9-year-old Phan Thi Kim Phuc, naked and horribly burned, running from a napalm attack, moved many Americans. But, for John Plummer, minister of Bethany United Methodist church in Purcellville, Virginia, that picture had special significance.

In 1972, he was responsible for setting up the air strike on the village of Trang Bang—a strike approved after he was twice assured that there were no civilians in the area. It was in that air strike that the Vietnamese child was burned. In June of 1996, he saw a network news story about Kim Phuc and learned she was not only alive but she was living in Toronto. When Plummer learned that she was scheduled to speak at the Vietnam Veterans Memorial in Washington, D.C. he made plans to attend.

As Kim Phuc addressed the crowd, she said that if she ever met the pilot of the plane she would tell him she forgives him and that they cannot change the past but she hoped they could work together in the future. Plummer got word to her that the man she wanted to meet was there. "She saw my grief, my pain, my sorrow," Plummer wrote in an article in the *Virginia Advocate*. "She held out her arms to me and embraced me. All I could say was, 'I'm sorry; I'm so sorry,' over and over again. At the same time she was saying, 'It's all right; it's all right; I forgive; I forgive.' " Plummer learned that Kim Phuc became a Christian in 1982.

The most wonderful words any of us can hear come from the lips of Jesus: "I forgive." Those are His words for anyone who will trust Him. There is no need for us to live our lives with guilt and condemnation.

James Garfield was a brilliant man. They say he was ambidextrous and could simultaneously write Greek with one hand and Latin with the other. In 1880, he was elected president of the United States. He was shot in the back while in the nation's capital on July 2, 1881, less than four months after taking office. The newly elected President died eleven weeks later on September 19, 1881. He never lost consciousness. At the hospital, the doctor probed the wound with his finger in an attempt to locate the bullet. He couldn't find it, so he tried a silver-tipped probe. Still the bullet eluded him.

Alexander Graham Bell devised a metal detector to aid in the search, but the metal detector was rendered ineffective by the metal bed frame on which the president was lying. When the President finally died in September it wasn't from the bullet, but from infection. The repeated probing, which the physicians thought would help the man, eventually killed him.

Too many people continue to dwell on their sins and failures. They probe and, instead of finding relief, do more damage. It is far better to let Jesus forgive us. That allows us to live.

83—Guilt or Grace

Guilt can be real. Paul Tournier, a Christian doctor, wrote a book called *Guilt and Grace: A Psychological Study.* In the book, he made a distinction between real guilt and false guilt. Real guilt concerns our sins against God. It is real and we want to deal with it. False guilt is a result of not keeping rules that others, not God, put on us. It is false and there is nothing we can do about it but disregard it.

For Tournier, grace is the answer to true guilt. God is willing to forgive us and free us from the condemnation that would cripple us for the rest of our lives if we let it.

All of us know what it's like to be tempted and all of us know the guilt and shame that accompanies failure. I have discovered that many believers feel shame and condemnation over past failures, even after God has forgiven them.

There are several ways to respond to failure. One way is to give up emotionally and expect to fail. Charlie Brown, in the popular cartoon *Peanuts*, is a prime example of a loser who has lost any expectation of winning. On one occasion, after striking out in a baseball game, he is consoled by Lucy. "That's all right, Charlie Brown. You win some, and you lose some," Lucy tells him. Charlie Brown, who never wins, replies, "That would be nice."

Bob Uecker, the former major league catcher, made a career out of describing his inabilities as a baseball player. In one of his appearances on Johnny Carson's *Tonight Show,* he mentioned that he had contributed to the St. Louis Cardinals' pennant drive in 1964. "What did you do?" asked Carson. Uecker explained, "I came down with hepatitis and had to be taken out of the lineup." "How did you catch hepatitis?" asked Carson. Uecker answered, "The Cardinals trainer injected me with it."

The sense of inevitable failure can lead us to cope with our weaknesses rather than finding grace and strength to overcome them. For example, there was a man on a diet who had given up buying coffee cake on his way to work in the morning. To help him overcome temptation he did not even drive by the bakery. One morning he came in with a huge piece of coffee cake. His fellow workers asked him what had happened.

"I accidentally wound up on the street with the bakery," he said. "So I prayed, God if it is your will for me to have some coffee cake this morning, have a space for me to park right in front of the bakery. And sure enough, on my eighth trip around the block, there it was."

No matter how we try to justify ourselves, our weaknesses remind us that we can fail. Even believers know the experience of failure. Paul describes the struggle each of us faces in his letter to the Romans. *"So I find this law at work: When I want to do good, evil is right there with me. For in my inner being I delight in God's law; but I see another law at work in the members of my body, waging war against the law of my mind and making me a prisoner of the law of sin at work within my members"* (7:21-23).

It seems hopeless, doesn't it? I want to do good, I delight in God's law, but there's this inconsistent behavior that plagues me. God wants me to be a winner, so why do I keep losing? I don't rob banks, but I can be unforgiving.

Clarence Darrow, the famous criminal trial lawyer, once said: "Everyone is a potential murderer. I have not killed anyone, but I frequently get satisfaction out of obituary notices."

I continually thank God for the eighth chapter of Romans. I know all about the conflict of Romans 7 but I want to know if there is any answer for my dilemma. Do I have to live with guilt?

Paul's answer, and the hope for all of us, is in Romans 8:1-2: *"Therefore, there is now no condemnation for those who are in Christ Jesus, because through Christ Jesus the law of the Spirit of life set me free from the law of sin and death."*

God's answer to guilt is the grace of Jesus Christ. God's grace comes to us because we are in Jesus Christ. Believers are not to be condemned, guilty and ashamed because we are "in Christ Jesus" by faith.

Denise Banderman described her experience with grace in *Leadership Journal*: "I needed more study time before my final exam in the youth ministry class at Hannibal-LaGrange (Missouri) College. When I got to class, everybody was cramming. The teacher, Dr. Tom Hufty, came in and said he would review with us before the test. Most of his review came from the study guide, but some things he said I had not heard. Dr. Hufty responded they were in the book and we were responsible for everything in the book. We couldn't argue with that.

"Finally it was time to take the test. 'Leave them face down on the desk until everyone has one, and I'll tell you when to start,' our professor instructed.

"When we turned them over, to my astonishment every answer was filled in. My name was written in red ink. The last page said: 'This is the end of the exam. All the answers on your test are correct. You will receive an A. The reason you passed the test is because the creator of the test took it for you. All the work you did in preparation for this test did not help you get the A. You have just experienced grace.'

"Dr. Hufty then went around the room and asked each student, 'What is your grade? Do you deserve the grade you are receiving? How much did all your studying for this exam help you achieve your final grade?' Then he said, 'Some things you learn from lectures, some from research, but some things you only learn by experience. You've just experienced grace. Years from now, if you know Jesus Christ as your personal Savior, your name will be written in a book, and you will have had nothing to do with writing it there. That is the ultimate grace experience.' "

Each of us has experienced guilt. We have all experienced condemnation. God never intended those to be the defining experiences of our lives. He wants us to be "*in Christ Jesus.*" There is no guilt there. We don't have to live with guilt and condemnation. God's grace is available to the weakest of us. All God asks of us is that we remain in Christ. That means that, in the biggest test of our lifetimes, we all get A's since the Creator took the test for us.

84—Spiritual Power

Muhammad Ali was seated in an airplane awaiting take off when the flight attendant asked him to fasten his seat belt. He looked at her and said, "Superman don't need no seat belt." She responded, "Superman don't need no airplane, either." At this, he fastened his belt.

None of us is Superman. We are all dependent on the power that comes from God.

I suspect that we have all tried, at some point, to live for God with the resources of our own strength. Our limitations bring frustration and we lower our expectations. We are, then, willing to "settle for" what we can do. After all, we think, others are more gifted and have an easier time than we have.

One of the problems with that kind of thinking is that it's never good to compare ourselves unfavorably with others. God knows the gifts and abilities He has invested in us and doesn't expect us to live up to anyone else's expectations. He never asked any of us to be Billy Graham. I am not expected to come up with a scientific concept as earthshaking as the theory of relativity. I don't have the ammunition necessary to produce that kind of fire power. God doesn't want any one of us living in depression because we aren't doing what someone else does. He wants us to do what He created us to do. And, we can't do that without His help.

Thinking that we are dependent only on our own resources means that our inabilities define our standards of success. We unconsciously begin to "settle for" our personal limitations.

There are encouraging Scriptures for us. One is found in Jesus' last words to His disciples. Before He ascended to heaven following His resurrection. He told them, *"But you will receive power when the Holy Spirit comes on you; and you will be my witnesses in Jerusalem, and in all Judea and Samaria, and to the ends of the earth"* (Acts 1:8).

We have been empowered by the Holy Spirit. He takes our unique personalities and strengths, and then adds His power so that we can effectively share our faith with others.

The apostle Paul was exceptionally gifted, but he also knew the limitations of his natural ability. In his first letter to the Corinthian church, he identified his weakness, but explained how he was able to compensate for his weakness through the enabling power of the Holy Spirit. He wrote, *"I came to you in weakness and fear, and with much trembling"* (2:3). J. B. Phillips paraphrased that verse this way: *"I was feeling far from strong. I was nervous and rather shaky."*

That sounds so human. Who of us hasn't been in a situation that jangled our nerves? Do we give up because we are "nervous and rather shaky?" Not if we know that God's power is available to us.

Paul continued with the solution that is available to all of us: *"My message and my preaching were not with wise and persuasive words, but with a demonstration of the Spirit's power, so that your faith might not rest on men's wisdom, but on God's power"* (2:4-5).

God's power is available to us. Acts 1:8 says that Jesus promised the power of the Holy Spirit to us to enable us to witness. Paul wrote the Corinthians and testified that the Spirit's power works. The problem I have is that too often I don't rely on that amazing resource God has made available.

I can be like the little boy who was trying, unsuccessfully, to lift a big rock. His father saw him struggling and asked him if he was having trouble. "Yes," the boy panted. "Have you tried everything?" the father questioned. "Yes," the boy grunted. The father continued, "Have you used all the resources available?" "Yes," the boy said as he struggled. "No you haven't," his father said, "you haven't asked me."

Too many times, I have tried to do God's work in my strength. He is waiting to bring His power into the picture if we only ask Him.

Or, maybe some of us treat God's power as a scarce commodity and use it sparingly. A Welsh woman lived in a remote valley in Wales. She went to a great deal of trouble to have electrical power installed in her home. When the employee of the power company checked her meter, he discovered that she wasn't using very much electricity at all. In fact, her usage was hardly measurable.

The company sent someone to check on the reason. The man went to the woman's door and said, "We've looked at the amount of your electrical usage. Don't you use electricity?"

"Oh yes" she said. "We turn it on every night to see how to light our lamps and then we switch it off again." This sounds like the way many Christians apply the power of God in their lives.

When I pastored in Virginia Beach a man named Dan came to me after a morning worship service. He asked if I would pray for him. I asked him what his need was and he told me that his girlfriend had left him and he wanted her back. I knew that the answer to Dan's problem was a relationship with Jesus, so I asked if he thought a relationship with Jesus might not be what he really needed. Maybe Jesus could fill the emptiness he felt.

Dan said that maybe that could be true. Then I asked if he would pray a prayer with me inviting Jesus into his life. He said he would and repeated the sinner's prayer after me. The next Sunday evening he came to me before the service and asked if he could say something during the meeting. I had no idea what he might say, but I gave him the microphone. He told the church, "I came for prayer to get my girlfriend back, but got saved instead. I didn't mention it to the pastor last week, but I've been out of work for three months with a bad back.

"Monday morning when I woke up my back wasn't hurting. I went to work for the first time in those three months. I stopped at a 7-11 on the way to work for some coffee. The place was full of people on their way to work. I announced, 'I received Jesus as my Savior yesterday and He healed my back. I'm going to work for the first time in months.' Then I bent at the waist and went through motions to show them I was healed."

We didn't even mention his back in prayer but God saved him and healed him. Isn't it wonderful when we do what we can do and find God's power is able to take us into the realm of the impossible and do what we cannot do?

85—Does God Understand?

No one is more misunderstood than God. Some people view Him as a harsh, unforgiving Ruler who has no compassion. That is so wrong. He is a holy God and judgment is not an option with Him. It is a part of His holy nature. The good news is that He judged sin when His Son died on the Cross. Jesus died so that everyone who believes in Him can live free from guilt. The apostle Paul explained this in Romans 8:1: *"Therefore, there is now no condemnation for those who are in Christ Jesus."*

It is difficult to understand why anyone who knows about Jesus would choose to ignore the salvation God so freely offers. Jesus showed us how much God loves us. The prophet Ezekiel explained clearly God's plan for us: *" 'Do I take any pleasure in the death of the wicked?' declares the Sovereign LORD. 'Rather, am I not pleased when they turn from their ways and live?' "* (Ezekiel 18:23).

Several years ago, a businessman found out about an elderly widow who was unable to pay her rent. He went to some of his friends and asked them if they would be kind enough to contribute something to help pay her bill. He went to the woman's house that week to deliver the money. He approached her door and knocked repeatedly, but she did not answer.

A couple of days later, he saw her, walked up to her and said, "Some friends of mine and I found out about your situation. We want to help. I came to your house to give you money for your rent. When I knocked several times I got no answer." She took a gasp of breath and put her hand to her face. She said, "Oh, I thought you were the landlord coming to evict me."

That is how some people view God. They won't open their hearts to Him because they're afraid He has come to punish them. God hasn't come to hurt us. He sent His Son to save us. He doesn't want any of us to perish. The Cross is God's proof that He has done everything He can to rescue us.

The first entire chapter of the Bible I memorized was Isaiah 53. I knew, even when I was young, that it was important to see God through the truth of this chapter. The words were burned so deeply into my heart that they changed forever my understanding of God. *"But he was pierced for our transgressions, he was crushed for our iniquities; the punishment that brought us peace was upon him, and by his wounds we are healed. We all, like sheep, have gone astray, each of us has turned to his own way; and the LORD has laid on him the iniquity of us all"* (Isaiah 53:5-6).

This passage talks about all of us. We've all messed up. But, *"the LORD has laid on him the iniquity of us all."* Any of us can be rescued from sin if we will only receive the salvation that comes through Jesus.

I've been in church long enough to know one objection that keeps people from faith. They wonder whether God really understands them. Have you ever thought, "God you can't know what it's like to be me—to suffer what I have had to endure!"

My wife, Gwen, and I visited the Holocaust Museum in Washington, D. C. The most moving part of the exhibit for both of us was the room full of shoes. They were all sizes from small to large and each represented a victim of the Holocaust. They painted a picture of unimaginable cruelty. Does God understand that?

Gwen was conceived by two sixteen-year-olds who weren't married. I know some of the struggle she went through to find an identity. How do people deal with feeling that they are accidents no one really wanted? Does God understand that?

I grew up in the South. I watched a deeply disturbing documentary on lynching that shocked me. I didn't realize that lynchings were announced in the papers and the public was invited. That era remains a tragic holdover of prejudice and injustice that is a blight on our history. Does God understand that?

In describing the importance of the death of Christ, Alister McGrath, in his *Studies in Christian Doctrine*, quoted from a playlet entitled, *The Long Silence*:

"Billions of people were scattered on a great plain before God's throne. Some of the groups near the front talked heatedly—not with cringing shame, but with belligerence. 'How can God judge us?' said one. 'What does He know about suffering?' snapped a brunette. She jerked back a sleeve to reveal a tattooed number from a Nazi concentration camp. 'We endured terror, beatings, torture, death!' In another group, a black man lowered his collar. 'What about this?' he demanded, showing an ugly rope burn. 'Lynched for no crime but being black! We have suffocated in slave ships, been wrenched from loved ones, toiled till death gave release.'

"Far out across the plain were hundreds of such groups. Each had a complaint against God for the evil and suffering He permitted in His world. How lucky God was to live in heaven where there was no weeping, no fear, no hunger, no hatred! Indeed, what did God know about what man had been forced to endure in this world? 'After all, God leads a pretty sheltered life,' they said. So, each group sent out a leader, chosen because he had suffered the most. There was a Jew, a black, an untouchable from India, an illegitimate, a person from Hiroshima, and one from a Siberian slave camp. In the center of the plain, they consulted with each other.

"At last they were ready to present their case. It was rather simple: before God would be qualified to be their judge, He must endure what they had endured. Their decision was that God should be sentenced to live on earth—as a man! But, because He was God, they set certain safeguards to be sure He could not use His divine powers to help Himself: Let Him be born a Jew. Let the legitimacy of His birth be doubted, so that none would know who is really His father. Let Him champion a cause so just, but so radical, that it brings down upon Him the hate, condemnation, and efforts of every major traditional and established religious authority to eliminate Him. Let Him try to describe what no man has ever seen, tasted, heard, or smelled—let Him try to communicate God to men. Let Him be betrayed by His dearest friends. Let Him be indicted on false charges, tried before a prejudiced jury, and convicted by a cowardly judge. Let Him see what it is to be terribly alone and completely abandoned by every living thing. Let Him be tortured and let Him die! Let Him die the most humiliating death—with common thieves. As each leader announced his portion of the sentence, loud murmurs of approval went up from the great throngs of people.

"But when the last had finished pronouncing sentence, there was a long silence. No one uttered another word. No one moved. For suddenly all knew—God had already served His sentence."

God does care. He does understand what we experience. And, He gave His Son, Jesus, to die in our place so we can live.

86—Seeing the Future Today

My father was a preacher. When I was born, he was pastoring a church in the coal-mining region of southwestern Virginia. I always had great respect for him and wanted to be like him. I grew up listening to his sermons and reading the books in his library. My father never went to college but he bought a Greek grammar and learned New Testament Greek on his own. His influence on me was so profound that from my childhood I wanted to be a preacher.

When I began to pastor, Dad was there to watch me learn. He was a reservoir of wisdom and gave me good advice as I got started. There came a time, after I had pastored for some time, that there was a subtle shift in our relationship. He began telling me stories designed to give me insight into the practical lessons he had learned. When I was in college studying engineering, we had a good relationship, but when I followed him into the ministry, he became a mentor. He made available to me the benefits of everything he had learned.

This same kind of transformation was taking place between Jesus and His disciples. The Twelve had been chosen very recently. They were totally confused by the direction Jesus was going. The first phase of ministry had ended with Peter's confession. They had expressed confidence in His identity. They now knew that He was the Christ, the Messiah that God had promised. The new phase began in Mark 8:31: *"He then began to teach them that the Son of man must suffer."* During the early phase of His ministry, He had not talked about His death.

Now that Jesus was nearing the final week of His life on earth, He entrusted His secrets to His twelve disciples. He was preparing them for His death and resurrection. It was with Good Friday and Easter in mind that Jesus took Peter, James and John with Him to the Mount of Transfiguration.

Among the lessons He wanted them to learn was the importance of seeing the glory of tomorrow on the other side of today's crisis. *"And he said to them, 'I tell you the truth, some who are standing here will not taste death before they see the kingdom of God come with power.' After six days, Jesus took Peter, James and John with him and led them up a high mountain, where they were all alone. There he was transfigured before them. His clothes became dazzling white, whiter than anyone in the world could bleach them"* (Mark 9:1-3).

It is natural for any of us to feel alarm when we face threatening circumstances. Our bodies react physically at events we can't explain. When the three disciples went to the top of the mountain with Jesus they saw something so outside their normal experience that there would have been alarm. That is a common emotion for those who encounter God's supernatural power. When angels appeared to people in the Bible the first thing they would say is, "Don't be afraid." There is something about the unknown that causes an adrenaline rush. Psychologists call it the "fight or flight" syndrome.

Suddenly, while the disciples were there with Jesus, Jesus' clothes lit up. That would cause anyone to take notice. They had heard Him talk of His upcoming death, now they got a glimpse of His glory. Whatever happened to Jesus was certainly going to affect them. He was going to die and they hadn't signed up to follow Him with His death in mind. It was important that, before their dreams were shattered, they got a glimpse of His divine nature.

While looking at what is happening today it is important for all of us to remember what God has promised for tomorrow.

Jesus had promised His disciples that some of them would see the kingdom of God come with power before they died. This was that promised moment. Jesus was transformed in front of three of them—Peter, James and John. It was necessary for them to see this. Jesus knew how devastating His death would be for them. He wanted to give them more than words to sustain them through the crisis. He wanted them to see a revelation of His glory. The gloom was impending. He was going to die. They needed to see His divine nature so they would not lose heart at His crucifixion.

Throughout the Gospels Jesus never spoke of His death without mentioning the Resurrection. His design for each of us is that we see through the immediate circumstances to the final result. What sustains us when times are tough? The promises He gives us. These three disciples were going to sit in on Jesus' funeral plans, but they were going to do it in the context of a manifestation of His glory. The Cross wouldn't defeat Him. Death wouldn't hold Him. They would need this experience to hold them steady in a few days.

We too often live under the tyranny of present circumstances. God wants us to have a hope that sees through immediate problems to the ultimate solution. The writer of the book of Hebrews says that Jesus was not at the mercy of what was about to happen. *"Let us fix our eyes on Jesus, the author and perfecter of our faith, who for the joy set before him endured the cross, scorning its shame, and sat down at the right hand of the throne of God"* (12:2).

Jesus saw through the cross to the joy and honor that would be on the other side. It is important for us to look at today through eyes that also see tomorrow.

Revelation from heaven can sustain us when information is inadequate. It is one thing to have someone explain to us something that he has seen. It is quite another thing to see it ourselves. It would be this scene that would stick in the memory of these three disciples.

There is a trite saying that a man with an argument is no match for a man with an experience. I love certain foods. I go to a Mexican restaurant and order number eleven by reflex. It is a taco, a burrito and an enchilada. I order that because I can't choose between them. If I sat across the table and watched a friend eat number eleven and describe it to me, I would trust him to tell me the truth: "This tastes good." But, I would much rather eat the "number eleven" myself. The information is no match for the experience.

Jesus understood the truth we will celebrate this Easter Sunday. Death could not keep Him down. He also knew the crisis the Cross would create for His disciples. He wanted His disciples to get a glimpse of Easter Sunday so they could face the challenge of Good Friday.

I could go on to say that there are many people who know about Jesus. They are familiar with the facts of His life, death and resurrection. That, however, is not the same as an experience with Him. One of our goals as believers is to help people see beyond the problems they face and experience the reality of the resurrected Christ who has defeated death and hell forever. That perspective on tomorrow can change anyone's life today.

87–Jesus Helps Us Get the Message

Communication is a challenge. Sometimes our muddled attempts to communicate can get out of control. There was an ad in the classified section of a newspaper one Monday: "FOR SALE: R. D. Jones has one sewing machine for sale. Phone 948-0707 after 7 p.m. and ask for Mrs. Kelly who lives with him cheap."

Shocked by the misleading ad, Mr. Jones asked the paper to rectify the situation with another ad on Tuesday. The paper published the following: "NOTICE: We regret have erred in R. D. Jones' ad yesterday. It should have read: One sewing machine for sale. Cheap. Phone 948-0707 and ask for Mrs. Kelly who lives with him after 7 p.m."

That only made matters worse. On Thursday, the paper published another distorted ad. So, on Friday, Jones ran the following ad: "NOTICE: I, R. D. Jones, have no sewing machine for sale. I smashed it. Don't call 948-0707 as the telephone has been taken out. I have not been carrying on with Mrs. Kelly. Until yesterday she was my housekeeper, but she quit."

Some miscommunication is less embarrassing. A mother, who had diabetes, explained to her 4-year-old daughter, Taylor, and 3-year-old son, Alex, what to do in an emergency. Trying to keep it simple, she told them to call 911 and tell the operator, "My mommy has diabetes." When she quizzed them to see if they understood, Taylor responded correctly and Alex answered, "I call 911 and say my mommy has beady eyes."

We can understand Jesus and His message clearly because He interjected stories into His teaching. He didn't leave us a difficult-to-read theology book because He wanted us to understand who He was and what He came to do.

When an expert in the law tried to argue with Jesus about who his neighbor was Jesus didn't argue fine points of the law. He told a story. And, in that story He effectively described Himself. Luke records that the expert in the law *"wanted to justify himself, so he asked Jesus, 'And who is my neighbor?' In reply Jesus said: 'A man was going down from Jerusalem to Jericho, when he fell into the hands of robbers. They stripped him of his clothes, beat him and went away, leaving him half dead' "* (Luke 10:29-30).

Then Jesus continued the story by describing two religious leaders, the priest and the Levite, who passed the man without offering help. To the amazement of those who heard Him speak, Jesus introduced the hero of the story—a Samaritan. It was a Samaritan who stopped and gave the man first aid, then took him to an inn where he could recover. Not only that, but the Samaritan paid all the expenses that would accumulate while the man recovered.

That simple story points out how easy it is to be religious without compassion. It also demonstrates the love Jesus has for those who have been beaten up by life. It would be difficult to miss the point because Jesus knew how to communicate.

There are many misunderstandings about Jesus in our world. To many people He is just irrelevant. We know that by the way they talk, think and live. Helmut Thielicke described God as many unbelievers see Him. They regard Him as the Cosmic Sheriff who has come to arrest them for their crimes and they purposely avoid Him. The Jesus we know is nothing like that. He is filled with compassion for us. He loves us beyond our ability to comprehend.

Stories are still helpful in enabling us to understand spiritual truths. Bob Weber, past president of Kiwanis International, told a story that helps us grasp what Jesus is like. Mr. Weber had spoken to a Kiwanis club in a small town and was spending the night with a farmer on the outskirts of the community. He had just relaxed on the front porch when a newsboy delivered the evening paper. The boy noted a sign in the yard, "Puppies for Sale." The paperboy got off his bike and asked the farmer, "How much do you want for the pups, mister?" "Twenty-five dollars, son." The boy's face dropped. "Well, sir, could I at least see them anyway?" The farmer whistled, and in a moment the mother dog came bounding around the corner of the house followed by four cute puppies, wagging their tails and yipping happily. Running behind them, another pup came straggling around the house, dragging one leg.

"What's the matter with that puppy, mister?" the boy asked. "Well, Son, that puppy is crippled. We took her to the vet and the doctor took an X-ray. The pup doesn't have a hip joint and that leg will never be right." To the amazement of both men, the boy dropped the bike, reached for his collection bag and took out a fifty-cent piece. "Please, mister," the boy pleaded, "I want to buy that pup. I'll pay you fifty cents every week until the twenty-five dollars is paid."

The farmer explained again, "But, Son, you don't seem to understand. That pup will never, never be able to run or jump. That pup is going to be a cripple forever. Why in the world would you want such a useless pup as that?" The boy paused for a moment, then reached down and pulled up his pant leg, exposing that all-too-familiar iron brace and leather knee-strap holding a twisted leg. The boy answered, "Mister, that pup is going to need someone who understands him to help him in life!"

Jesus can help us in life because He understands us. He accepts us as we are—our temptations, our discouragements and our fears. He even understands death because He died for us. Though we have been crippled by sin, the risen, living Christ has given us hope. By His resurrection, we have help in this life and hope for the life to come. It doesn't matter to Him how crippled we are, He loves us.

Men who were with Randolph Hearst in San Francisco remember the night he came into *The Examiner* office and heard of a man who had been seen on a half-submerged rock in the bay, with the tide rising and certain to overwhelm him. In the office, Hearst's employees were speculating about how the man got himself into such a predicament.

"What difference does it make how he got there?" Mr. Hearst cut in. "Get him off first and find out afterward. Charter tugs, call for volunteers and save his life—that's the main thing." They went out with the tugs (it was a wild night), and rescued the man just before the sea rose over the rock.

The Jesus we know is just like that. He rescues us first and then deals with the behavior that got us into trouble in the first place. If you are clinging to a rock and the water's rising, Jesus is on His way to rescue you. Like the Good Samaritan He will see that you become healthy again. Trust Him; He has your best interest in mind.

88—Someone Who Cares About Me

We are often in situations that call for dependence on someone else. That is evident in the availability of an emergency phone number. Sometimes we need to get help from somebody and calling 911 means that advice is only a phone call away. Usually those calls reflect a serious problem. At other times, the calls may seem frivolous. But, each call reflects someone's need for a listening ear. Just to understand what some people regard as emergencies, consider these recorded conversations:

Dispatcher: "9-1-1. What is your emergency?" Caller: "Hi, is this the police?" Dispatcher: "This is 9-1-1. Do you need police assistance?" Caller: "Well, I don't know who to call. Can you tell me how to cook a turkey? I've never cooked one before."

Dispatcher: "9-1-1. What is the nature of your emergency?" Caller: I'm trying to reach nine-eleven but my phone doesn't have an eleven on it." Dispatcher: "This is nine-eleven." Caller: "I thought you just said this was nine-one-one." Dispatcher: "Yes, Ma'am. Nine-one-one and nine-eleven are the same thing." Caller: "Honey, I may be old, but I'm not stupid."

Dispatcher: "9-1-1." Caller: "Yes, I'm having trouble breathing. I'm all out of breath. I think I'm going to pass out." Dispatcher: "Sir, where are you calling from?" Caller: "I'm at a pay phone. North and Foster." Dispatcher: "Sir, an ambulance is on the way. Are you an asthmatic?" Caller: "No." Dispatcher: "What were you doing before you started having trouble breathing?" Caller: "Running from the police."

We, as human beings, have a built-in desire for community. One of the important functions of the church is to connect us with other people. As much as we may feel independent, there are times when we want someone to know who we are and where we are. It didn't take the early Church long to figure that out. As soon as the believers were filled with the Spirit in Acts 2, there were 3,000 new Christians. Talk about changing the shape of things in one day! How did they handle the dramatic increase? The book of Acts reports that they began to build a community.

Luke, who wrote the book of Acts, told us how the Church began: *"All the believers were together and had everything in common. Selling their possessions and goods, they gave to anyone as he had need. Every day they continued to meet together in the temple courts. They broke bread in their homes and ate together with glad and sincere hearts, praising God and enjoying the favor of all the people. And the Lord added to their number daily those who were being saved"* (Acts 2:44-47).

This wasn't Communism, it was community. The message about the Church's beginnings is clear, they *"were together,"* they *"continued to meet together"* and were *"enjoying the favor of all the people."* The result of their commitment to the Lord and commitment to each other was the growth of the Church. "*The Lord added to their number daily those who were being saved."*

Just by looking at this Scripture, we can see that part of the Church's appeal was the fact that it offered satisfying relationships. The Church offers two benefits to people. First, it offers fellowship with God through Jesus Christ. Second, but also important, it offers membership in a family of caring believers.

William Barclay called these believers the "Church of people whom others could not help liking." It is significant that those first Christians enjoyed the favor of all the people. It meant that they were likable. Philip Yancey asked a provocative question in one of his books when he wrote: "People liked Jesus. Why don't they like us?" I would add to that, "They liked the early Church, too."

There has never been a more enthusiastic, world-changing group of believers than those Christians in the first century. I wouldn't go back and many more individuals are coming to faith now, but they touched their generation for Christ. Without radio, television, movies or slick brochures, they reached their peers. Without an army, they overthrew the mighty Roman Empire. Something about them compelled others to join their company.

Charles Swindoll, in his book *Dropping Your Guard*, wrote that relationships are important. He explained: "No one says, 'Our family is a family because we eat together.' We do that in restaurants and school cafeterias. Unguarded, open relationships within the Body of Christ are just as important as the dispensing of Scriptural truth."

A friend of ours was going through a family crisis when a fellow-Christian encouraged him. "Fellowship is two fellows in the same ship," his well-meaning friend told him. "I am in the boat with you." Our troubled fellow-believer responded with, "Well, row then, doggone it!" Somewhere in the history of most converts to Christianity, there's the story of a friend who showed up to help row the boat.

The first step in helping someone believe in Jesus is, in a word, love. Two soldiers had been released from a prison camp in Siberia following World War II. "We did our best," said an officer, "to repatriate the men as fast as possible, but many were still there when winter threatened to close up the port." Only a limited number could board the last small boat. Among those waiting to be transported were two who had been chums all through the war. One of them was selected, but the other seemed doomed to remain behind. An order was given that those who were leaving could take only one important item of luggage.

The heart of the man who was chosen went out to his buddy, so he emptied his duffle bag of his prized souvenirs and personal belongings and told his companion to get into the canvas sack. Then carefully lifting the bag on his shoulders, he boarded the ship with his friend as his single, most precious possession. That kind of love is irresistible.

Near Kingsport, Tennessee, a southbound bus made a scheduled midday stop so passengers could freshen up and get a bite to eat. One bus driver made an announcement as he brought his bus to a stop. "Folks we'll be stopping here long enough for you to get something to eat. This bus company has a strict policy that prevents us from recommending a restaurant by name, but if anybody wants me while we are here, I'll be eating a T-bone steak with French fries at Tony's first-class, spotlessly clean diner across the street."

There are some places I would go to eat simply because I trust the word of others who ate there. Two ways we can touch others is by lovingly committing ourselves to a relationship with them and by letting them see what Jesus means to us. They may choose to follow us to the restaurant that we frequent.

89—We Are Family

Dennis, from Katy, Texas, needed a same-day dry cleaners before he left on a trip. He remembered one store with a huge sign, "One-Hour Dry Cleaners," on the other side of town, so he drove out of his way to drop off a suit. After filling out the tag, he told the clerk, "I need this in an hour." She said, "I can't get this back to you until Thursday." He responded, "I thought you did dry cleaning in an hour." "No," she replied, "That's just the name of the store."

It makes one wonder how many churches just have the name "church" without a concept of what it means or what it's supposed to do. There are many things the Bible teaches about the Church, and one of those things is that when we become part of God's Church we become part of a very large family.

In the Apostle Paul's letter to the Ephesians he explained the concept of church. He told the Ephesians that a church is a family, a building and a temple: *"So now you Gentiles are no longer strangers and foreigners. You are citizens along with all of God's holy people. You are members of God's family. We are his house, built on the foundation of the apostles and the prophets. And the cornerstone is Christ Jesus himself. We who believe are carefully joined together, becoming a holy temple for the Lord. Through him you Gentiles are also joined together as part of this dwelling where God lives by his Spirit"* (Ephesians 2:19-22, NLT).

A unique characteristic of a local church is that it consists of people of different ages, from different backgrounds and with different geographical origins. It is made up of the tall and short, the large and the small and it calls them all family. That means that when someone comes to faith in Jesus Christ he or she is immediately part of a large, universal family. It also means that person becomes part of that universal family called the local church.

As someone once said, "You can pick your friends, but you're stuck with your relatives." My sister may not have chosen me, but when I was born, she had a younger brother. I have seen the miracle happen repeatedly in church. Someone responds to Jesus, is "born again" and immediately we have a new brother or sister.

An expectant mother had two sons, four and two years old. She asked the older one, Ben, if he would like to have a new brother. After careful thought, Ben replied, "No, let's just keep Brian." Of course, Ben didn't know it but he can have a new brother and still keep Brian.

Paul's explanation of the church makes certain things clear. There are no "outsiders" in God's family. No group has a special corner on Him. He dwells in His Church— which is one new creation. No local church can overlook the fact that it is in the same family with every other believer.

In Paul's world, "strangers" were regarded with suspicion and dislike. It's true in our world, too. There is a natural tendency to avoid people who are different. In a healthy local church, we take Paul's words seriously. People are no longer "strangers" and "foreigners." We become a beautiful mix of brothers and sisters that make up a wonderful family.

The world is already a village. We know that from sociologists who evaluate the population of our shrinking planet. What happens in Asia is broadcast in the Americas at warp speed. An epidemic of Swine flu or Bird flu can break out in Mexico or Southeast Asia and we are immediately affected. No one can dispute the fact that we are close to one another. God's goal is for us to be a family. That can only happen by our being born again into God's family. At that point, we have the same Father.

Fred Craddock, while lecturing at Yale University, told of going one summer to Gatlinburg, Tennessee, to take a short vacation with his wife. One night they found a quiet little restaurant where they looked forward to a private meal—just the two of them. While they were waiting for their meal, they noticed a distinguished looking, white-haired man moving from table to table, visiting guests.

The man made his way to their table and asked, "Where are you folks from?" They told him Oklahoma. "What do you do for a living?" he continued. "I teach homiletics at the graduate seminary of Phillips University," Craddock replied. "Oh, so you teach preachers, do you? Well, I've got a story I want to tell you." In addition, with that he pulled up a chair and sat down at the table with Craddock and his wife.

The man stuck out his hand. "I'm Ben Hooper. I was born not far from here across the mountains. My mother wasn't married when I was born so I had a hard time. When I started to school my classmates had a name for me, and it wasn't a very nice name. I used to go off by myself at recess and during lunchtime because the taunts of my playmates cut so deeply. What was worse was going downtown on Saturday afternoon and feeling every eye burning a hole through you. They were all wondering just who my real father was.

"When I was about 12 years old a new preacher came to our church. I would always go in late and slip out early. But one day the preacher said the benediction so fast I got caught and had to walk out with the crowd. Just about the time I got to the door I felt a big hand on my shoulder. I looked up and the preacher was looking right at me.

" 'Who are you, son? Whose boy are you?' I felt the old weight come on me. It was like a big black cloud. Even the preacher was putting me down. But as he looked down at me, studying my face, he began to smile a big smile of recognition. 'Wait a minute,' he said, 'I know who you are. I see the family resemblance. You are a son of God.' With that he slapped me across the rump and said, 'Boy you've got a great inheritance. Go and claim it.' "

The old man looked across the table at Fred Craddock and said, "That was the most important single sentence ever said to me." With that he smiled, shook the hands of Craddock and his wife, and moved on to another table to greet old friends. Suddenly, Fred Craddock remembered. On two occasions the people of Tennessee had elected an illegitimate to be their governor. One of them was Ben Hooper.

Christians are a family because everyone who believes in Jesus has the same Father. Whatever your background may be, whoever your ancestors were and whatever they did doesn't limit you. When we come to Jesus we are "born again" and get, not only a heavenly Father, but a huge number of brothers and sisters. The Bible calls that family the Church.

90—Mother's Day

Pastor Roger Matthews said that he and his family were traveling one summer in the Pocono Mountains of Pennsylvania. Like a good Presbyterian family, they attended church while they were on vacation.

One hot, lazy Sunday they found a little Methodist church and attended the worship service there. As Pastor Matthews described it, the day was hot and the people were nearly drowsing during the preacher's sermon. To wake everyone up, the minister suddenly said, "The best years of my life have been spent in the arms of another man's wife." The congregation let out a gasp and came to immediate attention. The dozing deacon in the back row dropped his hymnbook. Then the preacher added, "It was my mother." The congregation tittered a little and managed to follow along as the sermon concluded.

Matthews explained that he filed away this trick in his memory. The next summer, on a lazy Sunday, he was preaching and the flies were buzzing around and the ushers were sinking lower and lower in their seats in the back row until he could hardly see them. Then he remembered that experience in the Pocono Mountains. So he said in a booming voice, "The best years of my life have been spent in the arms of another man's wife." Sure enough, he had their attention! One of the ushers in the back row sat up so fast he hit his head on the back of the pew in front of him! He had them. But, he had a memory lapse and forgot what came next! All he could think to say was, "...and, for the life of me, I can't remember her name!"

As we celebrate Mother's Day this weekend, it would be good to remember how important they are to us. Children are the joy of a mother's heart, but they can sometimes be a challenge to a mother's sanity.

When asked, "What kind of girl was your mom?" two children gave their responses. One said, "I don't know because I wasn't there, but my guess would be pretty bossy." Another answered, "They say she used to be nice." I'm not sure the little girl meant that the way it can be taken.

Children sometimes tell more than we want them to say. When a child was asked, "How did you mom meet your dad?" she answered, "Mom was working in a store and Dad was shoplifting."

To the question, "Why did your mom marry your dad?" one daughter quoted her grandmother: "Grandma says that Mom didn't have her thinking cap on."

The family is the foundational structure of our society. It would be fair to say that mothers are an essential ingredient in that foundation. An example of how important a mother can be is portrayed in the accounts of Jesus' mother, Mary.

When the shepherds showed up at the birth of Jesus, they not only worshiped the Baby, but also recounted what they had seen in the field as the angels appeared and celebrated the birth of Jesus. Luke recorded an interesting comment about Jesus' mother, Mary: *"But Mary quietly treasured these things in her heart and thought about them often"* (Luke 2:19, NLT). One of the qualities mothers have is the ability to harbor thoughts about the destinies of their children.

Obviously, Mary held on to some things about Jesus that weren't common knowledge in the community as He grew into manhood. The neighbors didn't understand who Jesus was. Mark tells us that when Jesus began His public ministry the community in which He had been reared couldn't receive His message because they knew Him as an ordinary young man. *"Isn't this the carpenter? Isn't this Mary's son and the brother of James, Joseph, Judas and Simon? Aren't his sisters here with us?" And they took offense at him"* (Mark 6:3). Apparently, what Mary held in her heart about Him was held very close to her heart.

Mary's expectations for her Son, were not common knowledge.

The time came for Jesus to begin His public ministry. The occasion was a wedding and the organizers of the party ran out of wine. Some suggest Jesus' mother was the organizer. At least, she certainly took charge of the crisis. She had been holding onto dreams and expectations about her oldest Son for thirty years. He had done no miracles to this point. He had been a carpenter in Joseph's carpenter shop. But, Mary had "quietly treasured" the truth of His birth in her heart.

She went to Jesus and explained the problem. Then she went to the servants who were catering the wedding reception and told them, "*Do whatever he tells you*" (John 2:5). That was the catalyst for Jesus turning water into wine and launching a public ministry that changed the world.

While everyone else saw a carpenter, Mary knew that He was God's unique Son. She obviously did not spread the news, but she never lost sight of His destiny.

My mother didn't have a perfect son, as Mary did, but I suspect she had hopes and dreams about what I would become. None of our mothers had perfect children but perhaps those mothers, too, have treasured things in their hearts about us.

Gwen and I have three daughters and I am amazed at Gwen's maternal instinct. A sure way for me to get in trouble with Gwen is to let her think I am not treating one of her daughters fairly. On countless occasions, one of the girls would come to me and say, "Where's Mom?" Then off they would go to discuss some issue with her that could not be entrusted to me. They have found, in their mom, a person who would go to the ends of the earth to see their dreams fulfilled.

It is difficult for us who aren't mothers to understand the willingness of mothers to make sacrifices so their children can reach their destinies. On August 16, 1987, Northwest Airlines flight 225 crashed just after taking off from the Detroit airport, killing 155 people. One survived: a four-year-old from Tempe, Arizona, named Cecelia. News accounts say when rescuers found Cecelia they did not believe she had been on the plane. Investigators first assumed Cecelia had been a passenger in one of the cars on the highway onto which the airliner crashed. But, when the passenger register for the flight was checked, there was Cecelia's name. Cecelia survived because, even as the plane was falling, Cecelia's mother, Paula Chican, unbuckled her own seat belt, got down on her knees in front of her daughter, wrapped her arms and body around Cecelia, and then would not let her go.

Today is a good day to say thank you to all the mothers who have wrapped their arms around us and have refused to let us go. They move in the wonderful tradition of a mother who "treasured these things in her heart" and never let go of the Savior her Son was to become.

Unless noted otherwise all Scripture references are taken from the New International Version.

Scripture taken from the HOLY BIBLE, NEW INTERNATIONAL VERSION VERSION ® 1973, 1978, 1984 by International Bible Society. Used by permission of Zondervan. All rights reserved.

End Notes

1–Hope Keeps Us Alive

Michael Green, *Illustrations for Biblical Preaching*, p. 194.
Bruster & Dale, *How to Encourage Others*.
John Ortberg, *If You Want to Walk on Water, You've Got to Get Out of the Boat*, Zondervan, Grand Rapids, Michigan (2001), p. 159.

2–Where Do We Run?

Philip Yancey, *The Bible Jesus Read*, Zondervan: Grand Rapids, Michigan (1999), p. 145.
Stories From the Heart, compiled by Al and Alice Gray, Multnomah Publishers: Sisters, Oregon p. 245.

3–We Are Living Witnesses

Ibid. pp. 259-261.
Our Daily Bread, November 6, 1994. (sermonillustrations.com)

4–The Power of Water Baptism

Focus On the Family Magazine (Charles Foster, Elwood, Indiana)
sermonillustrations.com
Brown, S. W., Robinson, H. W., & Willimon, W. H. 1993. *A Voice in the wilderness : Clear preaching in a complicated world*. Mastering ministry's pressure points. Multnomah Books: Sisters, Oregon

5–The World Needs Love

James S. Hewett, *Illustrations Unlimited* (Wheaton: Tyndale House Publishers, Inc, 1988), p. 310.

William Barclay, *The Letters to the Galatians and Ephesians,* Revised Edition, Westminster Press, Philadelphia, PA

6—Don't Miss Your Moment

Teri Leinbaugh, Shelbyville, KY, *Christian Reader,* "Lite Fare."

Hewett, op. cit., p. 391.

Bruce Thielemann, "Dealing with Discouragement," *Preaching Today,* Tape No. 48.

7—Don't Worry

Paul Lee Tan, *Encyclopedia of 15,000 Illustrations,* p. 3297.

Rex Bonar in *Fresh Illustrations for Preaching & Teaching* (Baker), from the editors of *Leadership.*

Jacob M. Braude, *Complete Speaker's and Toastmaster's Library,* Vol. 3, Prentice-Hall, Inc.: Englewood Cliffs, New Jersey, p. 121.

Steve Chandler, *100 Ways to Motivate Yourself,* The Career Press, Inc.: Franklin Lakes, New Jersey (2004), p. 178.

8—The Challenge of Forgiving

e-Sword,net

Chicken Soup for the Christian Soul, Health Communications, Inc.: Deerfield Beach, Florida, pp. 9-10.

9—Amazing Grace

Progress Magazine, December 14, 1992.

10—A Turned-Around Life

Hewett, op. cit., p. 50.

Christianity Today, Vol. 35, no. 2.

From *In Other Words* (Mar/Apr 1993). *Christian Reader,* Vol. 33, no. 6.

Paul Lee Tan, *Encyclopedia of 15,000 Illustrations,* pp. 429-430.

12—Jesus Seeks the "Lost"

Hewett, op. cit., p. 243.

13—God Loves His Church

Stephen Olford, *Committed to Christ and His Church*, Baker Book House: Grand Rapids, Michigan, p. 92.

14—How Do I Get Right with God?

Paul LeeTan, *Encyclopedia of 7700 Illustrations*, p. 1226.
J. Rodman Williams, *Renewal Theology*, Vol. 2, Academie Books, Zondervan Publishing House: Grand Rapids, Michigan, p. 64.

15—Love Breaks Down Barriers

Jack Seberry, Grand Rapids, Michigan. *Christian Reader*, "Lite Fare."
Hewett, op. cit., p. 107.
Billy Graham, *Leadership*, Vol. 5, no. 4.
Hugh Duncan Boise, Idaho. *Leadership*, Vol. 16, no. 1.
Tony Campolo, *Let Me Tell You a Story*, Word Publishing (Thomas Nelson Publishing): Nashville (2000), pp. 120-121.

16—Trust in the Lord

Men of Integrity, Vol. 1, no. 2.
Sam Sasser, *Let's Continue to Lift Sister Smith's Leg in Prayer.* (publication information not known).
D.L. Moody, *Christian History*, no. 25.
Greg Asimakoupoulos, Naperville, Illinois. *Leadership*, Vol. 16, no. 4.

17—Thank You

Ariana Macksey, Olga, Washington, *Christian Reader*, "Lite Fare."
From the files of *Leadership*.
David A. Seamands, *Instruction for Thanksgiving*, *Preaching Today*, Tape No. 62.
Tan, (7700), op. cit.
Joel Gregory, *The Unlikely Thanker*, *Preaching Today*, Tape No. 110.

18—Disappointments Can't Break You

Hewett, op. cit., p. 230.
Ibid., p. 90.
Cartoonist Rob Portlock in *Leadership*, Vol. 13, no. 3.
Leadership, Vol. 16, no. 1.

19–God Makes It Work Out Right

Gary P. Uber, "Reader's Digest," June 1992.
Harry Emerson Fosdick, *Twenty Centuries of Great Preaching*,
    Vol. 9, Word, Incorporated: Waco, Texas, p. 56.
Dan Betzer, Ft. Meyers, Florida. *Pentecostal Evangel*.
Leadership, Vol. 12, no. 3.
Chery Walterman Stewart, *More Stories from the Heart*, op. cit.,
pp. 247-248.

20–A Savior Has Been Born

Tan, (15,000), op. cit., p. 1368.
Public Speaker's Humor, p. 153.

21–Who Do You Belong To?

Glenn Van Ekeren, *Speaker's Sourcebook II*, Prentice Hall:
    Paramus, New Jersey (1994), p. 155.
The Bible Jesus Read, Philip Yancey, pp. 205-206.
Hewitt, op. cit.
Tan, (15,000), op. cit., p. 423.

22–A Bumper Crop

Michael Green, *Illustrations for Biblical Preaching*, pp. 293-294.
Vic Pentz, "A Twinge of Nostalgia," *Preaching Today*, Tape No. 88.

23– Never Give Up

Charles E. "Tremendous" Jones, *Life Is Tremendous*
Green, op. cit., pp. 376-377.

24–Hope

Perfect Illustrations for Every Topic and Occasion, p. 131.

26–Grace

Green, op. cit., pp. 318-319.
Campolo, op.cit., pp. 22-23.

27—Saying "Amen" to God's Promise

Green, op. cit. pp. 212-213.
Perfect Illustrations for Every Topic and Occasion, pp. 36-37.

28—God Loves Us

Campolo, op. cit., p. 93.
Don E. McKenzie, Northway Christian Church, Dallas, Texas.
James S. Hewett, *Illustrations Unlimited* (Wheaton: Tyndale House Publishers, Inc, 1988), p. 316.
James S. Hewett, *Illustrations Unlimited* (Wheaton: Tyndale House Publishers, Inc, 1988), p. 324.

29—What Business Are We In?

Green, op. cit., p. 398.

30—Smoke Signals

Green, op. cit., p. 381.
John Yates, "An Attitude of Gratitude," *Preaching Today*, Tape No. 110.

31—Living In Freedom

Hewett, op. cit., p. 466.

32—The Week That Shook the World

Hewett, op. cit., p. 402.

33—He's Alive

varnam.org
Hewett, op. cit., pp. 165-166.
sermonillustrator.org

34—The Footsteps of Faith

James Montgomery Boice. James S. Hewett, *Illustrations Unlimited* (Wheaton: Tyndale House Publishers, Inc, 1988), p. 425.
Tan, op. cit., (15,000), p. 579.

35–Don't Stay Down

Van Ekeren, op. cit., p. 155.
Hewett, op. cit., p. 155.
Judy C. Knupke, Newton Lower Falls, Massachusetts.
Leadership, Vol. 12, no. 4.

38–You Can Make a Difference

Luis Palau, "Go to the Ends of the Earth," *Preaching Today*, Tape No. 124.

39–God is My Compass

Hewett, op. cit., p. 384.
Van Ekeren, op. cit., p. 12.

40–Mother's Deserve a Day

Hewett, op. cit., p. 376.
Ibid, p. 382.
Edythe Draper, *Draper's Book of Quotations for the Christian World* (Wheaton: Tyndale House Publishers, Inc., 1992). Entries 7841-7843.
Hewett, op. cit., p. 381.
Anthony Campolo, *The Power Delusion*. James S. Hewett, *Illustrations Unlimited* (Wheaton: Tyndale House Publishers, Inc, 1988), p. 380.

41–That's What Friends Are For

Hewett, op. cit., p. 227.
Ibid, p. 92.
Ibid, pp. 123-124.
pawprints.kashalinka.com
Hewett, op. cit., p. 228.

42–Don't Forget

Perfect Illustrations for Every Topic and Occasion, p. 41.

Paul Aurandt, "The Old Man and the Gulls," Paul Harvey's *The Rest of the Story*, 1977, quoted in *Heaven Bound Living*, Knofel Stanton, Standard, 1989, p. 79-80.
sermonillustrations.com

44–Courage

Perfect Illustrations for Every Topic and Occasion, pp. 52-53.
W. Frank Harrington, "It's Decision Time," *Preaching Today*, Tape No. 162.
Chicken Soup for the Soul

45–Get to Know God

Hewett, op. cit., p. 315.

47–The Value of Storms

Green, op. cit., p. 103.
Hewett, op. cit., p. 488.

48–The Key to Everything

Ibid, p. 75.

50–Regaining a Sense of Direction

Max Lucado, *No Wonder They Call Him Savior*.
Perfect Illustrations for Every Topic and Occasion, p. 306.

51–Love to the Limit

Children's Letters to God.

52–Hope for the Hopeless

Hewett, op. cit., pp. 291-292.
Ibid, pp. 114-115.
Ibid, pp. 289-290.

53–Changing Your World

John Casey, "Real Giving," *Preaching Today*, Tape No. 156.
Green, op. cit., p. 72.

55—We Are God's Masterpieces

Hewett, op. cit., p. 220.

56—It's All About Jesus

Ibid, p. 109.
Ibid, p. 408.
Haddon Robinson, "When Good Snakes Become Bad Snakes," *Preaching Today*, Tape No. 145.
e-Sword.net

58—Find Your Fastball

Hewett, op. cit., p. 232.
Van Ekeren, op. cit., p. 7.

60—Strength For Tough Times

Hewett, op. cit., p. 205.

61—Humility

Cartoonist Johns in *Leadership,* Vol. 12, no. 1.
Daniel, Decoder of Dreams, Donald Campbell, p. 22. (bible.org)
Green, op. cit., p. 198.
Our Daily Bread (higherpraise.com)

62—Who's Got Your Back

Tan, (15,000), op. cit. 2078.
Ibid, p. 1131.

63—Guidance by Surprises

Helen Roseveare, Living Faith. "Heart to Heart," *Today's Christian Woman*.

64—Our Ministry Begins

Van Ekeren, op. cit., p. 264.
Charles Swindoll. James S. Hewett, *Illustrations Unlimited* (Wheaton: Tyndale House Publishers, Inc, 1988), p. 489.

65—Enjoy the Ride

Leith Anderson, "The Lord Is My Shepherd," *Preaching Today*, Tape 136.
Hewett, op. cit., p. 363.
timshen.truepath.com

67–Thanksgiving

David Washburn (sermoncentral.com)
Van Ekeren, op. cit., p. 49.
Hewett, op. cit., p. 263.
Tan, (15,000), op. cit., p. 2948.

68–Faith That Grows With Time

Perfect Illustrations for Every Topic and Occasion, pp. 46-47.

70–Wise Men Still Seek Him

Perfect Illustrations for Every Topic and Occasion, p. 39.

71–The Human Side of a Miracle

Benjamin Reaves, "Living Expectantly," *Preaching Today*, Tape No. 65.

74–Love One Another

Campolo, op. cit., pp. 16-17.

75–Never Give Up

Craig Brian Larson, "Strong to the Finish," *Preaching Today*, Tape No. 155.

77–God's Surprise

Taped sermon by Joel Gregory.

78–The Life Worth Seeking

Taped sermon by Joel Gregory.

79–A New Nature

David Owens (sermoncentral.com)
Green, op. cit., pp. 269-270.

80—Do You Want to Get Well?

Corrie Ten Boom in *Each New Day*. *Christianity Today*, Vol. 36, no. 3.

81—Hope For the Rejected

higherpraise.com (Max Lucado, *God Came Near*, Multnomah Press, 1987, p. 57.)
Sent from Judy Vaught by way of internet.

82—Forgiveness

Tan, (15,000), op. cit., p. 901.
Roger Thompson (higherpraise.com)

83—Guilt or Grace

Van Ekeren, op. cit., p. 388.
Ibid, p. 149.

84—Spiritual Power

Hewett, op. cit., p. 295.

85—Does God Understand?

R. Larry Moyer, "Right Smack in the Middle of Sin," *Preaching Today*, Tape No. 148.
Hewett, op. cit., p. 302.

87—Jesus Helps Us Get the Message

Hewett, op. cit., p. 75.

88—Someone Who Cares About Me

Charles Swindoll, *Dropping Your Guard*.

89—We Are Family

Perfect Illustrations for Every Topic and Occasion, p. 277.

Jamie Buckingham, *Power for Living*. (sermonillustrations.com)

90–Mother's Day

Lowell Streiker, ed. *An Encyclopedia of Humor.* 1998, Hendrickson Publishers (e-steeple.com)
Perfect Illustrations for Every Topic and Occasion, p. 56.

Made in the USA
Columbia, SC
23 December 2018